5

(Scotland)

Robert the Bruce's Rivals:
THE COMYNS, 1212–1314

Robert the Bruce's Rivals:
THE COMYNS, 1212–1314

✛

Alan Young

TUCKWELL PRESS

First published in 1997 by
Tuckwell Press Ltd
The Mill House
Phantassie
East Linton
East Lothian EH40 3DG
Scotland

Reprinted 1998

ISBN 1 86232 017 9 (cased)
ISBN 1 86232 053 5 (paperback)

British Library
Cataloguing-in-Publication Data
A Catalogue record for this book is available on request from
the British Library

Typeset by Hewer Text Composition Services, Edinburgh
Printed and bound by Biddles Ltd, Guildford, Surrey

CONTENTS

ACKNOWLEDGEMENTS

As my research on the Comyn family started in 1970, it is a daunting, if not impossible, task to try to acknowledge all those who have assisted me since that date. The final push towards publication was helped immensely by a sabbatical semester. I am most grateful to the University College of Ripon and York St John for this opportunity to reflect on past research, explore some new avenues and finally complete the study. I would like to express my thanks to friends, colleagues and students in the Department of Historical Studies at the University College for their support and interest. In particular, I owe a great debt to my friend and colleague, Dr John Addy, whose infectious enthusiasm for research has constantly, over twenty years, provided stimulation and encouragement for my own research in medieval history.

Over many years, I have benefited from the advice, help and support of colleagues working in the field of Scottish and northern English medieval history. The Scottish Medievalists' Conference and B.A.R.G. (the Baronial Research Group) have consistently provided stimulating forums for the discussion of research on medieval Scottish and baronial history. In particular, I have appreciated the help and advice of Dr Grant Simpson, Dr Keith Stringer, Dr Alexander Grant and Mr Geoffrey Stell. Anyone involved in research on medieval Scottish history must acknowledge a debt to the immense work of Professor A.A.M. Duncan and Professor G.W.S. Barrow. I am, personally, greatly indebted to Professor Geoffrey Barrow who first encouraged me to undertake research on the Comyn family and who has always been willing to give me the benefit of his vast knowledge of Scottish history and geography. His guidance has been invaluable. He has also read all of this book in draft and I have benefited greatly from his many helpful suggestions as well as being saved from numerous errors. The opinions and errors which remain are my sole responsibility.

A number of libraries and record offices have given me tremendous assistance in my research. I owe thanks to the staff of the Scottish Record Office, the National Library of Scotland, the Public Record Office and the British Museum for their help. I am particularly grateful for the assistance of Mrs G.C.W. Roads and the Court of the Lord Lyon and Dr N. Mills of the Historical Search Room, Scottish Record Office for help in research on Comyn seals; and to Mr Joseph White of Historic Scotland and to staff of the architectural section of the National Monuments Record of Scotland (RCAHMS) for help in research on Comyn castle and abbey sites. Without the efficient support of the Inter Library Loan Service at the University College of Ripon and York St John, research could not have been as extensive and I am grateful for the help provided by Christie Edwards. I am also grateful for the speedy, efficient and cheerful way in which the final draft was put on disk principally by Mrs Hilary Hunt, with assistance from Mrs Janet Olsen. An author is fortunate to have such a patient and supportive publisher as John Tuckwell and I am most thankful for both his encouragement and patience.

My wife, Heather, has been a source of much encouragement and support throughout my research and writing and especially in the final stages of the work. Without the help and encouragement of my parents, it is unlikely that the research would have started. I owe them a tremendous amount for their support over many years and I am therefore dedicating this book to the memory of my mother and father.

ILLUSTRATIONS

PLATE SECTION

MAPS AND PLANS

The Comyn Family Tree

?

William Comyn the Chancellor d. c. 1160?

William d. 1144 · Richard m. Hextilda d. c. 1179 · Walter · Osbert d. 1144

Richard m. ? d. 1244x1249

William Earl of Buchan (styled c. 1212) d 1233 — m. (2) Marjory Countess of Buchan

(1) ?

Walter Lord of Badenoch m. Isabella Countess of Menteith c. 1234 d.s.p. 1258

William (clerk)

Jean m. William Earl of Ross

David m. Isabel de Valoniis

Alicia de Lindsay of Lamberton ? — (2) m. John I Lord of Badenoch d. c. 1277 — m. (1) Eva

William · Richard

William of Kilbride m. Euphemia d. c. 1283

(Four daughters – one named Alice)

? · ? m. Geoffrey Mowbray · ? m. Alexander Macdougall of Argyll

John II of Badenoch (Competitor) m. Eleanor, sister of John de Balliol d. c. 1302

Eva

William, Lord of Kirkintilloch m. Isabella · Alexander m. Eva

Edmund m. Maria d. 1314 · John d. before 1315

Euphemia m. William la Beche · Maria

Robert d. 1306 · John 'junior' d. c. 1295? · m. Richard Siward

John III of Badenoch m. Joan de Valence d. 1306

William ?

John m. Margaret d. 1314

Elizabeth m. Richard Talbot

Joan m. David Earl of Atholl

Adomar d. 1316

The Comyn Family Tree

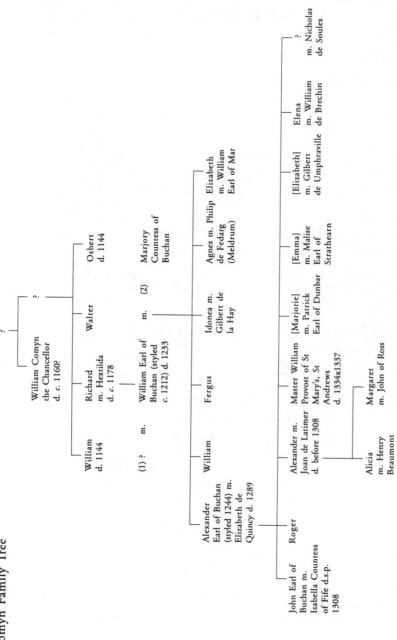

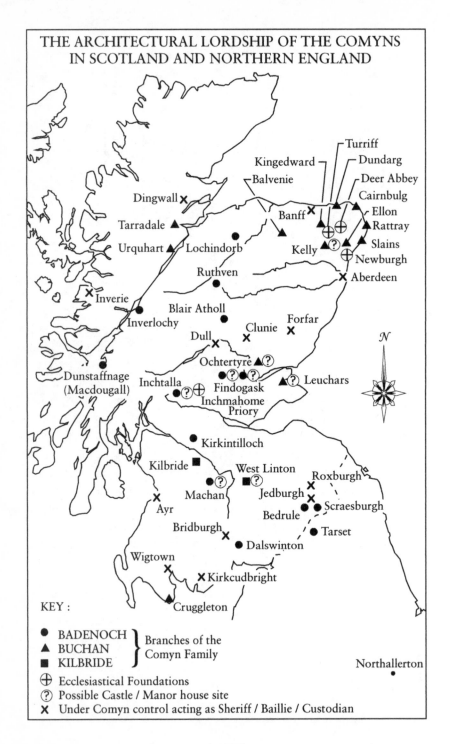

THE ARCHITECTURAL LORDSHIP OF THE COMYNS
IN SCOTLAND AND NORTHERN ENGLAND

Turriff
Kingedward
Dundarg
Balvenie
Deer Abbey
Dingwall
Cairnbulg
Banff
Ellon
Tarradale
Rattray
Urquhart
Lochindorb
Kelly
Slains
Newburgh
Ruthven
Aberdeen
Inverie
Blair Atholl
Inverlochy
Forfar
Clunie
Dull
Ochtertyre
Dunstaffnage
(Macdougall)
Inchtalla
Leuchars
Findogask
Inchmahome
Priory
Kirkintilloch
Kilbride
West Linton
Roxburgh
Machan
Jedburgh
Scraesburgh
Ayr
Bedrule
Bridburgh
Tarset
Dalswinton
Wigtown
Kirkcudbright
Cruggleton

N

KEY :

● BADENOCH ⎫ Branches of the
▲ BUCHAN ⎬ Comyn Family
■ KILBRIDE ⎭

⊕ Ecclesiastical Foundations
? Possible Castle / Manor house site
✗ Under Comyn control acting as Sheriff / Baillie / Custodian

Northallerton

CHAPTER ONE

Bruce, Wallace, Balliol and Comyn: Heroes and Villains in Scottish Tradition

The century of Scottish history culminating in the battle of Bannockburn (1314) was a dramatic one. The period – and especially the years 1290 to 1314 – produced heroes and villains now long established in Scottish tradition and legend. The names of Robert Bruce and William Wallace have emerged in this tradition as heroes and champions of Scotland in a time of need. William Wallace is seen as the first popular leader of Scottish nationalism, the tragic conclusion to his patriotic resistance making him also a martyr for that cause. Robert Bruce is viewed as Scotland's saviour following his dramatic seizure of the Scottish kingship and successful resistance to English imperialism. The names of Wallace and Bruce have captured popular imagination and hold a unique place in Scottish history. By contrast, the name of John Balliol has entered Scottish consciousness as 'Toom Tabard',[1] a Scottish king who abjectly surrendered his kingdom to Edward I in 1296. Similarly, the name of Comyn has long been associated in Scottish tradition with treachery – the family being involved in the infamous kidnapping of young Alexander III in 1257 and treachery against *both* Scottish heroes, Wallace at the battle of Falkirk in 1298 and Bruce in 1306.

The foundation for these traditions was firmly laid by Scottish writers of the fourteenth and fifteenth centuries. John of Fordun[2] wrote *The Chronicle of the Scots Nation* in the 1380s and this work has formed the main strand in the standard narrative account of Scottish medieval history. Fordun is increasingly acknowledged as an invaluable source of information for the century before Bannockburn because of his use of original thirteenth-century material not found elsewhere. His reporting of facts may be reliable but it should be emphasised that his information was set in a framework strictly governed by his chief themes: the growth of the Scottish nation, the need to keep it independent and the importance of monarchy in attaining these two objectives. Events were carefully selected – the extension and definition of the Scottish kingdom, the suppression of revolts and the fight against England for independence. The minority of Alexander III, 1249–1260, was used by Fordun to demonstrate the importance of having a king. The death of Alexander III was lamented all the more because the absence of strong kingship led to 'the evils of after times'.[3]

Fordun's framework was followed by Walter Bower,[4] abbot of Inchcolm (writing c.1440) and Andrew of Wyntoun,[5] prior of Lochleven (writing c.1420). The emphasis of all three on patriotism, the cause of Scottish independence and hostility to the tyranny of England is hardly surprising given the political instability of the fourteenth and fifteenth centuries.[6] After Robert I's death in 1329, Scotland suffered from another minority period as well as civil war; Edward III's support of Edward Balliol's attempt to gain the Scottish crown was a strong reminder of Edward I's earlier interference; Scottish government was further weakened following David II's capture by the English at Neville's Cross (1346) and his subsequent long captivity. Bower's elaboration of Fordun's work took place against the background of further political instability in Scotland, the country being once again divided following the murder of James I and another minority period.

Despite the sound reputations of Fordun and Bower as historians, fourteenth- and fifteenth-century anxieties and preoccupations naturally affected their interpretations of Scottish history in the century before Bannockburn. The century was viewed in a strongly monarchocentric way. Fordun in hindsight boosted the image of Alexander III and laid the foundation for the myth of the 'Golden Age' of Alexander III. His reign was used to create an ideal for the kind of kingship to be aimed at, a strong independent Scotland. The heartfelt laments on the death of Alexander III in Fordun, Bower and Wyntoun emphasise the point:

O Scotland, truly unhappy, when bereft of so great a leader
and pilot.[7]
... at all times after the king had reached the age of discretion, his

subjects lived in constant tranquillity and peace, and in agreeable
and secure freedom.[8]
Scotland, how sweet it is to remember your glory while your king
was alive.[9]

The role of the nobility in the century before Bannockburn was inevitably
viewed by Fordun, Bower and Wyntoun from their monarchocentric
standpoint. Emphasis was placed on the threat posed to the monarchy by
the faction and lawlessness of the nobility and their role as over-mighty
subjects. These factors were particularly stressed in the minority of
Alexander III and in the period after Alexander III's death as they laid
Scotland open to interference from England. In this context, the roles of
Bruce, Wallace, Balliol and Comyn were judged and heroes and villains
created. Thus Robert Bruce became the hero of the entire narratives of
both Fordun and Bower as he restored the ideals of kingship embodied
in the 'Golden Age' of Alexander III. William Wallace was portrayed
as a champion of Scottish nationalism resisting English imperialism.
The reputations of Robert Bruce and William Wallace were further
enhanced by works specifically dedicated to them. The poem, *The
Bruce*, written in 1375 by John Barbour,[10] archdeacon of Aberdeen, was
a very full account of Robert Bruce's life, written in the form of an epic
with Bruce as the chivalric hero. The vernacular poem, *The Wallace*,[11]
written in the 1470s by Henry the Minstrel, better known as 'Blind
Hary', fulfilled a similar purpose for William Wallace.

By contrast the Comyns were usually portrayed as overmighty subjects
posing a threat to the Scottish kingdom and Alexander III's kingship. As
rivals to both Robert Bruce and William Wallace, the Comyns were also
seen as endangering the achievements of both heroes. John Balliol was
also judged as a rival to Bruce and condemned as a weak, ineffectual
leader opening Scotland to English hegemony.

That propaganda was an important concern of Fordun, Bower,
Wyntoun, Barbour and 'Blind Hary' can be detected in their descriptions
of their heroes and villains. Adulation of Wallace first occurred in
Fordun:

From that time there flocked to him all who were in bitterness
of spirit and were weighed down beneath the burden of bondage
under the unbearable domination of English despotism, and
he became their leader. He was wondrously brave and bold,
of goodly mien, and boundless liberality ... and by dint of his

prowess, brought all the magnates of Scotland under his sway, whether they would or not.[12]

Bower added praise for Wallace:

> ... rightly striving until his death for faithfulness and his native land, a man who never submitted to the English.[13]

Perhaps the most memorable assessment of Wallace was given by Andrew Wyntoun:

> In all England there was not then
> As William Wallace so true a man
> Whatever he did against their nation
> They made him ample provocation
> Nor to them sworn never was he
> To fellowship, faith or loyalty.[14]

This viewpoint received elaboration from 'Blind Hary' who seems to have added to Wallace's achievements some of his own creation. The vilification of Wallace in English chronicles and songs[15] where he is portrayed as 'leader of these savages', 'a robber' and 'an unworthy man', and Wallace's savage death in London have served to heighten Wallace's reputation in Scotland as a hero and a martyr.

Whereas Wallace was a hero in defeat, to fourteenth- and fifteenth-century Scottish writers, Robert Bruce was undoubtedly *the* hero of these narratives from Fordun onwards. Fordun's attitude to Bruce is summed up in the following description:

> ... the English nation lorded it in all parts of the kingdom of Scotland ruthlessly harrying the Scots in sundry and manifold ways ... But God in His mercy, as is the wont of His fatherly goodness, had compassion...; so He raised up a *saviour and champion* unto them – one of their own fellows to wit, named Robert Bruce. The man ... putting forth his hand unto force, underwent the countless and unbearable toils of the heat of the day ... for the sake of freeing his brethren.[16]

The tone was followed by Bower:

> ... whoever has learned to recount his individual conflicts and particular triumphs – the victories and battles in which with the help of the Lord, by his own strength and his energetic valour as

a man, he forced his way through the ranks of the enemy without fear, now powerfully laying them low, now powerfully turning them aside as he avoided the penalty of death – he will find, I think, that he will judge none in the regions of the world to be his equals in his own times in the art of fighting and in physical strength.[17]

Bower himself acknowledged the role of John Barbour's *The Bruce* in chronicling Bruce's achievement in more detail 'with eloquence and brilliance, and with elegance'.[18] Indeed *The Bruce*, which is the most comprehensive life of any medieval king in the west, portrayed Robert Bruce as the hero of an epic poem.

The fourteenth- and fifteenth-century Scottish propagandists regarded the battle of Bannockburn as a fitting climax of a just, indeed a holy, war. Their narratives were heightened by frequent biblical references with the books of the Maccabees holding special relevance to Scotland in the late thirteenth and early fourteenth centuries.[19] The plight of Scotland at the hands of English imperialism was easily compared to that of Israel threatened by its more powerful neighbour, Syria. Thus Walter Bower compared Wallace to Mattathias who initiated the revolt in Israel as dramatically as Wallace led the fight for Scotland's liberty in 1297. Robert Bruce was seen as 'another Maccabeus', i.e. a great captain, by the author of the Declaration of Arbroath (1320).[20]

It is hardly surprising that the language used by fourteenth- and fifteenth-century Scottish chroniclers to describe the rivals or enemies of Bruce and Wallace is appropriate to their heightened views of their heroes. John Balliol, according to Fordun:

... did homage to Edward I, king of England, for the kingdom of Scotland, as he had before promised in his ear, submitting to thraldom unto him for ever.[21]

And

... upon the king of England coming to the aforesaid castle of Montrose, King John, stripped of his kingly ornaments, and holding a white wand in his hand, surrendered up, with staff and baton and resigned into the hands of the king of England all right which he himself had, or might have, to the kingdom of Scotland.[22]

Bower was more forthright, describing the Scottish kingdom as:

... abnormal in the time of this disastrous King John, and after his deposition, severely shaken and torn apart by very great instability and destruction for ten years on end.[23]

Bower details the abject nature of Balliol's surrender in Balliol's letter[24] to the king of England in which Balliol apologised for having 'grievously offended' and admitted that Edward:

... as superior lord duly enfeoffed ... could freely and of right undertake invasion and hostile suppression in this manner since we have denied his homage together with loyalty and fealty.

Again Andrew Wyntoun, perhaps more memorably, echoes Fordun and Bower:

> This Johun the Balliol dispoyilyeide he
> Off al his robis and royalte,
> The pellour that tuk out his tabart,
> Tuyme Tabart he was callit efftirwart
> Amd all othir insignyis
> That fel to kynge on ony wise,
> Bathe septure suerde, crowne and rynge,
> Fra this Johun, that he made Kynge,
> Hallely fra hym, he tuk thar
> And mad hym of his Kynrick bare.[25]

In Fordun and Bower, the criticisms of the Comyns as overmighty subjects start with the first Comyn government during Alexander III's minority:

But these councillors were so many kings. For he who saw the poor crushed down in those days, the nobles ousted from their inheritance, the drudgery forced upon citizens, the violence done to churches, might with good reason say 'Woe unto the kingdom where the king is a boy.'[26]

The Comyn's leading role in the kidnapping of young Alexander III in 1257 was particularly emphasised:

Walter Comyn, earl of Menteith and his accomplices, were more than once summoned before the king and his councillors, upon many grave charges; but they did not appear. But as they durst not await their trial according to the statutes of the kingdom, they

took counsel together, and with one accord, seized the king, by
night, while he was asleep in bed at Kinross, and before dawn,
carried him off with them to Stirling.[27]

The Comyn government was:

... disaffected men who did as they pleased and naught as was
lawful and reigned over the people right or wrong.[28]

Bower added his own moral indignation:

... the Comyns were in the lead among those who rose against
the king: as a consequence their name is now, so to speak,
obliterated in the land, despite the fact that at the time they were
multiplied beyond numbers in the ranks of the magnates of the
kingdom ... Therefore knights and magnates ought to pay greater
attention to the words of the apostle: 'Honour the king'.[29]

At the battle of Falkirk in 1298, the Comyns were blamed by Fordun
for the defeat of Wallace through their desertion:

William was put to flight ... For, on account of the ill-will,
begotten of the spring of envy which the Comyns had conceived
towards the said William, they with their accomplices forsook the
field and escaped unhurt...
... after the aforesaid victory which was vouchsafed to the
enemy through the treachery of Scots, the aforesaid William
Wallace, perceiving by these and other strong proofs, the glaring
wickedness of the Comyns and their abettors...[30]

Both Fordun[31] and Bower accused John Comyn of betraying Robert
Bruce to Edward I after an 'indissoluble treaty of friendship and peace'
had been made between Robert Bruce and Comyn in or shortly after
1304 in order to secure the 'deliverance of the Scottish nation from
the house of bondage and unworthy thraldom'. Instead of co-operation
with Bruce, John Comyn 'talked over Robert's death in earnest – and
shortly determined that he would deprive him of life in the morrow'.
According to Bower, John Comyn had:

... such a strong sense of greed and such a great and culpable
intensity of ambition that he broke his agreement and made null
his oath, meditating how to attack his faithful ally (who suspected
no ill)...

... Once Bruce had been thoroughly destroyed by the tyranny of
the king of England, he would occupy his position and take over
the kingdom which by rights belonged to Bruce and no-one else.
Behold a second Naboth, whose death was engineered so that a
wicked man might gain his vineyard.[32]

Comyn's murder in 1306 by Robert the Bruce in the church of the
friars at Dumfries was seen from a Bruce standpoint by both Fordun
and Bower:

... a day is appointed for him and the aforesaid John to meet
at Dumfries ... John is twitted with his treachery and belied
troth. The lie is at once given. The evil speaker is stabbed, and
wounded unto death, in the church of the Friars...[33]

Bower added that by Comyn's death, 'Edward, king of England, it is
believed, was cheated of his desire both marvellously and wonderfully'.[34]
Comyn's reputation was thus further tarred by emphasising his key role
in Edward I's ambitions in Scotland.

It is recognised by historians that Fordun's and Bower's works were
charged with patriotic fervour and nationalism and that the reputation
of Robert Bruce, also Fordun's hero, 'will always depend on how much
credence we give to Barbour ... we need to remember that for him Bruce
was the hero of a work of art ... His terms of reference forbade him to
write of shortcomings'.[35] The dramatic tale of Bruce's coup of 1306, as
told by the fourteenth- and fifteenth-century writers, is acknowledged
as a 'literary product, the final satisfying version of an originally much
simpler, at least less romantic story'.[36] It is also recognised that Bruce's
chief political rivals in Scotland, the Comyns, have suffered particularly
at the hands of Fordun and others, from 'the *necessity* of giving the
Comyns a bad name in post-Bruce Scotland'.[37]

It is certainly understandable that the history of the century before
Bannockburn was written from the perspective of the winners rather
than the losers. For all the recognition and acknowledgement of bias in
the fourteenth- and fifteenth-century histories, however, it remains true
that the figures of Balliol and Comyn still remain firmly in the shadows
of the traditional heroes Bruce and Wallace. Fordun and Bower, in fact,
echo the official Bruce government attitude to the years 1290 to 1306. It
has been remarked that the absence of references to King John in the
'Acta' of Robert I suggests that 'there seems to have been a pretence that

the Balliol kingship had never existed'.[38] The official Scottish attitude is further developed in the negotiations with the English at Bamburgh in 1321 when 'the whole Balliol episode is thus reduced to the level of malicious English fiction'.[39] It is recognised as misleading that John Balliol 'has gone down in history as Toom Tabard rather than as King John',[40] and a view from the Balliol perspective has at least helped to give more balance to the Bruce-oriented version of the Great Cause of 1291–2. The Bruce version of events, reinforced by later historians, has tended to emphasise the confrontation between Bruce and Balliol as the 'culmination of an ancient rivalry of heroic proportions'.[41] A view from the Balliol standpoint has revealed this as a misleading misrepresentation of the Balliols as there is no evidence to suggest that the Balliols had adopted any stance against the Bruces before 1286. A Balliol perspective also served to highlight their dependence on the political power of the Comyns.[42]

If it is misleading that the history of medieval Scotland has been written from a Bruce perspective rather than a Balliol perspective,[43] it is perhaps an even greater distortion of that history that a Comyn perspective is lacking for the century before Bannockburn. The Comyn family were the most powerful and influential noble family in thirteenth-century Scotland, through both extensive landholding and political office holding. This power was fully apparent by 1240 and was consistently revealed from that date until the murder of John Comyn of Badenoch, the head of the senior line of the family, by Robert Bruce in the church of the Greyfriars, Dumfries in 1306.[44] From a baronial standpoint, the Comyns rather than the English were the biggest losers at Bannockburn in 1314. Bruce's actions led to the demise of the Comyn family in Scottish politics between 1306 and 1314; the Bruce-oriented version of the century before Bannockburn has almost succeeded in writing them out of Scottish history. It has certainly given the family a one-dimensional character as traitorous rivals to the Bruces. According to Bower, the Comyns fell from power because of their actions against Scottish kingship, especially as leaders in the kidnapping of Alexander III in 1257, and 'as a consequence their name is now, so to speak, obliterated in the land'.[45] In fact, Bower and other proponents of the Bruce version of Scottish history have contributed significantly to the demise of the Comyn name.

The Comyns have suffered more than others from the problems and prejudices militating against a balanced view of the nobility in the century before Bannockburn. They have suffered from the monarchocentric writings of the fourteenth and fifteenth centuries which have placed them in the shadow both of Alexander III's 'Golden Age' and also of the Bruce and Wallace traditions. A monarchocentric viewpoint serves to highlight the role of the nobility as unprincipled aggressors and overmighty subjects in political crisis periods. The Comyns played a prominent part in both the minority of Alexander III, 1249–1260, and the long political crisis following Alexander III's death in 1286. The fact that both crises led to English intervention and indeed to the outbreak of war with England in the latter case has led to nationalist sentiments clouding commentary on the century before Bannockburn in general and the years 1290 to 1314 in particular.

A baronial standpoint is needed to balance the monarchocentric writings of Fordun, Bower, Barbour and Wyntoun; a Comyn perspective is needed to balance the Bruce-oriented version of the century before Bannockburn; a viewpoint from the thirteenth century is needed to counteract the political bias and nationalism of fourteenth- and fifteenth-century commentaries.

The inadequacy and inconsistency of the monarchocentric approach to Scottish politics is revealed in Fordun's attitude to Walter Comyn in 1249 and 1257. In 1249, Walter Comyn, earl of Menteith is portrayed as 'a man of foresight and shrewdness of counsel'[46] and praised for his strong support of Alexander III's kingship:

> ... he went on to say that a country without a king was, beyond doubt, like a ship amid the waves of the sea, without rower or steersman ... he moved that this boy be raised to the throne as quickly as possible.[47]

Yet in 1257, Walter Comyn and his accomplices in the kidnapping of Alexander were 'disaffected men, who did all as they pleased and nought as was lawful, and reigned over the people, right or wrong'.[48] Traditional accounts of the century before Bannockburn leave a lot of questions to be answered about the role of the nobility, but a view from the standpoint of the most powerful thirteenth-century baronial family, the Comyns, should contribute substantially to the debate. What was the relationship between the Comyns and William Wallace in their support of John Balliol's kingship? What was the Comyn perspective on the rise of the Bruces in the late thirteenth century and when did their rivalry start? What was the relationship between the Comyns and the Scottish kings in the century before Bannockburn? What was the relationship between the

Comyns and the English kings in the same period? The Comyns did not have the equivalent of John Barbour for Robert Bruce and Blind Hary for William Wallace to praise their actions. Yet some chronicles did take a more favourable view of Comyn activities than Fordun, Bower and their fourteenth- and fifteenth-century contemporaries. Thus the pro-Comyn *Melrose Chronicle* can help to balance anti-Comyn writings for Alexander III's reign; the *Chronicles of Lanercost* and *Guisborough* as well as Thomas Gray's *Scalacronica* give some balance to the period 1286 to 1314.

The century before Bannockburn saw very significant political developments in Scotland – the definition of the kingdom, the development of kingship and the constitution, the growth of national consciousness and the idea of the community of the realm. Yet the Comyn family's political power in this period was such that the thirteenth century has been called the 'Comyn century'.[49] An investigation into the Comyns' contribution to this most formative period is long overdue. A Comyn perspective is necessary to test the Bruce-oriented version of thirteenth-century Scottish history and the Comyns' traditional role in it as traitorous rivals to Robert Bruce.

NOTES

1. G.G. Simpson, 'Why was John Balliol called 'Toom Tabard?', *Scottish Historical Review* (hence *S.H.R.*) XLVII (1968), pp.196–9.
2. John of Fordun, *Chronica Gentis Scotorum*, ed. W.F. Skene (Edinburgh, 1871–2) (henceforth *Chron. Fordun*).
3. *Chron. Fordun* I p.309 (II p.304).
4. *Scotichronicon by Walter Bower* (General Editor D.E.R. Watt) (henceforth *Chron. Bower* (Watt), Vol. V, ed. Simon Taylor, D.E.R. Watt and Brian Scott (Aberdeen, 1990). Vol. VI, ed. Norman F. Shead, Wendy Stevenson and D.E.R. Watt with Alan Borthwick, R.E. Latham, J.R.S. Phillips and the late Martin S. Smith (Aberdeen, 1991).
5. *The Oryginale Cronykil of Scotland by Andrew of Wyntoun*, ed. D. Laing (Edinburgh, 1879) (henceforth *Chron. Wyntoun* (Laing).
6. A useful survey of these writers is contained in Norman H. Reid, 'Alexander III: The Historiography of a Myth', in *Scotland in the Reign of Alexander III 1249–1286*, ed. Norman H. Reid (Edinburgh 1990), pp.186–94.
7. *Chron. Fordun* I p.310 (II p.304).
8. *Chron. Bower* (Watt), V p.423.
9. *Ibid.* p.427.
10. J. Barbour, *The Bruce*, ed. W.M. Mackenzie (London, 1909).
11. Blind Hary, *The Wallace*, ed. M.P. McDiarmid (2 vols.) (Edinburgh, 1968).
12. *Chron. Fordun* I p.328 (II p.321).

13. *Chron. Bower* (Watt), VI p.317.
14. Cited in A. Fisher, *William Wallace* (1986), p.132.
15. Peter Coss (ed.), *Thomas Wright's Political Songs of England* (1996), pp.160–180.
16. *Chron. Fordun* I p.137 (II p.330). The italics are my own.
17. *Chron. Bower* (Watt), VI p.319.
18. *Ibid.*
19. G.W.S. Barrow, 'The Idea of Freedom in Late Medieval Scotland', in *Scotland and its Neighbours* (1992), p.19.
20. A.A.M. Duncan, *The Nation of Scots and the Declaration of Arbroath (1320)*, Historical Association, General Series no. 75 (1970), p.35; also *Chron. Bower* (Watt), VI p.301.
21. *Chron. Fordun* I p.321 (II p.315).
22. *Ibid.* I pp.32, 6–7 (II p.320).
23. *Chron. Bower* (Watt), VI p.53.
24. *Ibid.* VI P.79.
25. *Chron. Wyntoun* (Laing), II p.337.
26. *Chron. Fordun* I p.297 (II p.292.)
27. *Ibid.* I p.298 (293).
28. *Ibid.*
29. *Chron. Bower* (Watt), V p.323.
30. *Chron. Fordun* I p.330 (II p.323.
31. *Ibid.* I p. 338–9 (II pp.330–1).
32. *Chron. Bower* (Watt), VI p.305.
33. *Chron. Fordun* I p.340 (II p.333).
34. *Chron. Bower* (Watt), VI p.313.
35. G.W.S. Barrow, *Robert Bruce* (3rd edition, Edinburgh 1988), pp. 312–13 (henceforth Barrow, *Bruce*).
36. *Ibid.* p.140.
37. *Ibid.* (my italics), p.140.
38. N.H. Reid, 'Crown and Community under Robert I', in *Medieval Scotland, Crown, Lordship and Community* (*Essays Presented to G.W.S. Barrow*), eds. Alexander Grant and Keith J. Stringer (Edinburgh, 1993), p. 204.
39. *Ibid.* p.205.
40. R. Nicholson, *Scotland, the Later Middle Ages* (1974), p.44.
41. G. Stell, 'The Balliol Family and the Great Cause of 1291–2', in *Essays on the Nobility of Medieval Scotland*, ed. K.J. Stringer (Edinburgh, 1985), p.151; Barrow, *Bruce* Ch.3, 'Bruce *versus* Balliol'; G. Neilson, 'Bruce *versus* Balliol 1291–2), *S.H.R.* XVI (1919), pp.1–14.
42. G. Stell, 'The Balliol Family and the Great Cause of 1291–2, p.151.
43. R. Nicholson, *Scotland, the Later Middle Ages*, p.44.
44. A. Young, 'The Political Role of Walter Comyn, Earl of Menteith, During the Minority of Alexander III of Scotland', in *Essays on the Nobility of Medieval Scotland*, ed. K.J. Stringer, p.132; A. Young, 'Noble Families and Political Factions',

in *Scotland in the Reign of Alexander III* 1249–1286, ed. N.H. Reid, pp.8–10, 23–4; A. Young, 'The Earls and Earldom of Buchan in the Thirteenth Century', in *Medieval Scotland: Crown, Lordship and Community*, eds. Alexander Grant and Keith J. Stringer, pp.174, 198.

45. *Chron. Bower* (Watt), V p.323.
46. *Chron. Fordun* I p.293 (II p.289).
47. *Ibid.*
48. *Ibid.* I p.298 (II p.293). The discrepancy may be caused by Fordun taking material from a pro-Comyn source as well as an anti-Comyn one.
49. Grant G. Simpson, 'Kingship in Miniature: A Seal of Minority of Alexander III, 1249–1257, in *Medieval Scotland: Crown, Lordship and Community*, eds. Alexander Grant and Keith J. Stringer, p.131.

CHAPTER TWO

The Foundation
for the 'Comyn Century'

The depth of the rivalry between Comyns and Bruces can be gauged by the severity of Bruce's 'herschip' or harrying of the Comyn base of Buchan in 1308.[1] Without the destruction of this power base in the north, Robert Bruce's kingship over Scotland as a whole could not be a reality. The 'herschip' of Buchan and the still impressive visible symbols of Comyn lordship in Badenoch and Lochaber, especially the castles of Inverlochy and Lochindorb, might give the impression that the Comyns were an exclusively Highland and northern Scottish power in the late thirteenth and early fourteenth centuries. Yet Robert Bruce's infamous murder in 1306 of his great rival, John Comyn, head of the senior Badenoch branch of the family, took place in the Greyfriars' church, Dumfries, close to the important southern Comyn base at Dalswinton in Nithsdale. This hints at a rather broader basis to Comyn power. The process of dismemberment and redistribution of Comyn estates in the years after 1308 amply confirms that, while the greatest concentration of Comyn landed power was in the north, their territorial strength and influence was, indeed, wide-ranging, extending into almost every part of Scotland.

The foundation for this pervasive power had been laid by 1212 with significant further consolidation occurring in the 1220s and 1230s. To understand not only the full extent of Comyn power but also its nature and why it led to a 'Comyn century' of influence in Scottish history from c.1212 to 1314, it is necessary to analyse the establishment of the Comyn power base.

In the first half of the twelfth century, the Comyns were in the vanguard of the Anglo-Norman 'invasion' of the Scottish royal household.

This process was actively encouraged by David I, a 'Scot by birth, a Norman by adoption',[2] throughout his reign, 1124 to 1153. William Cumin (Comyn), the first member of the family to make an impact in Scotland,[3] was chancellor of Scotland from c.1136. He had been a clerk in the English chancery of Henry I from c.1121, being a protégé and pupil of Geoffrey Rufus who became chancellor of England in 1123. Rufus became bishop of Durham in 1133 and it is possible that Cumin followed his mentor to Durham though he was already by this time archdeacon of Worcester. The Comyns, unlike the Bruces, Morevilles and other members of the 'new aristocracy' in Scotland, were not noble families in origin with substantial estates in Normandy or northern France. It is probable, in fact, that William Cumin belonged to one of the families of clerks which originated from cathedral towns such as Bayeux and Rouen.[4] From this relatively obscure clerical and ecclesiastical base, William Cumin sought to secure the family's secular fortunes in Scotland through his nephews who were already well established in the Scottish royal court by 1140.[5] The alliance of mutual self-interest between William Cumin and the Scottish monarchy was to become a typical feature in the rise of the Comyns. William Cumin participated in David I's invasion of northern England in 1138 and was captured when the Scottish army was defeated at the battle of the Standard near Northallerton.[6] On his part, David I gave full support initially when William Cumin attempted to gain the bishopric of Durham following the death of his mentor, Geoffrey Rufus, in 1141.[7]

In 1144, Cumin was forced to relinquish his claim to the bishopric of Durham after three years of hard fighting during which Cumin's favourite nephew, another William, died. Cumin's loyalty to the Angevin cause in the English civil war enabled him to return to southern England and regain the archdeaconry of Worcester by 1155.[8] Yet the family's social climbing in Scotland continued after 1144 through William's remaining nephew Richard who benefited from the patronage of King David and especially his son, Earl Henry, to become the real founder of the Comyn family's landed fortunes. Between 1144 and 1152 David and Earl Henry, acknowledged at this time as exercising general control over England north of the Tees, granted to Richard Cumin the important lands of Walwick, Thornton, Staincroft and Henshaw in Tynedale (south-west Northumberland, west of Hexham) on marriage to Hextilda, daughter to Uhtred, Waltheof's son.[9] These lands, the first secular base of the Comyn family, were confirmed in Comyn possession by Henry II and

Henry III[10] and remained in Comyn hands until their political eclipse in the early fourteenth century. The lands were not simply a direct grant from the Scottish king but a gift on marriage to Hextilda, from a leading Northumbrian landowning family. This marriage, the first of many 'good' marriages in the family's rise to power, was ultimately of more significance than the Tynedale land initially gained. It not only provided Richard Cumin with a valuable alliance with an important Northumbrian family but gained for that family, through Hextilda, a connection with Scottish landholding and the old Scottish princes. Hextilda was the daughter of Uhtred of Tynedale and Bethoc, only daughter of Donald Ban, brother of Malcolm Canmore and son of Duncan I, king of Scots.[11] The fact that Hextilda was Donald Ban's granddaughter gave Richard Cumin's descendants a legitimate, if not the strongest possible, claim to the Scottish throne. Richard was, therefore, not only the founder of the secular fortunes of the Comyn family but also of the claim of his great-great-grandson, John Comyn the Competitor, to the Scottish throne during the 'Great Cause' 1291–1292.

Just as his uncle, William Cumin, had been in the vanguard of the Anglo-Norman invasion of the Scottish royal household, Richard Cumin (d.1179) became a leading member of the 'new' Scottish aristocracy as he was at the forefront of the Anglo-Norman social invasion of Scottish landholding. The first Scottish lands on record as being granted to Richard Cumin by the Scottish royal house were those of West Linton in Peeblesshire, granted sometime before 1152 by David's son, Earl Henry.[12] Subsequent grants define Richard's lands more thoroughly,[13] indicating that by 1152 he possessed a substantial area of land in north-west Peeblesshire. Richard's marriage with Hextilda also led to the family possessing the important lordship of Bedrule (Roxburghshire) which was certainly in the possession of the Comyn family before 1280.[14] The land of Bedrule or Rulebethoc derived its name from 'the lands on the river Rule of Bethoc' wife of Radulf, the son of Dunegall lord of Nithsdale. This Bethoc was the mother of Hextilda, wife of Richard Cumin. The lands on the River Rule were Bethoc's rather than Radulf's and it seems that Radulf was Bethoc's second husband. Bethoc predeceased Radulf (d. c.1185) – there is no evidence of Radulf succeeding to Bedrule – and Richard Cumin, through his wife Hextilda, seems to have succeeded to Bedrule on Bethoc's death, probably between c.1150 and 1170.

Another lordship in Roxburghshire, Scraesburgh (alias Hunthill), was in Comyn possession in the late thirteenth century[15] but in this case there is no evidence linking Scraesburgh with Richard Cumin and it seems probable that Scraesburgh passed into Comyn hands some time later, perhaps in the early thirteenth century. There is plenty of indirect evidence showing Richard Cumin's significance as a landowner in Roxburghshire. The witness lists to his charters were dominated by either churchmen or other landowners from Roxburghshire.[16] It is also significant that Richard's son John, and his lord, Earl Henry, were buried at Kelso abbey before 1152.[17] Richard Cumin's marriage to Hextilda was most significant for the expansion of the Comyn family's landholding in Roxburghshire and it seems probable that the family's possession of Dalswinton in Nithsdale – certainly held by Richard's descendants before 1250[18] – may also have derived from this source.[19] Radulf son of Dunegal (second husband of Bethoc, mother of Hextilda) had been lord of Nithsdale and probably at the same time lord of Dumfries. He died c.1185, however, and if his land did pass to the Comyn family, it was after Richard Cumin had died.

By the 1160s Richard Cumin was a landowner of importance in northern England and, perhaps more significantly for the future of the Comyn family, had a firm footing in southern Scotland. His landed wealth and priorities are well represented in endowments to religious houses in both northern England and southern Scotland.[20] Hexham priory and the abbeys of Rievaulx, Kelso and Holyrood all received gifts but it is clear that Hexham priory and Kelso abbey held special favour. The fact that Richard's son John was buried at Kelso abbey along with Richard's lord, Earl Henry, signifies both the importance of his southern Scottish holding and also the significance of Scottish royal patronage. Complementary to this patronage was royal service. Richard Cumin was, by his death c.1179, a counsellor of long experience to the Scottish monarchy. He is known to have witnessed at least six charters of Malcolm IV,[21] the earliest one being 1159, and thirty-three charters of William the Lion.[22]

The frequency and prominence of Richard's appearances at the royal court demonstrated his increasing importance to the Scottish monarchy. This was more tangibly demonstrated by William the Lion's bestowal of the office of justiciar of Lothian on Richard Cumin in the 1170s.[23] The office was an important one, the justiciar being the leading judicial officer of the crown in his area and an increasingly significant administrative adviser to the king.[24] The role of justiciar before 1200 was probably similar to that described in the treatise on the Scottish king's household c.1292: the justiciar was to dispense justice evenly to all the king's subjects and to determine all crown pleas except the most solemn or difficult ones, and there were to be three justiciars, i.e. for Scotia, Lothian and Galloway. Richard Cumin appeared in witness lists as justiciar between 1173 and 1178 but it is impossible to be precise about his period of office as charter clerks often failed to give the title of 'justiciar' to a man holding office. It is difficult to say whether he held the office for a brief term or shared the duties of justiciar with Robert de Quinci, Robert Avenel, Walter Olifard and Geoffrey de Melville between 1173 and 1178.[25] However, as four men – Richard Cumin, Robert de Quinci, Robert Avenel and Geoffrey de Melville – witnessed a number of royal acts dealing with Scotland south of the forth between c.1170 and c.1178, it seems at least possible to assign to them, either in succession or simultaneously, the justiciarship of Lothian.

Richard Cumin's position as justiciar can be seen as both a cause and result of his importance in southern Scotland. It was usual for justiciars to be either important barons or at least important landowners before gaining office[26] – Richard Cumin, with his lands in Peeblesshire and Roxburghshire, easily came into the latter category. The office can also be seen as increasing the prestige of Richard Cumin and linking his family more firmly to Scottish royal interests. In 1174, for example, Richard Cumin was in close attendance on William the Lion when the Scottish king furthered his claim to the English northern counties. Richard was prominent in the list of attendant knights with the king when he was surprised and captured while besieging Alnwick.[27] He was, indeed, regarded as of sufficient importance to be one of the hostages for the performance of the Treaty of Falaise (December 1174) whereby William the Lion became Henry II's liegeman for Scotland and for all his other lands.[28] Richard Cumin closely identified himself with the Scottish king's interests in 1174 in much the same way as his uncle, William Cumin, the king's chancellor, had in actively supporting David I's invasion of northern England in 1138. A further link between the Comyns and the Scottish Crown can perhaps be seen in the reference in 1179 to Richard Cumin having a hunting station in Selkirkshire. It seems possible that Richard held the office of keeper of the royal forest.[29]

Both Comyns and Bruces were part of the new aristocracy 'of royal service' in twelfth-century Scotland. The Bruces, through Robert I de

Bruce, were granted the lordship of Annandale by David I as early as 1124 but the family had already become established as lords of Cleveland in north Yorkshire and had served Henry I as justice, i.e. chief royal agent, in northern England.[30] The problem of personal allegiance to competing kings was exposed in 1138 at the Battle of the Standard, near Northallerton, when Robert de Bruce, lord of Cleveland, fought on the side of Thurstan archbishop of York against a Scottish invasion force led by David I and including Bruce's son, Robert de Bruce of Annandale.[31] The Comyns, by contrast, did not receive their first landed grants in Scotland until between 1144 and 1152. Although part of the same 'new' aristocracy in Scotland, Comyns were very dependent on the Scottish monarchy for their empire-building whereas the Bruces, because of their fairly well developed links in England, were perhaps the least dependent of the new knightly families in Scotland. This was shown in 1173–74 when Robert de Bruce II of Annandale supported Henry II against William the Lion's invasion of northern England.[32]

Under Richard Cumin's heir, William Cumin (Comyn), the impetus of the family's growth in landed power and influence increased at the same rate as William's involvement in the administrative and judicial affairs of the kingdom. The natural emphasis on the Comyns becoming the first Anglo-Norman earls in Scotland on the marriage of William Comyn to Marjorie, heiress of the earl of Buchan, in 1212 has tended to detract from the consolidation of Comyn power in the south before that date. William Comyn had inherited lands in Tynedale and Peeblesshire but had substantially improved upon his inheritance before 1212. He was granted c.1200 the lordship of Lenzie (to the north of Glasgow) by William the Lion for the service of one knight,[33] the first instance on record of a royal grant to a member of the Comyn family for a specifically stated military service. The charter is significant in that it reflected the divergence between Scottish and English feudal practice. In England, the king often gave out sizeable estates in return for the service of scores of knights, whereas in Scotland the king mainly granted out land in return for a single knight's fee. Nevertheless, the man who held land in Scotland for only one knight's fee had an equivalent status in society to the man who held land in England for many knights' fees. By c.1200, William Comyn was clearly recognised as one of the king's major barons. It is also clear that William Comyn was lord of Kirkintilloch[34] (also north of Glasgow) as well as Lenzie by c.1200, indicating an important northerly expansion of the family's landed interests. The Comyn lordship of

Kirkintilloch was further strengthened by William the Lion's grant, of 2nd October 1211, to William Comyn and his heirs of the right to have a burgh at Kirkintilloch and a market every Thursday.[35] This was yet another important royal privilege for the family and, incidentally, the earliest surviving charter grant of a baronial burgh. It is perhaps the simplest form of burghal privilege on record.

To add further weight to growing Comyn landed interests in the Glasgow area, it is apparent that William Comyn also held an important area of land south of Glasgow – in Machan (in the Clyde valley) and around Lesmahagow. The lands of Machan are only known for certain to have belonged to John Comyn of Badenoch (d.1306) as they were forfeited to Robert Bruce (Robert I) and then redistributed to Walter fitz Gilbert in the early fourteenth century.[36] The fact that Machan was in Comyn hands, however, in William Comyn's time is indicated by a dispute between William and the abbot of Kelso which was settled c.1189×1193.[37]

William Comyn's increasing status in Scotland and at the Scottish court was also apparent before 1212. He was a frequent witness to royal charters[38] – from his first appearance in 1178 he witnessed eighty-eight charters of William the Lion, many of them being in the 1190s when his position in these lists showed a growing prominence. It is probable that he had been made sheriff of Forfar by c.1190. He was certainly sheriff by 1213[39] but his period of office is uncertain as there is a great gap in the records for this sheriffdom between c.1161 and c.1211. It is, however, possible to draw conclusions from the evidence of witness lists. Between c.1180 and c.1211 William Comyn witnessed at least twenty-six charters at Forfar, Montrose and Arbroath with the vast majority at Forfar. Most of these charters dated from c.1195 to c.1211[40] and it is perhaps reasonable to suggest that he was sheriff of Forfar in these years and perhaps even earlier. It was by no means unusual for sheriffs not to be given that title when witnessing charters in their own sheriffdoms.

The office of sheriff was an important royal appointment.[41] He was the right hand of the king in the localities and his duties were all embracing, encompassing military, financial, judicial and administrative affairs. The sheriff, therefore, played a crucial role in the king's attempt to define and control the country. William Comyn was fairly typical of the Scottish sheriff in the late twelfth and early thirteenth centuries; like the majority of sheriffs in this period, he was a Norman, a substantial landowner and a royal servant. Other sheriffs of baronial or knightly status included John son of Orm and Walter Corbet (Roxburgh), Alexander of St Martin (Haddington) and William Freskin II (Nairn). Although there was a tendency for sheriffdoms to become hereditary in the early thirteenth century, Forfar did not pass to any of William Comyn's sons and heirs.

William Comyn's status at the royal court was further demonstrated between 1199 and 1200 when, along with the abbot of Arbroath and William Giffard, he was sent as one of the king's messengers on a friendly mission to King John of England soon after his accession to the English throne.[42] The apparent purpose of this mission was to arrange for the Scottish king's visit to London and his safe conduct in England over which matter a misunderstanding had taken place. William Comyn's role as trusted royal servant entered a new level, however, when he was promoted to the office of justiciar of Scotia, i.e. the area north of the Forth, c.1205.[43] This office, the premier justiciarship in Scotland, represented the most senior royal administrative office in the north.[44] Promotion to this office was both a natural extension of the royal service shown by William Comyn in his role as sheriff of Forfar as well as a continuation of the Comyn family's association with the office of justiciar – William's father, Richard, had been justiciar of Lothian. William Comyn's promotion to the justiciarship of Scotia c.1205 was the first major sign of a deliberate royal policy to involve the family in the consolidation of royal authority in the north. The justiciarship was the 'most significant bridge between the king's court and the localities'.[45] It is a remarkable testimony to the family's role as pillars of the Scottish monarchy that the Comyns were justiciars of Scotia for no fewer than 66 of the 100 years between c.1205 and 1304.[46]

Undoubtedly, William Comyn's status after 1205 is reflected in his increased prominence in royal witness lists. He also played an important role in the treaty of peace between King John and William the Lion in 1209.[47] According to the Liber Pluscardensis,[48] this treaty occurred after John demanded satisfaction from King William for once more advancing Scottish claims to the English northern counties. In order that the terms of the treaty might be fulfilled, two knights were chosen on behalf of the two kings and charged with the duty of taking an oath on the agreement with their hands on the Holy Gospel by the souls of the two kings. William Comyn, justiciar of Scotia, swore on behalf of William the Lion. As part of the terms of the treaty, thirteen hostages were delivered into the hands of the English king's councillors at Carlisle. One of these hostages was a son of William Comyn, probably either Richard or Walter, the two elder sons.

In his capacity as justiciar, William Comyn was probably in charge of the operation between 1211 and 1212 to suppress the rebellion of Guthred son of Donald Macwilliam who landed in Ross in January 1211 to lead a rebellion through Ross and Moray.[49] Moray had proved to be a consistently difficult region to control throughout the twelfth century. Despite the planned settlement of Moray in David I's time, Highland rebellions continued to be a danger to the throne as well as to all royal attempts to define and consolidate Crown authority in the north. Donald Macwilliam claimed the throne from the 1160s until 1187 and rebellions, in fact, continued until 1230. The rebellion of 1211 was met by a large royal army of 4,000 men who were sent into Ross under the leadership of William Comyn, the earl of Atholl, and representatives of the two families claiming the earldom of Mar, Malcolm son of Morgrund and Thomas Durward. Bower's description of William Comyn as 'warden of Moray' seems to indicate that Comyn was given this office on a short-term, temporary basis. The expedition under Comyn's leadership was successful and Guthred Macwilliam was captured, but it is clear from William the Lion's actions that the rebellion was treated very seriously as it had some support from the nobility in the north. William the Lion himself came north to Moray to make a treaty of peace with the earl of Caithness whose daughter he took as hostage. More importantly for the Comyn family, King William reacted to the events of 1211–12 by reviewing completely royal policy in the north, looking for new ways to reinforce it more effectively.

Professor Barrow has remarked that lack of royal demesne in the north of Scotland meant that William the Lion was 'conspicuously absent'[50] from this region. Despite the establishment of some sheriffdoms in northern Scotland,[51] royal presence in the north and north-east was still in need of bolstering in 1212. William Comyn's elevation to the earldom of Buchan c.1212 on marriage, his second, to Marjorie, the only child and heiress of Fergus earl of Buchan, was significant for a number of reasons. The marriage meant that William Comyn became the first 'Norman' earl of Buchan; he became, in fact, the first 'Norman' earl in Scotland. The marriage was of great importance, therefore, for social and institutional reasons. By 1286 only five earldoms were in the hands of families of Anglo-Continental origin[52] – by comparison with the Comyns, the Umphravilles did not acquire the earldom of

Angus until 1243 and the Bruces did not gain the earldom of Carrick until 1272. The marriage was perhaps of even greater importance for its political impact – for both the Comyns and for Buchan. Given the political circumstances of 1211–12 in the north, it seemed to provide further evidence of a royal intention to use the Comyn family (and Buchan) to represent royal interests in the north. It was more than a little convenient for the crown to introduce a powerful royal agent, his justiciar, into the north-east next to areas of uncertain loyalty and establish him hereditarily in the earldom of Buchan. The exact date of William Comyn's elevation to the earldom is uncertain[53] but it is possible to see his marriage to the heiress of Buchan as reward for his efforts against the Macwilliam rebels in Ross and Moray in 1211–12. As earl of Buchan and consequently one of the most powerful landowners in northern Scotland, William Comyn was well placed to counter any other threats from those areas.

By 1212, the Comyns had real power – the Comyn century had begun! To the already sizeable possessions accumulated by Richard and William Comyn before 1212 – principally the lordships of Kirkintilloch and Lenzie plus Machan (in the Glasgow area); West Linton (Peeblesshire); Bedrule (Roxburghshire); Dalswinton (Dumfriesshire) and important lands in Tynedale – William Comyn in 1212 added practically the whole of Buchan, a vast area in north-eastern Scotland. The extent of William Comyn's newly acquired landed wealth in Buchan is reflected in the charters of Fergus, last Celtic earl of Buchan, William Comyn and his wife Marjorie. A charter of Earl Fergus mentioned his court at Ellon, evidently the caput of the earldom.[54] Other land referred to as being in Earl William's possession[55] included Slains and Cruden (on the south-east coast of Buchan); Fechil (in Ellon parish); Tarves (west of Ellon); Old Meldrum (south-west of Tarves); Rattray (on the coast between Peterhead and Fraserburgh); Strichen (inland west of Rattray); Deer (south of Strichen) and Turriff (west of Deer). A fuller picture of the extent of the earldom of Buchan as it developed in the thirteenth century with its organisation around key castle sites can be obtained (see Map 2) by examining later thirteenth-century charters supplemented by using later material, dating from and after Robert I's dismemberment of the earldom.[56] This evidence will be explored when the Comyns' political power in the crisis years at the end of the thirteenth century is examined.[57]

The landed possessions of William Comyn as earl of Buchan were

This page gives details of the Comyn earls' lands, in sections, listing the probable demesnes of the earldom (with National Grid references), derived from the lands which were component parts of the new fourteenth-century baronies; Map 2 shows these lands and also feudal and ecclesiastical tenancies.

I. Probable Demesnes of the Earldom of Buchan

	ABERDOUR/Dundarg	NJ8964		KELLY	NJ8634
A1	Ardlaw	NJ9363	Ky1	Asleid	NJ8441
A2	Auchlin	NJ9163	Ky2	Auchmaliddie	NJ8844
A3	Auchmacleddie	NJ9257	Ky3	Auchnagatt	NJ9341
A4	Bodychell mill	NJ9562	Ky4	Barrack	NK8941
A5	Coburty	NJ9264	Ky5	Cairngall	NK0447
A6	Drumwhindle (Little)	NJ9236	Ky6	Gonarhall	NJ8658
A7	Glasslaw	NJ8559	Ky7	Knaven	NJ8943
A8	Memsie	NJ9761	Ky8	Logierieve	NJ9127
A9	Pitsligo	NJ9367	Ky9	Newburgh	NJ9925
A10	Pittulie	NJ9567	Ky10	Saithlie	NJ9756
A11	Quilquox	NJ9038	Ky11	Tillydeak	NJ9536
A12	Rathen	NK0060			
	KINGEDWARD	NJ7256		**PHILORTH**	NK0063
K1	Byth	NJ8156	P1	Ardglassie	NK0161
K2	Castleton	NJ7156	P2	Ardmachron	NJ9861
K3	Faithlie	NJ9967	P3	Ashogle	NJ7092
K4	Fishry	NJ7658	P4	Auchentumb	NJ9258
K5	Fortrie	NJ7359	P5	Auchmacleddie	NJ9257
K6	Kinharrachie	NJ9231	P6	Balchers	NJ7158
K7	Scattertie	NJ6957	P7	Blackton	NJ7257
K8	Tyrie (Easter)	NJ9363	P8	Bracklawmore	NJ8458
			P9	Brakans	NJ7553
			P10	Cairnbulg	NK0163
			P11	Cairneywhing	NJ8757
	RATTRAY	NK0858	P12	Delgatie	NJ7550
R1	Cairnglass	NK0462	P13	Drumwhindle	NJ9236
R2	Crimond	NK0557	P14	Fintry	NJ7554
R3	'Crimondbell' [Bilbo?]	NK0656	P15	Inverallochy	NK0462
R4	Crimongorth	NK0455	P16	Kinbog	NJ9962
R5	'Rothnathie'[1]	NK0360	P17	Kinglasser	NJ9963
R6	Tullikera	NK0259	P18	Luncarty	NJ7153
	'Kindolos'	unidentified	P19	Plaidy	NJ7254

1   'Rothnathie' is not on the modern map, but is on that of Gordon of Straloch (1580–1661).

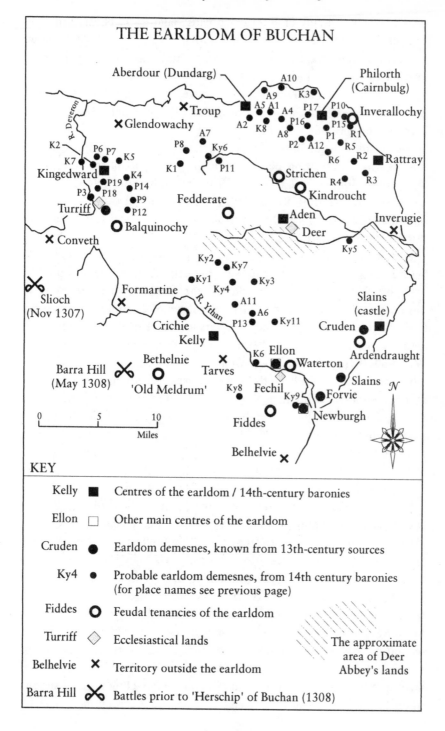

THE EARLDOM OF BUCHAN

Aberdour (Dundarg)

Philorth (Cairnbulg)

A10

✗ Troup
A9   K3
A5 A1
A2   A4   P17   P10
K8   A8   P16   P15   Inverallochy

✗ Glendowachy
A7

K2
P6 P7
K5
P8   Ky6
P2   A12   R5
R1

K7
K1   P11
P1   R6   R2   ✗ Rattray

Kingedward
K4
P19   P14
Strichen   R4   R3

P3   P18
P9   Kindroucht

Turriff
P12   Fedderate

Balquinochy
Aden
Deer   Inverugie

✗ Conveth
Ky5

Ky2   Ky7

Ky1   Ky3
Formartine   Ky4

✗ Slioch
(Nov 1307)   ✗
A11   Slains
(castle)

Crichie   P13   A6   Ky11

Kelly   Cruden

Ardendraught

Bethelnie   K6   Ellon
Barra Hill   ✗   Tarves   Waterton
(May 1308)   'Old Meldrum'   Ky8   Fechil   Slains   𝒩
Ky9   Forvie

0   5   10
Fiddes   Newburgh

Miles

Belhelvie ✗

KEY

Kelly	■	Centres of the earldom / 14th-century baronies
Ellon	□	Other main centres of the earldom
Cruden	●	Earldom demesnes, known from 13th-century sources
Ky4	•	Probable earldom demesnes, from 14th century baronies (for place names see previous page)
Fiddes	○	Feudal tenancies of the earldom
Turriff	◇	Ecclesiastical lands
Belhelvie	✗	Territory outside the earldom
Barra Hill	✂	Battles prior to 'Herschip' of Buchan (1308)

The approximate area of Deer Abbey's lands

not, however, limited to Buchan. The Comyn earls of Buchan held considerable lands elsewhere. Earl William had, for instance, landed interests in Strathisla (Banffshire), about ten miles west of Kingedward.[58] Further to the west he also held a small piece of land in the town of 'Dunbernyn' (probably Dumbennan) just west of Huntly in Strathbogie.[59] Earl William also had property to the south of Buchan in or near the Durward barony of Coull, in Mar.[60] It is apparent that William's wife Marjorie and presumably her father, Earl Fergus, held Fordoun, in the Mearns,[61] indicating perhaps that they had part of the thanage of Kincardine. South of the Tay, Earl William and his wife held substantial lands in Fife including Kennoway, Kilrenny, Fithkil (now Leslie) and Balmullo (Leuchars) which had probably come to the Celtic earls of Buchan through Earl Colban.[62]

Despite extensive land ownership in other parts of Scotland both before 1212 and after, 1212 perhaps sees the beginning of a natural process whereby William Comyn transferred the centre of his attentions to the north-east. This is reflected in a charter of excambion[63] whereby Earl William exchanged land in Gartshore in Kirkintilloch for some land in the town of Dumbennan, just west of Huntly. After 1212, William's Tynedale lands were passed to his son and heir Richard. The importance of these lands, however, was still apparent in 1221 when Henry III granted William an important privilege, a weekly market at his manor of Thornton, perhaps indicating the foundation of Newbrough as a borough.[64] Perhaps more visibly, William Comyn's new status in the north of Scotland was marked by his foundation of the Cistercian house of Deer in 1219.[65] Unfortunately, the foundation charter is not known to exist (it was probably destroyed in the 'Harrying' of Buchan by Bruce in 1308) but it apparently conveyed to the brethren the churches of Deer and Inverugie St Peter (or Peterhead).[66] The abbey was, subsequently, liberally endowed with large areas of land. In Buchan also, Earl William endowed the chapel of the Blessed Virgin Mary in Rattray with two stones of wax annually.[67] Undoubtedly, Earl William had become a magnate of the first order in 1212. His prominence in royal service, which had gained him recognition and reward in 1205 and 1212, was further evidenced after 1212. He witnessed many royal charters in first or second place,[68] and the number of charters witnessed suggests he was in almost constant attendance at the royal court at Edinburgh, Perth, Forfar, Stirling, Scone, Fyvie, Cluny, Elgin, Clackmannan, Dundee, Linlithgow, Aberdeen, Kinross, and in England at York and Accrington. In 1214 he was one of seven earls who, on the day after William the Lion's death, took the king's son Alexander, a youth of 16½, brought him as far as Scone and raised him to the throne, according to Fordun, with more grandeur and glory than anyone until then.[69] In 1221 Earl William was again prominent when he witnessed, at York, the marriage contract between Alexander II and Joan sister of Henry III of England.[70] In another charter involving a royal marriage on 10th March 1229, Earl William was an important witness to Alexander II's charter to Margaret his younger sister granting her the whole of Tynedale for her marriage.[71] The value of Earl William's support to the Scottish king was revealed by the terms of the charter in which the king reserved to himself the homages and services of William and his heirs.

As justiciar of Scotia, Earl William continued, after 1212, to perform duties in the judicial field[72] but, perhaps more significantly, continued to perform the military/political role in the north which he had fulfilled so successfully against the Macwilliam rebels in 1211–12. As earl of Buchan after 1212, he was well placed to counter other threats from Ross and Moray. When the rebellious Macwilliam family, this time represented by Gilleasbuig, disturbed the peace of Moray again c.1229–30 (burning some wooden fortification and killing a baron, Thomas de Thirlestane), William's success in 1211–12 prompted the king to appoint him again to the wardenship of Moray as 'a special emergency office' and furnish him with a great force of troops.[73] The dependence of the crown on strong baronial support in the north is emphasised by the fact that it was after the king himself unsuccessfully campaigned against Gilleasbuig that he placed the earl of Buchan in charge of Moray and made him responsible for Gilleasbuig's capture. Gilleasbuig and his two sons were killed and their heads brought to the king.

After the rebellion of 1211–12, the elevation of William Comyn, already by that time a prominent royal servant, to the earldom of Buchan can be seen as a long-term stabilising measure for royal authority in the north. In 1229 the replacement of the temporary expedient of a warden of Moray by a hereditary lordship, the lordship of Badenoch, represents a further extension of royal influence in the north through the Comyn family. The lordship of Badenoch, perhaps part of the estates forfeited by Gilleasbuig because of his rebellion (or at least land under Gilleasbuig's control), was in the highest part of Moray and probably the most difficult for the crown to control. Though not a rich region, it was of great strategic value[74] for its dominance of the principal passes from both the North and

West Highlands into the basin of the Tay. William Comyn's son, Walter, second son by his first marriage, was in possession of the lordship between 1229 and 1234[75] – whether as a gift from Alexander II (which seems most likely in view of Earl William's age), a gift from his father or as an hereditary possession on his father's death in 1233 is not certain.

The Comyns were clearly seen from 1211–12 to 1230 as performing the role of *key* royal agents in the north to counter the threat of the Macwilliam clan to the Scottish throne and at the same time to consolidate royal authority in the north of Scotland. The success of this Crown policy seems to have been proven by the fact that there were no more challenges to the established royal line from the Macwilliams. As for the Comyn family, the hereditary control of Badenoch and Buchan, together with the justiciarship of Scotia, meant that the Comyns' power in the north became almost viceregal.[76] Since Badenoch went together with Lochaber,[77] this meant Comyn power stretched right across northern Scotland from Buchan in the extreme east to Loch Linnhe on the west coast. Richard Cumin and his son William Comyn earl of Buchan, through royal service and 'good' marriages, gave their successors the means to dominate the Scottish political scene from the 1230s to 1314. Their landed strength in the north, so quickly and decisively built up between 1212 and 1229, was added to extensive landholding in central and southern Scotland and important possessions in Northumberland. The wide-ranging nature of Earl William's landed influence was reflected also in his ecclesiastical patronage – the foundation of Deer abbey in Buchan and patronage of the chapel of the Blessed Virgin Mary at Rattray being matched elsewhere in Scotland by patronage to the religious houses at St Andrews and Arbroath, in particular, but also those at Dryburgh, Cambuskenneth and the church of St Kentigern, Glasgow.[78]

Perhaps the greatest legacy of Richard and William Comyn was the political support which they left for their successors. Walter Comyn, earl of Menteith (c.1234–1258), and Alexander Comyn, earl of Buchan (1244–1289), successive leaders of the Comyn family, made political capital out of the number and strength of this support. Whoever was to lead the Comyn family after 1233 was assured of family support, strong in influence and number (see family tree). The Comyns proved to be strongly 'clannish' – every bit as clannish as their Gaelic predecessors and their late medieval successors. Support for the children of William Comyn's first marriage came from Richard, the eldest son (d. c.1244×1249) and his son John, the first John Comyn of Badenoch; Walter lord of Badenoch who became chief of the Badenoch branch of the family and gained the earldom of Menteith (c.1234) by marriage with Isabel, heiress of Menteith;[79] David who formed an important third branch of the family by gaining the important lordship of East Kilbride (before 1215) on marriage to Isabel de Valognes, lady of East Kilbride[80] (this also gained for the family landed interests in England – in Northumberland, Norfolk, Suffolk, Essex and Hertford); and Jean, who married William earl of Ross (styled 1251–1274). From William Comyn's second marriage to the heiress of Buchan, there was Alexander, heir of Buchan, who married Elizabeth, one of the three co-heiresses of the great Anglo-Scottish baron, Roger de Quincy;[81] his two brothers, William and Fergus; Idonea who married Gilbert de la Hay;[83] Agnes who married Philip de Fedarg, founder of the family of Meldrum of Meldrum;[83] and Elizabeth, who married William earl of Mar.[84] Earl William Comyn's sister, Idonea, married Adam fitz Gilbert.[85] Other members of the Comyn family whose relationship to Earl William is uncertain include John Comyn earl of Angus[86] (d.1242), Robert Comyn and William Comyn of Suttenfield or Surdenfield. Influence over yet another earldom, Atholl, came through Richard Cumin I and lasted through most of the 1230s until 1242[87] – after Richard's death, his wife Hextilda took as her second husband Malcolm earl of Atholl, and a second link between the Comyns and Atholl was that Earl Patrick of Atholl's mother Isabella was probably connected to the Comyn family by her mother. Thus Earl Patrick of Atholl (styled 1237) was the great-grandson of Hextilda.

Outside the family members of the Comyn support group, there were other families closely attached to the Comyns through either affinity or a feudal connection. Deriving from Richard Cumin's time were strong links with the Bonekil family in particular, but also the Ridel and Umphraville families.[88] Landowning families in William Comyn's circle were the Grahams, the Mowats, the Boscos, the Pauntons, the Prats, the Sinclairs, and the Wardroba families.[89] A notable feature of William Comyn's affinity was continuity with that of his Celtic predecessor, Earl Fergus[90] – these included sons of former earls of Buchan, William of Slains, Robert de Montfort, John son of Uhtred and Cospatric Macmadethyn, the latter the recipient of a charter from Earl William granting him Strichen and Kindroucht in feudal form.[91] Earl William's officials were usually Celtic.

It would appear that the Comyns combined the Celtic system of organisation based on personal relationships with the Norman feudal system based on tenure, each supporting the other. In 1212 the foundation for the Comyn century was in place. By 1233 a Comyn 'party' was also in existence and the stage was set for Comyn influence to be fully felt on the political scene.

NOTES

1. Young, 'The Earls and Earldom of Buchan', in *Medieval Scotland*, eds. Grant and Stringer, p.174.
2. R.L.G. Ritchie, *The Normans in Scotland* (Edinburgh, 1954), p.179.
3. *Regesta Regum Scottorum (R.R.S.)*, 1 p.157; for William Cumin's early career, see Alan Young, *William Cumin: Border Politics and the Bishopric of Durham 1141–1144*, Borthwick Paper No.54, Borthwick Institute of Historical Research, University of York 1978, pp.2–8. 'Cumin' was the twelfth century form, 'Comyn' the thirteenth century form of the name.
4. *Ibid.* p.5; it is possible that the family came from Bosc – Bernard Commin (Dept Eure) near Rouen; see G.W.S. Barrow, *The Anglo-Norman Era in Scottish History* (Oxford, 1980), p.175.
5. Young, *William Cumin*, p.7.
6. *Chronicles of the Reigns of Stephen, Henry II and Richard I*, ed. R. Howlett (Rolls Series III, 1884–9), p.169 (henceforth *Chron. Stephen*); *The Chronicle of Melrose*, A.O. Anderson and others (1936), p.33 (henceforth *Chron. Melrose*).
7. Young, *William Cumin*, p.10.
8. *Ibid.* pp.26–7.
9. *Cal. Charter Rolls II (1257–1300)*, pp.40–41.
10. *Ibid.*
11. E.L.G. Stones and Grant G. Simpson, *Edward I and the Throne of Scotland 1290–1296* (Oxford, 1978), II p.138; cf. *Chron. Wyntoun* (Laing), II p.309 lines 1085–88.
12. *Kelso Liber* I, p.226 No. 274.
13. *Holyrood Liber* pp.210–11; *Morton Registrum* II, p.4.
14. *Glasgow Registrum* I, p.195; *Origines Parochiales Scotiae* (Bannatyne Club 185–55), I p.348 (henceforth *O.P.S.*).
15. *Cal. Docs. Scot.* II Nos. 766, 823, 1816.
16. *Holyrood Liber* p.211; *Kelso Liber*, I p.226 (*R.R.S.*, II p.190); *Hexham Priory*, II p.85; *R.R.S.*, I pp. 92, 158, 284.
17. *Kelso Liber*, I p.11.
18. *Melrose Liber* pp.280–1.
19. *Kelso Liber*, I p.11.
20. *Hexham Priory*, II pp. 27, 84–5, 113; *Rievaulx Cart* pp. 187, 214–15; *Kelso Liber*, I p.226; *Holyrood Liber* pp.210–11.
21. *R.R.S.*, I pp. 194, 273.
22. *Dunfermline Reg.* p.39; *R.R.S.*, II pp. 152, 174, 204, 219; *Melrose Liber*, I p.13; *Newbattle Registrum* p.288.

23. *Newbattle Registrum* p.289; *Melrose Liber* pp.12-13.
24. *R.R.S.*, II p.46; see esp. G.W.S. Barrow, *The Kingdom of the Scots* (London, 1973), ch.3, pp. 93, 121–3.
25. *Ibid.* p.137.
26. *Ibid.* pp.122–3.
27. *Roger of Hoveden*, II pp. 63, 81.
28. E.L.G. Stones, *Anglo-Scottish Relations, 1174–1328* (Oxford, 1965), p.7.
29. *R.R.S* II p.264.
30. Barrow, *Robert Bruce* pp.20–21.
31. *Ibid.* 21.
32. Anderson, *Scottish Annals*, p.247; G. Stell, 'The Balliol Family and the Great Cause of 1291–2', in Stringer (ed.), *Essays on the Nobility of Medieval Scotland*, p.162 n.18.
33. S.R.O. G.D. 101/1.
34. *R.R.S.*, II pp.406–7.
35. *R.R.S.*, II pp.454–5; G.S. Pryde, 'Two Burgh Charters', *S.H.R.*, Vol.29, 1949–50 pp.64–6.
36. *R.M.S. (1306–1424)*, No.72 App.I; No.109 App.II; No.604.
37. *Kelso Liber* p.17 No.13; p.10 No.9; also *R.R.S.*, II pp. 364, 440.
38. *R.R.S.* II for the earliest charter (1178); *ibid.*, II p.27.
39. *Ibid.* p.463.
40. *Ibid.* p.40; C.A. Malcolm, 'The Office of Sheriff in Scotland', *S.H.R.*, Vol.II (1922–3), p.292.n.
41. *Arbroath Liber* p.5; Malcolm, 'Office of Sheriff', pp. 130–1, 141; *R.R.S.*, II p.41.
42. Anderson, *Early Sources*, II p.535; *Arbroath Liber* pp.329–30.
43. *Moray Registrum* p.14; *R.R.S.*, II p.429; Anderson, *Early Sources*, II p.362.
44. Barrow, *Kingdom of the Scots*, ch.3, pp. 128, 134–5.
45. A.A.M. Duncan, *Scotland, The Making of the Kingdom* (Edinburgh, 1975), p.595.
46. See the table in G.W.S. Barrow, *Kingdom of the Scots*, pp.137–8.
47. *Chron. Pluscarden*, I pp.46–7.
48. *Ibid.*
49. Young, 'Earls and Earldom of Buchan', in Grant and Stringer, *Medieval Scotland*, pp.175–6.
50. *R.R.S.*, II p.5.
51. The sheriffdoms of Aberdeen and Banff had come into existence in William the Lion's reign (*R.R.S.*, II p.36), if not earlier.
52. Barrow, *The Anglo-Norman Era*, pp.157–8.
53. Young, 'Earls and Earldom of Buchan', p.177.
54. *Aberdeen–Banff Colls.* pp.407–9.
55. *Aberdeen–Banff Illus.*, II 408–10, 427–8; S.R.O. G.D. 33 Section 3, 1; *Aberdeen–Banff Coll.* 560; *Aberdeen Reg.*, I pp.14–15; *Arbroath Lib.* pp.6–8 S.R.O. RH 1/2/31.
56. See *Scots Peerage*, II pp.258–61; Barrow, *Robert Bruce*, pp.271–4.
57. See pp. 148–9.
58. *Aberdeen–Banff Illus.*, II p.427.

59. S.R.O. RH 1/2/32.
60. S.R.O. RH 1/2/31.
61. *Arbroath Liber*, I No.132.
62. Young, 'Earls and Earldom of Buchan', pp. 179–80, 194.
63. S.R.O. RH 1/2/32.
64. *C.D.S.*, I No.809; P.R.O. C134 file 97 (2) (Inquisitiones Post Mortem).
65. I.B. Cowan and D.E. Easson, *Medieval Religious Houses: Scotland* (2nd edn., London, 1976), p.74.
66. *Aberdeen–Banff Illus.*, II p.410; Young, 'Earls and Earldom of Buchan', pp.185–6; see map p.201.
67. *Aberdeen Reg.*, I pp.14–15.
68. E.g. *Arbroath Liber* p.76; S.R.O. GD 45/26/4.
69. *Chron. Fordun*, I p.280.
70. *Cal.Pat.R.* (1216–1225), p.309.
71. *C.D.S.*, I No.1113; *Cal.Chart.Rolls*, I p.127.
72. *Coupar Angus Chrs.*, I pp.78–9.
73. *Chron. Bower* (Watt), V pp.142–3; see Young, 'Earls and Earldom of Buchan', pp.177–8.
74. G.W.S. Barrow, 'Badenoch and Strathspey, 1130–1312', *Northern Scotland* Vol.8 (1988), p.6; Barrow, *Feudal Britain*, p.247.
75. *Moray Reg.* pp.82–4.
76. Young, 'Earls and Earldom of Buchan', p.178.
77. G.W.S. Barrow, 'The Highlands in the Lifetime of Robert the Bruce', in *Kingdom of the Scots* (London, 1973), p.378.
78. *St Andrews Liber* pp.251–4; *Arbroath Liber* pp. 6–8, 92–4; *Dryburgh Liber* pp.11–12; *Cambuskenneth Reg.* pp.xxx–xxxi; *Glasgow Reg.*, I p.101.
79. *Scots Peerage*, VI p.127.
80. *C.D.S.*, I No.632.
81. *Cal.Close Rolls* (1268–72), p.8.
82. S.R.O. RH 1/2/31.
83. *S.H.S. Misc.*, Vol. IV pp. 318, 347–8.
84. N.L.S. Adv. 16.2.29; *Chron. Fordun*, II 109.
85. *Morton Reg.*, II pp.4–5.
86. *Chron. Melrose* p.90; J.H. Round, 'The Comyns of Snitterfield', *Ancestor*, Vol.IX pp.146–9.
87. A.A.M. Duncan, 'The earldom of Atholl in the 13th Century', *Scottish Genealogist*, Vol.VII No.2, April 1960, pp. 2–10; *Rievaulx Cart.* p.215.
88. *Kelso Liber*, I p.226; *C.D.S.*, I Nos. 2671–2; *St Andrews Liber* pp. 251–4; *Hexham Priory*, II p.85.
89. *Morton Reg.*, II pp.4–5; *Newbattle Reg.* p.7; S.R.O. RH 1/2/32; *St Andrews Liber* pp.250–3; *Arbroath Liber* pp.93–4; *Cambuskenneth Reg.* p.xxxi; *Coupar Angus Chrs.*, I p.90; NLS Adv. 34.1.10, Vol.II p.34; S.R.O. GD 101/2; *Aberdeen Reg.*, I, p.15; *Morton Reg.*, II p.5; *Glasgow Reg.*, I p.101.

90. *Aberdeen–Banff Illus.*, II pp. 427, 428; *Glasgow Reg.*, I p.101; S.R.O. GD 101/2; S.R.O. RH 1/2/31.
91. *Aberdeen Reg.*, I pp.14–15.

CHAPTER THREE

A Testing Time: Comyns, Bissets, Durwards and the English, 1230–1260

The Comyns had achieved a very solid power base in Scotland by 1233 through a combination of royal patronage and good marriages. This trend continued after the death of William Comyn, earl of Buchan, in 1233, with the principal beneficiary being Walter Comyn, second son of William Comyn's first marriage. It was under Walter Comyn's leadership that Comyn empire building was further consolidated between 1233 and 1242. Walter Comyn acquired the earldom of Menteith c.1234 on marriage to Isabella, daughter and heiress of Maurice, third earl of Menteith. His first recorded appearance as Earl was on 9th January 1234 and it seems that the marriage with Isabella took place between 30th June 1233 and that date.[1] Given the fact that by 1286 only five earldoms were in the hands of families with Anglo-Continental origins, the acquisition of *two* earldoms (through marriage) by the Comyns – Buchan (c.1212) and Menteith (c.1234) – suggests that the family was unusually favoured. Was the acquisition, through marriage, of the earldom of Menteith encouraged by Alexander II in the same way as the acquisition of the earldom of Buchan had apparently been supported by William the Lion?

It is certainly true that Walter Comyn was present at the royal court from as early as 1211×1214,[2] the last few years of William the Lion, and was a regular and increasingly prominent witness to royal charters in the early years of Alexander II, witnessing at Clunie (in Stormont), Kincardine, Kinross, Aberdeen, Clackmannan, Selkirk, Alyth, Stirling and Perth. In 1220, along with his father, Earl William, he was in attendance on Alexander II at York and was one of his barons who swore that Alexander's promise to marry Joan, sister of Henry III, would be fulfilled.³ Even before his elevation to the earldom of Menteith, Walter Comyn held the title of lord of Badenoch between 1229 and 1233. Given his already long service at the royal court and the age of his father, Earl William, it is very probable that the lordship of Badenoch came to Walter Comyn by the gift of Alexander II, soon after his father's successful campaign against Gilleasbuig Macwilliam's rebellion in Moray in 1229. Through Walter, therefore, the Comyns continued their role as the main agents of royal authority in the north.

It is certainly possible that Alexander II favoured a further enhancement of Walter Comyn's status in his acquisition of the earldom of Menteith c.1234. Following the death of Walter's father, Earl William of Buchan, in 1233, the Comyns did not have the status of Scottish earls – Alexander Comyn, heir to Buchan, did not have the title and status of earl of Buchan until c.1244 – and the marriage of Walter Comyn to the heiress of Menteith could be seen as a swift remedy to that situation. The fact that Walter Comyn was to play a key role in establishing royal authority in both Caithness and Galloway in the following year, 1235, once more emphasises the close relationship, indeed interdependence, between Comyns and monarchy in the first three decades of the thirteenth century.

In 1235 Walter Comyn appeared briefly as earl of Caithness.⁴ This is significant as Walter's role as lord of Badenoch and, in practice, royal agent for the Moray region of northern Scotland was being extended further north. Scottish kings had found Caithness a consistently difficult region in which to establish their authority in the twelfth and thirteenth centuries. Royal military expeditions had been launched against the region, and the family of de Moravia (Morays) had been promoted into territorial, administrative and ecclesiastical offices to try to loosen the grip of the earls of Caithness and promote royal interests.⁵ Scottish kings by the early thirteenth century were beginning to look for more permanent solutions to the problems of royal authority in northern Scotland. It is interesting to note that the Comyn family were thoroughly involved in the attempts at permanent solutions to the problem of Caithness as well as to Moray.

With regard to Caithness, King William significantly took as hostage the daughter of Earl John Haraldson of Caithness after he had dealt with a rebellion in Moray in 1214. This showed that rebellion in Moray had

had support from Caithness. William sought a permanent solution to the problem of Caithness, consolidating the treaty of peace with Caithness by tying the earldom's family through marriage with one of his own vassals, a member of the house of Angus. After the murder of Earl John in 1231, the title to the earldom of Caithness and Orkney would eventually (after 1239) come to the house of Angus. The Comyn family were to play a significant role in the settlement.[6] Walter Comyn himself briefly held the title to the earldom of Caithness in 1235 but the family's involvement did not stop there. One heiress was married to a member of the Comyn family, John Comyn earl of Angus (he was killed in 1242), while another heiress was married to Freskin de Moray, a Comyn ally. Comyns and Morays together played key roles on behalf of the Scottish crown in the establishment of a new regime in Caithness. William de Moray became earl of Sutherland in 1235 and it was probably intended that William's nephew Freskin would become earl of Caithness.

Walter Comyn was rather more directly involved in another trouble spot for royal authority in 1235 – Galloway. Having obtained a victory over rebels there in 1235, Alexander II found that business in other parts of his kingdom demanded his presence. He entrusted Walter Comyn with the task of tranquillising Galloway and bringing it to order.[7] It is possible, though there is no definite proof, that Walter acted as justiciar of Galloway or equivalent at this time.[8] English chroniclers accused Walter of fortifying a castle in Galloway sometime before 1244, and Walter was also implicated by the English in harbouring English outlaws and pirates, the de Marisco family[9] – this also points to involvement in Galloway. It is also worth noting that Walter Comyn's nephew and heir, John Comyn, certainly held the office of justiciar of Galloway in 1258, in the period 1266×1272 and also in 1275.[10] Given the tendency of the Scottish monarchy to confer hereditary titles and offices on the Comyn family in the thirteenth century – the earldom of Buchan, lordship of Badenoch and the virtually hereditary justiciarship of Scotia – it does seem as if Walter Comyn's role in Galloway could, indeed, have been an official one, justiciar or quasi justiciar after 1235.

In 1235 Walter Comyn appeared in a similar role to his father in 1211–12 and 1229–30 – the Comyns appear to have become the official 'trouble-shooters' of the Scottish monarchy in the first three decades of the thirteenth century. The tangible rewards for this key role were obvious – two earldoms (Buchan and Menteith), the lordship of Badenoch and numerous 'good' marriages bringing further power and influence.

The Comyns had risen in a remarkably short time to the forefront of the Scottish aristocratic establishment. Earl Walter's influence as the most powerful baron in Scotland was clearly demonstrated in 1237 at the Treaty of York.[11] It was Walter Comyn alone who took the formal diplomatic oath on the king's soul to keep the agreement whereby the Scottish king formally renounced the centuries-old Scottish claims to the counties of Northumberland, Cumberland and Westmorland. In 1238 Walter Comyn gave a very visible sign of his own status in Scotland as earl of Menteith by his foundation of the impressive Augustinian house of Inchmahome on an island in the Loch of Inchmahome. (see Illustrations)[12] The English chronicler, Matthew Paris, showed, too, that Earl Walter's status was fully appreciated in England.[13]

Yet Earl Walter's status was not just a reflection of his own powerful personality and undoubted leadership qualities so well documented in Scottish and English chronicles. His power was, above all, based on his leadership of a Comyn 'party' which had emerged by the 1240s. He was leader of a tightly knit family group consisting of three branches – the Badenoch, Buchan and Kilbride lines – which, with their affinities, held vast territorial influence. They had direct control, for instance, over the earldoms of Menteith, Buchan and, before 1242, Angus; they had influence over three further earldoms, Ross and Mar, and again, before 1242, Atholl; they held the important lordships of Badenoch, Lochaber, Kirkintilloch, Lenzie, Machan, East Kilbride, Bedrule and Scraesburgh as well as Tarset and Thornton in Tynedale. Through family and feudal connections their influence spread yet wider and deeper.

It was not until 1242 that this pervasive Comyn power came to be questioned. The Comyns were the prime example in the late twelfth and early thirteenth centuries of a family rewarded for royal service. Yet it is important to realise that they were not the only 'frontiersmen' in this period who contributed to and benefited from the expansion of royal authority in northern Scotland. The Morays seem to have worked in alliance with the Comyns in the north but this was not the case with two other empire builders, the Bissets and the Durwards. Rivalry in the north between the Bissets and Durwards on the one hand, and the Comyns on the other, is fundamental to an understanding of the political crisis which engulfed Scotland between 1242 and 1258 (see Map 3). Rivalry with the Comyns was important because it did not remain a local difficulty, nor even a solely Scottish problem – it provoked interference from the English king in Scottish affairs in 1244 and gave Henry III further opportunities to intervene in Scottish affairs during the minority crisis following the sudden death of Alexander II in 1249.

The Comyns were not the only family involved in the successful suppression of the Macwilliam revolt in Moray and Ross in 1211–12. The team, probably under William Comyn's leadership, as justiciar, included the earl of Atholl and representatives of two rival claimants to the earldom of Mar, Thomas the Durward (Doorward) and Malcolm, son of Earl Morgrund.[14] As a result of the success of the operation, *all* leading figures or their kindred and dependants were rewarded with office and land in Moray. It seemed that they were to fulfil the role previously, and perhaps inadequately, fulfilled by the earls of Fife. The Comyns' reward seems to have been the nearby earldom of Buchan c.1212, while the crown began the process of granting out to other families royal offices as well as the shires and thanages of Moray to be held as knight service fiefs or in feu-ferme. By the 1220s large parts, but not all, of Moray had been distributed in this way.

The Durward family was one of the chief beneficiaries of this process.[15] By 1226 Thomas Durward was sheriff of Inverness. Gilbert Durward became lord of Boleskine on the eastern shore of Loch Ness, while by 1230 Thomas Durward's son Alan Durward held the lordship of Urquhart on the western shore of Loch Ness. It seems probable that Alan Durward marked his presence in the area by starting to build Urquhart Castle, one of the most impressive castles in thirteenth-century Scotland. Thus the Durward family had been given a great boost in the north in the 1220s. The family, like the Comyns, had risen through royal service – their name was derived from the family's role as king's usher or doorward – and they were very prominent at the royal court in the 1230s.[16] The original name of the family was 'de Lundin', from the original lordship of Lundie in Angus in the early thirteenth century. Marriage to a daughter of Gilchrist, earl of Mar, gave Malcolm of Lundie other land but also gave his descendant Thomas the Durward a claim to the earldom itself. He pursued this actively during the vacancy between 1222 and 1228 – he failed to gain the earldom but in partial recompense he received a substantial area of land in Mar between Don and Dee.[17] This lordship was based on the castle at Lumphanan which he perhaps built, with probably another at Coull, north of Aboyne.

The Comyn rise to power had been sealed by the acquisition of an earldom (Buchan) in 1212. The Durwards similarly strove to gain an earldom in order to break into the forefront of the Scottish aristocracy.

Thomas Durward had put forward a claim to the earldom of Mar during the vacancy between 1222 and 1228. This claim was thwarted and the earldom came under the influence of the Comyns when William, earl of Mar, of an alternative line of earls, married a daughter of William Comyn, earl of Buchan, c.1242–4. The grant of a substantial lordship in Mar to the Durwards did not prevent Thomas's son renewing the claim when circumstances were more propitious.

Another source of rivalry building up in the 1220s and 1230s between the Comyns and Durwards related to the earldom of Atholl.[18] For a time, 1233–37, Alan Durward held the title earl of Atholl, after Thomas of Galloway. It is not known how he gained this title but it is possible that his right was based on either wardship of the heir or marriage to the heiress, Forueleth. The earldom, like Mar, was to come under the control of the Comyn family between 1237 and 1242 through their relative Patrick of Atholl, son of Isabel and Thomas of Galloway. Thus Durward ambitions to two earldoms had been thwarted by the Comyns.

Another empire-building family trying, and succeeding with royal approval, to establish a power base in northern Scotland were the Bissets. They had originally come to Selkirkshire from Nottinghamshire before 1200 but in the first three decades of the thirteenth century had become well established in northern Scotland.[19] By 1220 Walter Bisset was lord of Aboyne; he was to become lord of Stratherrick south of Inverness and also held Arran before 1251. In the second and third decades of the century, Walter's nephew, John, became well established west of Inverness. His lands included the lordship of the Aird – this included Redcastle. John's other lands in the same area apparently included Lovat, Kirkhill, Glenconvinth and Kiltarlity. John Bisset's presence in the north was further consolidated by his foundation of a Valliscaulian priory at Beauly and a leper house at Rathven (near Banff). John's brother, William, added to the family's presence in the north, becoming lord of Abertarff at the south of Loch Ness. The Bisset family, especially Walter and William, figure prominently in witness lists of Alexander II.[20] Walter Bisset witnessed many charters of Alexander II after 1223, and Walter and William attest numerous royal charters up to 1240. William was sheriff of Dumbarton in 1237. A Robert Bisset, probably of Upsettlington, a cousin of Walter Bisset, is also found witnessing Alexander II's charters in 1241 and 1242.

It is worth noting that Durwards and Bissets were neighbours in both Mar and Moray. The Bisset lordship of Aboyne adjoined the Durward

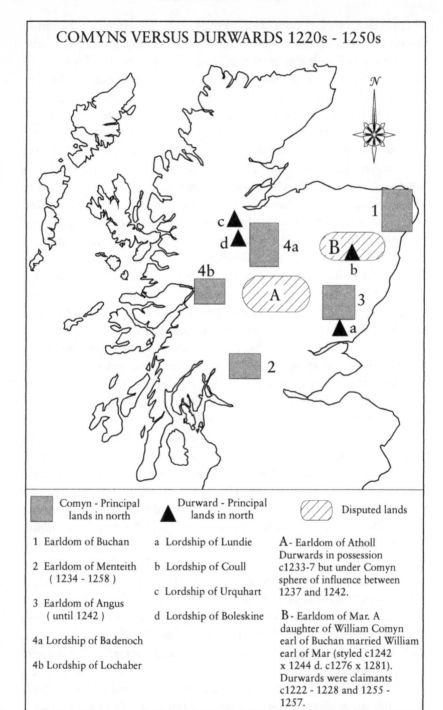

COMYNS VERSUS DURWARDS 1220s - 1250s

Comyn - Principal lands in north

Durward - Principal lands in north

Disputed lands

1 Earldom of Buchan

2 Earldom of Menteith (1234 - 1258)

3 Earldom of Angus (until 1242)

4a Lordship of Badenoch

4b Lordship of Lochaber

a Lordship of Lundie

b Lordship of Coull

c Lordship of Urquhart

d Lordship of Boleskine

A - Earldom of Atholl Durwards in possession c1233-7 but under Comyn sphere of influence between 1237 and 1242.

B - Earldom of Mar. A daughter of William Comyn earl of Buchan married William earl of Mar (styled c1242 x 1244 d. c1276 x 1281). Durwards were claimants c1222 - 1228 and 1255 - 1257.

lordship of Coull; an even closer territorial connection was present in the Moray area. Bisset lands were adjacent to the Durward lordships of Urquhart and Boleskine. Both families had reason to be jealous of the pervasive territorial influence of the Comyns. The Comyns held land in Mar close to Coull and Aboyne. The promotion of the Comyns to the hereditary lordship of Badenoch (and Lochaber went with Badenoch) in 1229 would certainly have been resented by both Bissets and Durwards who, only a short time before this date, had acquired the lordships of the Aird, Stratherrick, and later Abertarff (Bissets) and the lordships of Urquhart and Boleskine (Durwards). Durward rivalry with the Comyns over the earldoms of Mar and Atholl exacerbated this territorial rivalry. It would appear from their actions in the political crisis of the 1240s and 1250s that the Bissets and Durwards were allies against the Comyns.

The festering territorial rivalries and competing ambitions of three 'frontier' families burst into the open in 1242 with the suspicious death of Patrick, heir to the earldom of Atholl. According to Matthew Paris and the *Melrose Chronicle*,[21] Patrick was killed in his lodging at Haddington and the crime was covered up by fire 'so that those who were within should appear not to have been killed, but to have perished in a fire accidentally kindled'. Rumour implicated the Bissets in this death. Chroniclers put forward a number of motives.[22] Paris believed Walter Bisset, 'vigorous in arms, but crafty',[23] was the murderer in vengeance for the fall he had received at the hands of the young Patrick at a tournament on the previous day. The Melrose chronicler thought John Bisset was the criminal, with his uncle the accomplice. Bower thought that William (an error for Walter) was responsible through his knights and believed the crime was a 'result of long standing hostility between their predecessors'. The northern (English) Lanercost chronicler added another twist, stating that the inheritance of Thomas of Galloway was at the root of the murder – Patrick was murdered 'because he was expected to become great lord of a certain inheritance which descended to him and although he had been warned on that day by a letter from the wife of his murderer'. In 1233 Walter Bisset married the sister of Alan of Galloway and thus became Patrick of Atholl's uncle by marriage; it was probably Patrick's aunt who tried to give a warning. It appears, therefore, that there was more to Patrick's death than simple revenge for a tournament fall and that an inheritance was at the heart of the trouble. The Scottish king's court came to the decision on 26th November 1242 that the Bissets, Walter and John, were guilty and should be disinherited and exiled.[24]

It is important to examine the episode clearly because the reaction to Patrick of Atholl's death caused a political crisis in Scotland. In particular the harrying of the Bissets by the Comyn family, relatives of Patrick, has been seen as marking the beginning of ' "The Challenge of the House of Comyn", when the famous Anglo-Scottish family ... performed the more fearful role of overmightly subjects'.[25] There is a danger, however, in following the more extreme interpretation of Comyn actions in these years given by Walter Bower: 'the common report rang in everyone's ears that the kingdom was being undermined by the Comyns' reign of terror'.[26] Bower's writings strongly reflected the political instability and disorders in Scotland in the 1440s rather than the 1240s.

A Comyn perspective is unlikely to be given by the monarchocentric Bower, but there is a need to balance Bower's powerful and influential view. From a Comyn viewpoint, 1242 marked a challenge *to* the family's position. The family's rise to the forefront of the Scottish aristocracy – so strongly supported by the Scottish monarchy – was threatened when two earldoms, Angus and Atholl, slipped from their influence in 1242. John Comyn, earl of Angus, died in that year[27] and inevitably there would be a strong family reaction when their relative Patrick of Atholl, heir to the earldom of Atholl, died in such suspicious circumstances, removing that earldom from Comyn influence too. The harrying of Walter Bisset's lands at Aboyne by Alexander Comyn, heir of Buchan, and John Comyn (son of Richard Comyn), 'a keen fighter and a most outstanding participant in all knightly encounters',[28] was perhaps a hot-headed over-reaction by two younger members of the Comyn family to the loss of a relative of similar age. Behind this, however, was perhaps a deeper family quarrel between Bissets and Comyns, both relatives of Patrick of Atholl, over the inheritance of Thomas of Galloway. Bissets and Comyns were rival landowners in both Mar and Moray, and Patrick of Atholl's death may simply have been the trigger setting off an open display of Comyn resentment against ambitious newcomers who were also ingratiating themselves with the Scottish royal family.

Thus the Comyns' reactions should be seen in the 1240s context of retaliation against threats to the family's position rather than in the 1440s context of unprincipled aggression. It cannot be denied that in 1242 the Comyns fully used the vast power they had accumulated as agents of the Scottish monarchy but the Comyns did not act in isolation. The year 1242 saw the emergence of *two* well-defined and powerful groups who separately launched attacks on the Bissets. In fact, the first group to make a response against the Bissets was the one led by Patrick, earl of Dunbar, the king's cousin.[29] What is clear is the Scottish king's struggle to control the situation and secure the safety of Walter Bisset in the face of the pressure exerted by the two baronial groups. The Comyn party's influence at the royal court might have secured the decision desired by the Comyns – a disinheritance and exile of the two principal members of the Bisset family suspected of involvement in the death of Patrick of Atholl, Walter and John Bisset – but the matter was not to end there as Comyn power was soon to be tested by the English king.

The pro-Comyn *Melrose Chronicle* perhaps understandably denounced Walter Bisset as a 'most abominable traitor' who 'desisted not from pouring the poison of discord into the ears of Henry, the king of England until [Henry] collected his army, and caused [it] to come as far as Newcastle against lord Alexander, king of Scotland'.[30] Yet Matthew Paris[31] also gives a similar, though more detailed, account of Walter's part in fomenting troubles between Alexander and Henry: Walter Bisset hastened to be king of England and complained that the king of Scotland 'had disinherited him unjustly'. Walter and his nephew, moreover, seem to have raised important questions about the jurisdictional rights of the English king in Scotland: 'He added, moreover, that since the king of Scotland was the liegeman of the lord king of England he could not disinherit or irrevocably exile from his land one so noble, especially unconvicted, without the king of England's assent'.[32] The Bissets, once in England, would undoubtedly have pointed a finger at the Comyns as being chiefly responsible for their plight. Walter Comyn was certainly seen as a major threat to Henry III by English chroniclers. In particular, he was accused of fortifying two castles in Galloway and Lothian.

Matthew Paris strongly suggests, however, that Walter Comyn's fortification of these castles was used as an excuse by Henry III to interfere in Scottish affairs.[33] So what was the role of Walter Comyn prior to the serious confrontation which took place between large Scottish and English armies in August 1244? As for the two castles in Galloway and Lothian, these appear to have been Caerlaverock by the Nith and Hermitage in Liddesdale, the work of John or Aymer Maxwell and Nicholas de Soules respectively.[34] Both Maxwell and Soules were seen to be in the Comyn following in the 1240s and 1250s, and in addition Walter Comyn may still have been involved in an official capacity in Galloway. The Close Rolls record that prior to 1244 Walter Comyn himself had strengthened the family's castle of Tarset in Northumberland.[35] According to Matthew Paris, castle building in the border areas was 'to the prejudice of the king of England and contrary to the charters of [Alexander's] predecessors'.[36] Paris's writings consistently speak of wider issues such as these and they seem to reflect Henry III's attitude to Scotland in the wider context of Angevin foreign affairs.

In 1237 and the years afterwards, financial restraints and continuing continental ambitions caused Henry III to compromise with northern security.[37] In 1242 he had, as a matter of diplomatic policy, established good relations with Scotland while he crossed the sea to fulfil his landed ambitions on the Continent. He had even committed the defence of the northern counties bordering Scotland to the Scottish king while he was abroad. The events of 1242–1244 and the political instability in Scotland showed how risky this policy could be. Henry III feared disloyalty from his northern nobles and, after the death of his sister Joan, wife of king Alexander II, in 1238, the subsequent marriage between the Scottish king and a French noblewoman, Marie de Coucy, and the birth of their heir, the future Alexander III, in 1241, also feared a Franco-Scottish alliance. To these factors were added the accusations that the Scottish kingdom was harbouring members of the de Marisco family who had turned pirate and were attacking English shipping in the Irish Sea.[38]

No doubt the words of the Bissets easily fed Henry III's paranoia and provoked his march to the border in 1244 to seek remedy. By 1243 Walter Bisset was firmly established in English royal service.[39] According to Bower, he had sworn to go to the Holy Land in order to ingratiate himself with the English king.[40] Walter Bisset and his heirs were granted the manor of Lowdham in Nottinghamshire (this was confirmed in 1246) by Henry III until their Scottish lands were recovered. For five years, Bisset served Henry III while his nephew John was sent as the king's messenger to Ireland.[41]

Given the power of Walter Comyn in court circles in 1237, Matthew Paris's suggestion that Henry III used Walter's castle-building activities on the border as an excuse for intervening in Scottish political affairs seems to underplay the Comyns' role in the broader issues which concerned Henry. It is difficult to prove, but Walter Comyn's activities in Galloway from 1235 may have meant that he was involved in the harbouring of the Marisco pirates operating in the Irish sea. In 1244, Henry III forced two powerful groups of Scottish nobles, one led by

Patrick earl of Dunbar, the other led by Earl Walter Comyn, to swear by a bond of good behaviour – this bond implies such a link.[42] Perhaps the Comyns, too, were suspected of seeking to establish closer links with France; they were the predominant aristocratic power in Scotland when Alexander II took as his second wife the French noblewoman, Marie de Coucy, and it is possible that they were suspected of inviting a French force under John de Coucy to Scotland in 1243 or early 1244.

What is clear is that the power of the Comyns in Scotland could not be ignored by either Alexander II or Henry III in 1244. Both acted to try to curb Comyn power. Henry III forced a treaty of friendship from both the Scottish king and his magnates and, as we saw, received a bond of good behaviour from the two powerful groups which had emerged in 1242 under the leadership of Earl Patrick of Dunbar and Earl Walter of Menteith. Henry III probably saw himself as 'protector and overseer of affairs in Scotland'.[43] Alexander II similarly acted to curb Comyn power. The two justiciars of Scotia in 1242, Robert Mowat and Philip de Melville, had been ineffective in bringing order to northern Scotland when the Comyns sought vengeance against the Bissets in 1242. This is hardly surprising, given that Robert Mowat was very prominent in the Comyn following and Philip de Melville was probably under Comyn influence also.[44] Alexander II replaced them by Alan Durward as justiciar of Scotia and David de Lindsay as justiciar of Lothian, neither of whom were of the two parties which had emerged in 1242. It is important to note that the change in the justiciarship of Scotia took place before Alexander's confrontation with Henry III.[45]

From 1244 it seems that Alan Durward took over from Walter Comyn as the chief adviser of Alexander II and head of a totally non-Comyn government. Durward was a neighbour of Walter Bisset in Mar and he may have been involved with the army of Mar in the king's attempt to rescue the Bissets from the Comyn attacks on the family at Aboyne in 1242. Durward was, of course, already a territorial rival of the Comyns in Mar and Moray, and the family had also clashed with the Comyns in their attempts, before 1242, to remove the earldoms of Atholl and Mar from Comyn influence. Walter Comyn must have resented the fact that Durward, who had little political influence before 1244, had such an important position in government. He must have resented even more the return of Walter Bisset to the Scottish royal court by November 1247.[46] Durwards and Bissets certainly seem to have been allies in 1242 and afterwards.

The Comyns' meteoric rise to power seemed to have been halted. Patrick earl of Dunbar was recognised, at his death in 1248,[47] as the leading noble in the country but the decline in Comyn power was, in fact, more apparent than real. Walter Comyn's prominence in the witness lists of Alexander II's charters in the period 1244–9 hardly denotes a full political eclipse.[48] The nature of the Comyn 'party' which had made Earl Walter such a powerful figure in 1237 was well demonstrated in 1244.[49] The list of forty men named in the following of Earl Walter in that year demonstrates a tightly knit family group, with all three man branches (the Badenoch, Buchan and Kilbride lines) represented with their connections. This made a 'party' formidable in both numbers and influence. In the list there were, in addition to earl Walter, three bearing the Comyn name – John Comyn, David Comyn and Robert Comyn. Others linked by marriage were Gilbert de la Hay and two other members of the de la Hay family (both named William), also William de Valoniis (probably a relative of David Comyn through his marriage to Isabel de Valoniis before 1215). Nicholas de Soules, lord of Liddesdale and probable builder of Hermitage castle, was to be linked with the Comyn family by marriage – either this Nicholas or perhaps his son was to marry a daughter of Alexander Comyn earl of Buchan.

Lack of charter evidence prevents an accurate assessment of the place held by feudal tenants in Earl Walter's following, but Alexander de Stirling was certainly in Earl Walter's feudal following,[50] and was probably one of several important tenants in Earl Walter's support. Gilbert de la Hay's tie through marriage to the Buchan branch of the Comyn family was strengthened by a tenurial link.[51] Without evidence of feudal links, it is possible to identify individuals or families in the 1244 list who were regularly in attendance on Earl Walter and the other branches of his family. Hugh de Erth (Airth, near Stirling) and his family were regular followers of the main branch of the Comyn family.[52] The Mountfichets or Muschets (latinised *de Monte Fixo*) held land in Cargill on Tay and Kincardine in Menteith (west of Stirling) and were probably in the Earl's regular following. The influential Bonekil family, represented in the 1244 list by Ranulf and Walter, were regularly in the following of Richard Cumin and his father William Comyn earl of Buchan.[53] Members of the de Bosco family, represented in the 1244 list by William de Bosco, were also in the following of William earl of Buchan.[54] The Graham family were in the following of William Comyn both before and after he became earl, and Henry de Graham, mentioned in the 1244 list, was to be found in the following of both William Comyn, earl of Buchan, and William Comyn of Kilbride.[55] Alexander Uvieth or Eviot continued to be a political supporter of the Comyns in the 1250s, while Ralf Paunton was in the Countess of Buchan's circle in 1236.[56] There is no known connection of the Vieuxpont (Veteri Ponte) family with the Comyns but two members of the family, Ivo and William, were in the 1244 list. The family held land in Lothian and in Tynedale and it is perhaps the common Tynedale connection that links the Comyns and Vieuxponts in the 1244 list.

The 1244 list of Earl Walter's supporters gives a good cross-section of his 'party' at that time but it does not give a complete picture of his support. It is interesting to note, for instance, that Alexander Comyn, certainly active in the Comyn cause in 1242, and a most prominent member of the Comyn 'party' in the 1250s, was not in the 1244 group although the Buchan branch of the family was represented through its connections. The Mowat (or Monte Alto) family were certainly in the following of the Comyns of Buchan at the time. They had their base in the earldom of Ross – Jean, daughter of William Comyn, earl of Buchan, married William, earl of Ross. Given this Comyn affinity, it is hardly surprising that Robert Mowat, joint justiciar of Scotia 1241–44 with Philip de Melville (probably also under Comyn influence), was so ineffective in bringing order to Mar when the Comyns sought vengeance on the Bissets in 1242. The episode showed that lack of formal political office was no real bar to the political influence of the Comyns. The strength of the Comyn 'party' showed that their power could not easily be eclipsed. Yet both Alexander II and Henry III tried to curb Comyn influence in 1244. In 1244 it was Alan Durward, Henry de Balliol, David de Lindsay and William Giffard who swore on Alexander II's soul to keep the terms of the treaty of peace made between the Kings of Scotland and England.[57] It was Alan Durward who was to take the key position of justiciar of Scotia. Henry III obtained a bond of good behaviour from Earl Walter and his following in 1244 as well as ordering Hugh de Bolbec, sheriff of Northumberland, to take charge of the Comyn castle of Tarset and force Walter to demilitarise the castle.[58]

Yet Walter Comyn's real power, far from being extinguished after 1244, would emerge once more when Alexander II's death in 1249 left a political crisis in Scotland with the young Alexander III a minor and political groups in Scotland, France and England anxious to influence the young king. There is no evidence for any formal arrangements with regard to the government of Scotland during Alexander III's minority, and this strongly implies that it was Alexander II's intention that Alan Durward should remain as the main adviser to the king and in practice head of Scottish government.[59] Durward had been justiciar of Scotia since 1244 and had, at about the same time, entrenched himself firmly in the Scottish royal circle by marrying Alexander II's illegitimate daughter, Marjory. Soon after Alexander II's death, he appears to have sought to formalise and make more secure his position as head of the minority government. This is suggested by his attempt to knight the young Alexander before he was enthroned; in similar circumstances in England in 1216, Henry III had been knighted by William Marshal who was then asked by the English knights to take the office of 'rector regis et regni'.[60] However, it soon became apparent that Durward did not have enough authority over the Scottish nobility to execute his plan successfully. The majority of Scottish nobles were suspicious of Durward, and at this point Walter Comyn's authority and political leadership firmly emerge. The generally anti-Comyn chronicler, John of Fordun, admirably sums up Earl Walter's accepted leadership of the Scottish aristocracy:

> While they were arguing, the lord Walter Comyn, earl of
> Menteith, a man of foresight and shrewdness in counsel, answered
> and said that he had seen a king consecrated who was not yet a
> knight ... and he went on to say that a country without a king
> was beyond doubt, like a ship amid the waves of the sea without
> rower or steersman. For he had always loved king Alexander, of
> pious memory, now deceased – and this boy also for his father's
> sake. So he moved that this boy be raised to the throne as quickly
> as possible ... and by his advice, the said bishops and abbot, as
> well as the nobles and the whole clergy and people, with one
> voice, gave their consent and assent to his being set up as king.[61]

Earl Walter's argument had little substance about it though the sentiment is certainly more in keeping with the Comyns' role as pillars of the monarchy from 1200 to 1240 than with their usual depictions by Fordun and Bower as irresponsible aggressors and enemies of the monarchy during the minority. Walter Comyn's authority was clear-cut, his advice was acted upon immediately and his leadership was generally accepted as he led Alexander to the throne, successfully thwarting Alan Durward's plan. Yet Alan Durward's marriage gave him a special place in the royal circle and thus made Walter very wary as Durward's royal connection was the only real advantage which he held over him.

Durward was clearly keen to make the most of his authority in 1249. This can perhaps be seen in the change of seals on Alexander III's letters in 1250.[62] There were two seals in operation in 1250 – the small seal, or seal of minority, and the great seal (with the enthroned monarch on one side, the monarch as a mounted knight on the other). Two authorities on the seal of minority agree that the great seal was 'a token that the king was now considered of age to grant secure titles and to be represented as exercising government' and that 'this change [of seal] ... represents a decisive shift of power into the hands of Alan Durward'.[63] Although chroniclers are not the most reliable sources for exact titles given to officials, evidence from the seals seems to add veracity to Fordun's description of Alan Durward as 'justiciar of all Scotia' in 1249.[64] Durward was seeking a post with equivalent status to the English justiciar. He was seeking, by various means, in 1249 and 1250, to enlarge his political authority.

Earl Walter was worried by Durward's royal connections and perhaps this explains Comyn attempts to associate with the Bruce family both before and after Alexander II's death.[65] In view of the later rivalry of the Comyns and Bruces at the end of the thirteenth century, it is particularly interesting to speculate that the Comyns may have been seeking an alliance with Robert de Bruce (d. 1295) in the late 1240s. Robert de Bruce, if we can believe a partisan Bruce source, had been named as successor to Alexander II in 1238 when Alexander II, still childless, went to war in the Isles.[66] According to this source, Bruce's designation as heir occurred in a formal parliament of the magnates – during the 'Great Cause' 1291–92, Robert Bruce as Competitor asked for a search to be made for the document recording that decision. Such a document is not known ever to have existed but if such a designation had been made in 1238, the Comyns, acknowledged leaders of the aristocratic body at the time, would have been most aware of it. Whether or not an alliance with the Bruces was, in fact, sought, the Bruces tended to support the Durwards in the 1250s.

Lack of Bruce support, however, did not prevent Earl Walter and his party from being recognised as the dominant political force in Scotland in the period 1249–51. The fact that the Durward government could not ignore Earl Walter's power at this time is shown by Walter's attendance as a leading witness to several of Alexander III's charters.[67]

The Durwards had office but not power; they had insufficient support to control the country. It seems that the Scottish nobility in the middle of the thirteenth century was already well entrenched; Comyn leadership of this community seems generally to have been accepted, while forceful aspirants to that elite were treated with great suspicion.

It was Durward government's lack of control in the country that led to the intervention of Henry III in Scottish affairs late in 1251. It was, in fact, a joint magnate/clergy[68] deputation which went to Henry III asking for aid and, more especially, for Henry's intervention in Scottish affairs. The role of the church in Scottish political affairs during the minority period should not be underestimated. There were complaints to Alexander III that laymen were despoiling the priory of St Andrews and that the Durward government was affording it no protection.[69] It is not clear who was responsible but it is known that the priory of St Andrews was supported by the Durwards in their litigation with their neighbours in St Andrews, the provost and canons of the Church of St Mary of the Rock who usually looked to the Comyns for support.[70] Complaints to the king were followed by complaints to the pope, Innocent IV.[71] Again the charges seem to have been aimed chiefly at Scottish government, i.e. the Durward-led counsellors: excommunications had been revoked by royal command, cases about church possessions and church patronage had been summoned before secular courts and recourse to papal judges delegate had been forbidden. The papal response was to ask the bishops of Lincoln, Worcester and Lichfield to inquire into these complaints against the Scottish king and counsellors.

The Comyns, as leaders of the Scottish magnates, were closely involved with the clergy in sending a deputation to ask for Henry III's intervention. Walter Comyn had first-hand knowledge of Henry's intervention in 1244, had seen its decisiveness, and wanted this support in 1251. He also saw the value of church support. Church support for the Comyns in 1251 added breadth and stability to their following. The Comyns had established a good reputation with the Church mainly through the munificence of William Comyn earl of Buchan, and his son Walter was careful to maintain this reputation.

Henry III proved very willing to accept the invitation by Comyns and clergy to intervene in Scottish affairs. His decision was, no doubt, helped by the papal refusal, inspired by Durward pressure, of Henry III's demands that the Scottish crusading tenth should be used to further his royal ambitions in Sicily.[72] Durward pressure seems also to have been behind papal refusal of Henry's demand that the Scottish king should not be anointed or crowned without his consent.[73] Henry III was no doubt keen to act and build further on the authority he had established in Scottish political affairs in 1244. The Comyn/clergy invitation gave him the perfect opportunity to act once more as overseer of Scottish affairs in 1251.

At Christmas 1251 Henry III's intervention was sealed by the marriage, at York, of the young king of Scotland (aged ten) to Henry's young daughter, Margaret (aged eleven).[74] At a stroke, worries about a possible French marriage alliance (so apparent in Henry III's actions in 1244) were quelled. The year 1251 also had a major significance for Anglo-Scottish relations. It soon became clear that Henry took his new role as father-figure seriously, not only in regard to the welfare of the young couple but also the welfare of the Scottish kingdom. Henry used the special occasion of the wedding at York to implement changes to the Scottish government.[75] Hardly was the wedding ceremony over, when Walter Comyn, showing his political opportunism to the full, accused Alan Durward of trying to set up himself and his family as rulers of Scotland. According to the pro-Comyn *Melrose Chronicle*, Durward had sent messengers and gifts to the pope in an attempt to legitimise the daughters born to his wife, illegitimate half-sister of the new king, in order to secure further his family's position within the royal circle, and even make succession to the throne a possibility.[76]

After enquiring into Walter's accusations, Henry III – in Alexander III's name – made changes in the Scottish government's offices. Thus the chief officers, the justiciar, chancellor and chamberlain, were deprived of their offices in York in 1251; the Comyns were placed in power and Alan Durward was forced into exile. Earl Walter's return to power was finally realised when Robert, abbot of Dunfermline and chancellor of the Durward government, gave up the seal and Gamelin became chancellor.[77] Henry III's intervention and actions as overseer of Scottish affairs in 1251 could be seen from a crown standpoint as a blow to the development of an independent Scottish kingdom, for which the nobility deserved censure. However, in the political crisis which the minority caused, there seems to have been a common regard by the magnates of Scotland for the English king as an agent of stability. Even the respected chronicler, John of Fordun, who had as his main theme the growth of an independent Scottish kingdom, reflected this in his praise of Henry III,[78] 'for, nearly the whole time of his reign, he was looked upon by the kings of Scotland, father and son, as their most faithful neighbour and adviser'. This rather charitable view perhaps reflects the need at the time for stability in a crisis, but Henry's actions from 1244 clearly reflect a new phase in Anglo-Scottish relations, with Henry intending to exploit his dominance: in 1244 and 1251 at York the important matter of the Scottish king owing homage for the kingdom of Scotland as well as his English lands appears to have been raised.[79]

The Comyn party supporting Earl Walter in government in 1251[80] had the same basic nucleus as in 1244, with Walter at its head and Alexander Comyn earl of Buchan, William earl of Mar and John Comyn as its inner core. Still in the group from 1244 were Nicholas de Soules, John Le Blund and Alexander Vinet (Uvieth). Influential men gained from the Dunbar following after 1244 were David de Graham and Thomas de Normanville, both members of important noble families. Other men supporting the 1251–55 Comyn government were Hugh and William Gourlay (William was a feudal tenant of William Comyn of Kilbride), Thomas son of Ranulf (perhaps connected to the Bonekil family), Aymer de Maxwell and Mary his wife, David de Lochore and John de Dundemore. Very notable among supporters of the Comyn government in 1251 were the leading bishops of Scotland; they included William Bondington, bishop of Glasgow, Clement, bishop of Dunblane, Gamelin, bishop-elect of St Andrews, and William Wishart, archdeacon of St Andrews (his brother Richard was also named in the Comyn following). With such broad-based support, Walter Comyn seemed to have the general support of the country behind him. It is perhaps surprising given the political use made of that office by his rival Alan Durward that Walter Comyn himself did not take on the most important position in government, the justiciarship of Scotia, which his own father had held. Perhaps he had to placate his supporters: Alexander Comyn, since 1244 earl of Buchan, became justiciar of Scotia from at latest 1253; William earl of Mar became chamberlain in 1252; Gamelin, under Comyn patronage and probably a relative of William Comyn earl of Buchan by marriage, had custody of the small royal seal but was not mentioned as chancellor before February 1254; and Thomas de Normanville was justiciar of Lothian by c.1251.[81]

There was a common regard by the Scottish nobility in 1251 for the English king as a source of stability. Without that stability no-one, including the Comyns, could enjoy the rewards of power. The years 1251 to 1255 were to test fully Walter Comyn's political leadership of the

Scottish aristocracy; this leadership was to be tested also by the English king's firm intention to oversee Scottish affairs. Henry III was, of course, aware of the power of Earl Walter's party from his intervention in 1244 but he must have been influenced in his attitude to the Comyns in 1251 by the fact that they had come to him for help and that they had, moreover, the support of the leading clergy and the majority of the Scottish nobility. This augured well for stability in Scotland under the Comyns and it was stability that Henry wanted most of all in 1251. Henry too must have felt that he could ensure control over the Comyn government. He appointed two experienced Anglo-Scottish barons, namely Robert de Ros, lord of Wark, Helmsley and Sanquhar (and the King's cousin), and John de Balliol,[82] as guardians of the young king and queen – and no doubt his own interests – between 1251 and 1255. In addition he used other Anglo-Scottish barons such as Roger de Quincy and Malise earl of Strathearn on frequent embassies between the two countries during the minority period.[83] Henry also ensured that the great seal, by which Durward had tried to enlarge his authority, was broken and replaced by a small seal.[84] It appears too that Geoffrey de Langley was sent to Scotland as the queen's counsellor.[85] Henry seemed to regard the government in Scotland as subject to his overriding authority, and this is confirmed by the fact that his next intervention in Scottish affairs took place exactly on Alexander III's fourteenth birthday.

Yet 1251–5 represented a victory, in practice, for Walter Comyn's political leadership and diplomacy which effectively denied to Henry III the real control of the Scottish political scene which he desired. The Comyns strengthened their own influence over the church by pushing successive claims of two of their supporters, Abel of Gullane in 1253 and Gamelin in 1255, to the see of St Andrews.[86] This was doubly important as control over the premier see in Scotland was vital and Durward influence in the cathedral chapter could be effectively quashed. The Comyns were also successful in having their candidate, Henry, abbot of Holyrood, elected in 1253 to the bishopric of Galloway.[87] This case is also illuminating as it showed Comyn dominance over one of the two guardians of the young Scottish king and queen, John Balliol. The Comyn candidate in Galloway was elected despite the opposition of John Balliol in the name of the lordship of Galloway. The election of Henry abbot of Holyrood was upheld at York in 1255. By Henry III's later actions against his two guardians, it is apparent that he had envisaged them as guardians of the kingdom as well as of the king and queen. This plan was, however, effectively quashed by Earl Walter; the records of the period 1251–5 show that, in practice, the two guardians had no special precedence and little involvement in government activities. While Earl Walter's dominance over John Balliol had already been demonstrated, the other guardian, Robert de Ros, occupied a lowly position when he witnessed occasional Alexander III charters. This reflects his lack of status with regard to the Comyn government.[88] It is apparent that Walter Comyn was also behind the scheme to remove Geoffrey de Langley, the queen's counsellor, from Scotland, again with common consent.[89]

The black picture of the Comyn government 1251–55 painted by John Fordun and Walter Bower[90] has been seized upon by later writers and has tended, until recently,[91] to dominate analysis of this period. Fordun's charge against the Comyn government that 'these councillors were so many kings' was in sharp contrast to his praise for Earl Walter's actions against Durward's plans in 1249. Yet Walter Comyn's authority had been accepted by the clergy and most of the nobility in 1249 and 1251. Other charges by Fordun and Bower that the period 1251 to 1255 saw 'the poor crushed down … the nobles ousted from their inheritance, the drudgery forced upon citizens, the violence done to churches' are riddled with inaccuracies. The Comyn government was certainly guilty of hounding the recalcitrant Robert of Kenleith, chancellor of the previous government, out of office[92] but the Comyns, because of their vast influence throughout Scotland, had probably less need to pursue factional interest than their rival, Alan Durward, would have had from 1255 to 1257. The description of Comyn excesses against the church should also be set against the consistent church support for Walter Comyn in 1249, in 1251 and again in 1255.

Opposition to the Comyn government of 1251–55 came, in fact, from outside the country in the form of Alan Durward – this was a markedly different situation from the internally organised plot which was to oust Durward in 1251. Given the climate of the time, i.e. a political crisis, in which a dominant party would naturally try to secure stability by advancing its supporters, there is no evidence to suggest Walter Comyn's conduct of affairs from 1251–5 was more than usually culpable; there is no evidence that the Comyns were working against the interests of the kingdom.

General support in Scotland, however, was not enough for the Comyn government. The successful counter-coup of Alan Durward in

1255 proved that the continued confidence of the king of England was a necessity for any governing group in Scotland during the minority of Alexander III. Alan Durward, like Earl Walter in 1251, realised the necessity of Henry III's support and as an exile from Scotland soon ingratiated himself into the English king's favour by serving with him in Gascony at a time when such support was difficult to find.[93] Durward, in fact, volunteered to perform the service due in Gascony by the earl of Strathearn because of the English lands he held. English chancery records reflect his rewards for such service.[94] By 1255 he was regarded as one of Henry III's 'beloved friends'. Like Walter Bisset in 1242, Durward found Henry III receptive to the complaints he made about the Comyn government. To support a counter-coup by Durward suited Henry III after he returned to England at the end of 1254. He had his own reasons to be dissatisfied with the situation in Scotland – he had under-estimated the Comyns and was now aware of the ineffectiveness of his two guardians, Robert de Ros and John de Balliol, whom he was to accuse of failing in their duty.[95] Henry was also very attentive to the young queen's complaints and to the physician Reginald of Bath's criticisms of his daughter's medical treatment in Scotland.[96] Thus Henry III intervened once more, supporting Alan Durward and virtually giving a licence to rebel to opponents of the Comyns in Scotland, among whom were Patrick earl of Dunbar, Robert de Bruce, Malise earl of Strathearn and Alexander Stewart.[97]

The plan to overthrow the Comyn government was well conceived and ended successfully c.4th September 1255 when the young king and queen were secured at Edinburgh from under the noses of the Comyns and brought to Roxburgh.[98] The English king and queen had come north to Wark on Tweed to await them. The Comyn government was taken unawares, perhaps too complacent in the apparent security of their broadly based administration. Earl Walter and his party suddenly found themselves out of government and out-manoeuvred; they were unable to prevent the assembly of seventeen lay and eight ecclesiastical magnates who approved the appointment of a new council of fifteen to govern Scotland. The desire of Henry III to make firmer, more final arrangements than in 1251 – a named council of fifteen to serve for seven years (the remaining years of minority)[99] – was a sure sign that Walter Comyn had exercised more political influence from 1251 to 1255 than Henry had intended.

The group seems to have been led by Patrick earl of Dunbar.[100] But it was Alan Durward who once more took the key office of justiciar of Scotia[101] with Walter de Moray (of Bothwell) becoming justiciar of Lothian and David de Lindsay chamberlain. It is hardly surprising given the almost vice-regal power and influence of the Comyns in northern Scotland that the names of the fifteen councillors supporting the removal of the Comyn government have more of a southern and south-western bias. This, of course, applied to the Bruce and Stewart families, particularly strong in the south-west. Malcolm earl of Fife, Patrick earl of Dunbar and Neil earl of Carrick were also predominantly lords of the southern half of Scotland, as was de Meyners (Menzies) at this time. While Durward and Hay, the bishops of Dunkeld and Aberdeen, all represented strong northern interests, Durward's renewed attempts to gain the earldom of Mar showed his great desire (demonstrated since the 1230s) to alter the balance of power in the north which strongly favoured the Comyns.[102] Durward seems once more to have attempted to use the high office of justiciar of Scotia to increase his power and status. He tried to discredit the Comyns for their actions in government and also renewed his family's claim to the earldom of Mar by challenging the legitimacy of the earl of Mar's father and grandfather. Durward, however, was unable either to gain the earldom of Mar after a papal enquiry, or to prevent the consecration of Gamelin, the Comyn government's chancellor, to the see of St Andrews. In fact Gamelin so won the pope's support in this matter that the Durward government, which had outlawed him, was excommunicated.[103] Walter Comyn and his party still had important backing from the clergy and it is noticeable that only two bishops, those of Aberdeen and Dunkeld, were members of the 1255 council and only four abbots supported the Comyns' removal.

It soon became apparent that the new government in Scotland could not control the Comyn 'party'. Indeed, Earl Walter and his party refused to put their names to the document setting up the new council.[104] Comyn reaction was once more to seek Henry III's support. In Scotland, the Comyns, encouraged by Gamelin's consecration and angered by Durward's strong-arm tactics against their supporters, put pressure on the council and in 1257 forced it to pass on to Henry III a draft document which no doubt advocated the reintroduction of Comyn members to the Scottish government.[105] Henry III sent the prominent Anglo-Scottish magnate Roger de Quincy, earl of Winchester, to mediate but apparently with instructions not to change the rigid structure set up in 1255.[106] Henry had previously sent John Maunsell north in 1256 to try to sort out the troubles in Scotland. By 1257 it was clear that Walter Comyn's tactics of trying to regain power through the English king were failing. Henry III regarded himself as the principal counsellor of the Scottish king and felt he had a better chance of controlling Scottish affairs by using a number of Anglo-Scottish barons to safeguard his interests. As well as Anglo-Scottish nobles used on embassies between the two countries, there were three particular members of the council of fifteen who had strong links with the English crown, Malise earl of Strathearn, Robert Bruce, and Alan Durward. Henry showed too that he was ready to use his northern officials, the archbishop of York, the bishop of Durham and the sheriffs of York and Northumberland to help restore order in Scotland.[107]

The year 1257 marked a significant change in Comyn tactics. Having failed since 1255 to persuade Henry III to intervene on his behalf, and under pressure from the Durwards, Earl Walter decided to use the still considerable power at his disposal to achieve his ends. Members of the Comyn party kidnapped the Scottish king at Kinross and thus regained control of the government. The pro-Comyn *Melrose Chronicle* claimed that the Comyns seized control because the leaders of the Durward government had been excommunicated and that as a result the country was dishonoured.[108] Certainly the Comyn cause was helped by church support and by the pope's disapproval of the Durward government, but rather more pragmatic reasons probably provoked the kidnapping. Walter Comyn's political shrewdness enabled him to realise that Henry III was in a difficult situation in 1257–58 – he was preoccupied with events in Sicily, the baronial reform movement in England, the successful rebellions of the Welsh and the illness of the queen. These issues were probably taken into account when Earl Walter organised the 1257 coup and then in 1258 took positive action in strengthening his party's position by allying with Llewelyn, prince of Wales, and his supporters.[109] Although it was the Welsh who seem to have taken the initiative in seeking such an alliance, it says much for the political initiative of Walter Comyn that the two sides came together.

It soon became clear, however, that in 1257 the Comyns lacked general support for their actions – by contrast with 1251, Walter Comyn did not have the support of Henry III, nor that of the majority of the Scottish nobility. Comyn supporters named in the 1258 treaty included seven members of the Comyn government of 1251–5 – Alexander Comyn earl of Buchan, William earl of Mar, John Comyn, named in 1258 as justiciar of Galloway, Aymer de Maxwell, John de Dundemore, David de Lochore and Hugh de Berkeley. The list also included other regular members of the Comyn following: Freskin de Moray, Hugh de Abernethy, two members of the Mowat family, Bernard and William, William de Airth and Reginald Cheyne. The list, which seems to have been padded out with younger members of the family such as William and Richard, brothers of John Comyn, also included William earl of Ross, a relative who had played little part in previous Comyn activity. The 1258 Comyn group were still a powerful, closely knit group but they had less general support and little outside the Comyn affinity. The terms of the treaty showed that the Comyns were conscious that they did not have majority support and extremely hesitant to act without the backing of the king:

> If it should happen that we are compelled to enter into a peace
> or truce with the king of England or anyone else opposed to
> Llewelyn, by command of our lord king of Scotland we shall
> strive to see that this is done to Llewelyn's honour and advantage,
> nor shall we do anything contrary to the league unless it be by
> our lord the king's strictest compulsion, but rather we shall do our
> best to bring the lord our king into this alliance.[110]

The terms of the treaty give a strong impression that the Comyns did not control Alexander III and were desperately trying to win the support of their young king; in fact, they suggest that the Comyns had overreached themselves and were trying to draw back. Walter Comyn's influence as the leader of a large and close-knit family unit with its affinity was enough to secure *de facto* command for a while, yet Walter realised that this control would be short-lived unless he could win over the king and have real constitutional authority.

The alliance with the Welsh had been an inspired attempt to broaden the base of his support, but only three months after the treaty was made the Welsh made peace with Henry III. The Comyn government's lack of effective control was seen when they lost the great seal; it is further emphasised by the freedom which Alexander III had in writing to King Henry and by the freeing of Queen Margaret from Comyn custody. Compromise was in the air by the summer of 1258, with Alexander III coming more into the political picture, and seeking a measure of reconciliation between the Comyn and Durward factions.

That compromise was achieved was partly due to Henry III. He had played a forceful role in Scottish affairs since 1244 but in the summer of 1258 was in no position to insist that the arrangements he had made in Scotland in 1255, i.e. a seven-year council of fifteen governing Scotland, should be continued. On 2nd May 1258 Henry promised reform to his barons, and following the parliament of Oxford in June the baronial reform movement began and Henry was no longer in charge of English government. In September a reconciliation in Scotland was apparently agreed, a document of November 1258 issued by the English baronial council recording a compromise council of ten with four key members of the Comyn party (Walter Comyn earl of Menteith, Alexander Comyn earl of Buchan, William earl of Mar, and Gamelin bishop of St Andrews) and four members of the Durward party (Alan Durward, Alexander Stewart, Robert Meyners (Menzies) and Gilbert de Hay). The naming of Queen Marie and her new husband John of Acre as the other two members may have been a sop to Henry III, giving the impression that Alexander III's minority still continued. It is interesting to note the absence of prominent members of the 1255 (supposedly seven-year) council of fifteen – these included the earls of Dunbar, Strathearn and Fife as well as Robert de Bruce.

Walter Comyn, earl of Menteith, must still have been the leading political figure in Scotland when he died in late October or early November 1258, apparently as a result of a fall from his horse.[111] He had been chief witness to a charter of Alexander III on 16th October.[112] The suddenness of his death and the reactions to it in both Scotland and England indicate the effect he had had on the political affairs of both countries in the 1240s and 1250s. Messengers came to Henry III at St Albans on 23rd November especially to report his death. Matthew Paris described him as the 'most powerful earl in Scotland'.[113] In Scotland, even the largely anti-Comyn chronicler, John of Fordun, described him as 'a man of foresight and shrewdness in council'.[114] To the Comyn 'party' the loss of Earl Walter's leadership resulted in fear of loss of power similar to that shown in 1242. This was reflected in Walter Comyn's nephew and heir, John's, violent seizure between 1260 and 1261 of the earldom of Menteith from Walter's widow, Isabella, and her new husband John Russell, an English knight, amid accusations that Walter Comyn had been poisoned.[115]

Earl Walter's political significance in a crisis period of Scottish history has led to a number of extreme views about his role and that of the Comyns. To the influential but monarchocentric fourteenth- and fifteenth-century chroniclers John of Fordun and Walter Bower, Walter Comyn was seen largely as an unprincipled leader of an over-mighty faction, threatening the monarchy itself.[116] However, his actions should also be seen in the context of his leadership of a family caught up in a national crisis. Examples can be found, particularly in the period 1242–44, when the family used the immense power at their disposal in their own interests rather than in the interests of the state. However, when one considers that family interests were threatened and that Earl Walter's actions were, in the main, an attempt to stabilise the Comyn position rather than expand it, a fairer picture emerges. It would certainly be unwise to generalise about the family's political role in the minority crisis of 1249 to 1258 by using the years 1242–4 as a guideline. A better context for the Comyn role in the political crisis period 1242–58 would be their acknowledged place as key royal agents and pillars of monarchy in Scotland between 1205 and 1237.

There is clear evidence that Earl Walter was generally regarded as leader of the Scottish political community after the minority crisis began in 1249: he acted largely with the support of the Scottish nobility and the Scottish church. In fact, the only time when Walter Comyn acted without majority support during the king's minority was when he seized control of the young king himself in 1257. Even then, the terms of the treaty made with the Welsh in 1258 show that he was keenly aware of the king's position in society and that he was unwilling, even when he had *de facto* command, to do anything without the young king's permission. This was hardly unprincipled leadership. Even in 1257 and 1258 Comyn reverence for royal authority was unmistakable. The relationship between crown and nobility which had benefited the Comyns more than most noble families was placed under great strain during the minority – yet it survived.

At the other extreme from the depiction of Earl Walter Comyn as the unprincipled leader of a resentful faction is his elevation to the leadership of the 'patriot' party. It was probably Matthew Paris who first saw Walter Comyn's seizure of the king and government in 1257 as the wresting of power by native subjects from the hands of foreigners. The fact that the Comyns, the first noble family of Anglo-Continental origin to gain control of an earldom in Scotland, c.1212, could be regarded as 'native' is perhaps a tribute to the adaptation of the Comyns to Scottish society.

The Comyns were certainly 'patriots' in the sense that they were pillars of the Scottish monarchy, but they benefited immensely from their key role as royal agents – and in government they pursued a pragmatic rather than a patriot policy. The nobility of Scotland including the Comyns showed a clear awareness between 1249 and 1258 that political support from Henry III was necessary for any governing group in Scotland to secure stability. Walter Comyn certainly pushed Henry III's two guardians, Robert de Ros and John de Balliol, into the background during the period of Comyn government from 1251 to 1255. Yet the Comyns did not antagonise Henry III by pursuing 'national' policies. Earl Walter's government accepted, apparently without much struggle, the allocation of crusading taxes raised in Scotland for Henry III's own royal schemes in Sicily, nor is there evidence that Earl Walter pressed at the papal curia for Alexander III's anointment at a coronation ceremony. It was the Durward government, usually stigmatised by writers as pro-English, which raised these matters. It would be more realistic to describe the crisis in Scottish politics between 1249 and 1258 in terms of a pro-Comyn party and an anti-Comyn party than of a 'national' party and pro-English party.

NOTES

1. *Holyrood Liber* p.52; NB. it is possible that Walter Comyn received a charter of the earldom *R.M.S.* I Appendix 2 No. 4 though there is no date given and it may have been granted after his marriage to Isabella.
2. *Arbroath Liber* pp. 8, 21; *S.H.S.* Misc. Vol. IV pp.313–14, *Holyrood Liber* pp. 48, 50.
3. *Cal. Docs. Scot.*, I No. 1762.
4. Barbara E. Crawford, 'The Earldom of Caithness and the Kingdom of Scotland', in Stringer (ed.), *Essays on the Nobility of Medieval Scotland*, p.34.
5. *Ibid.* pp.30–3.
6. *Ibid.* p.37.
7. *Chron. Melrose* (Stevenson) p.146.
8. Barrow, *Kingdom of the Scots*, 'The Justiciar', p.107.
9. Paris, *Chron. Majora*, IV V. p.380; F.M. Powicke, *King Henry III and the lord Edward* (Oxford, 1947), p.744.
10. Barrow, *Kingdom of the Scots*, p.107.
11. Stones, *Anglo-Scottish Relations*, p.50.
12. *Liber Insule Missarum* (Bannatyne Club, 1847) pp.xxix–xxxii.
13. Paris, *Chron. Majora*, V p.724.
14. Young, 'Earls and Earldom of Buchan', in Grant and Stringer (eds), *Medieval Scotland*, p.175.

15. This section owes much to G.W.S. Barrow, 'Badenoch and Strathspey I', *Northern Scotland*, Vol.8 (1988) p.4.
16. Duncan, *Making of the Kingdom*, p.188.
17. *Ibid.*
18. Duncan, 'The Earldom of Atholl in the Thirteenth Century', *The Scottish Genealogist*, VII (1960) pp.2–10.
19. Duncan, *Making of the Kingdom*, pp. 188, 197; Barrow, *Anglo-Norman Era* pp. 32, 68; Barrow, 'Badenoch and Strathspey', *Northern Scotland*, p.5.
20. *Coupar Angus Chrs*, I pp.111–12.
21. Matthew Paris in Anderson, *Scottish Annals from English Chroniclers*, p.349; Chron. Melrose in Anderson, *Early Sources of Scottish History*, p.530.
22. For discussion of this see especially Duncan, *Making of the Kingdom*, pp.544–5; *Chron. Bower* (Watt), V pp. 179, 280–2.
23. *Scottish Annals from English Chroniclers*, p.349.
24. *Chron. Bower* (Watt), V pp. 183–4, 282.
25. D.E.R. Watt, 'The Minority of Alexander III of Scotland', *T.R.H.S.* 5th Series, XXI (1971) pp.1–2.
26. *Chron. Bower* (Watt), V p.181.
27. Chron. Melrose in Anderson, *Early Sources of Scottish History*, p.530.
28. *Chron. Bower* (Watt), V p.181.
29. Matthew Paris in Anderson, *Scottish Annals*, pp. 349–50.
30. Chron. Melrose in Anderson, *Early Sources of Scottish History*, p.536.
31. Matthew Paris in Anderson, *Scottish Annals*, p.350.
32. *Ibid.; Chron. Bower* (Watt), V n.17 p.284; Barrow, *Bruce*, pp.336–7 n.1.
33. Paris op.cit. p.353.
34. G.W.S. Barrow, 'The Army of Alexander III's Scotland' in Norman H. Reid, *Scotland in the Reighn of Alexander III* (1960), p.132 and n.3.
35. *Cal. Close Rolls* (1242–7) p.222. Walter Comyn himself was not known to own land in Tynedale but his elder brother Richard and Richard's son John inherited the family's Tynedale lands (including Tarset).
36. Paris in *Scottish Annals*, p.353.
37. Young, 'The North and Anglo-Scottish Relations in the Thirteenth Century' in J. Appleby and P. Dalton (eds), *Government, Society and Religion in Northern England* 1000–1700 (1997) pp.84–5.
38. *Ibid.;* F.M. Powicke, *King Henry III and the lord Edward* (1947) p.744.
39. *Cal. Docs. Scot.* I no.1621.
40. *Chron. Bower* (Watt), V p.185.
41. Anderson, *Early Sources*, p.536 n.3; *Chron. Bower* (Watt), V p.284 n.17.
42. *Cal. Docs. Scot.* nos.2671–2; Geoffrey de Marisco was, apparently, the nephew of the Archbishop of Dublin, John Comyn, and this explains the presence of a Maurice and Eustace Comyn in his company (Powicke, *Henry III and the Lord Edward*, p.744. There is no direct evidence to link the Irish Comyns with Scottish affairs.

43. Watt, 'The Minority of Alexander III of Scotland' p.3.
44. S.R.O. RH 1/2/32; *St Andrews Liber* pp.250–3, see Young, 'The Political Role of Walter Comyn, earl of Menteith' in Stringer (ed.), *Essays on the Nobility*, p.132.
45. *Chron. Bower* (Watt), V p.283 n.66.
46. *Coupar Angus Chrs*, I p.III.
47. Matthew Paris in *Scottish Annals* p.361.
48. Young, 'The Political Role of Walter Comyn, earl of Menteith' p.133.
49. *Cal. Docs. Scot.* nos.2671–2.
50. *Arbroath Liber* p.265; *Cambuskenneth Reg.* p.297; *Moray Reg.* pp.98–9.
51. S.R.O. RH 1/2/31.
52. Hugh de Airth was a bailiff of John Comyn in the 1280s (Stevenson, *Documents*, I pp. 262, 286).
53. *Kelso Liber*, p.226; *St Andrews Liber*, pp.251–4.
54. *Arbroath Liber*, pp.93–4; *Coupar Angus Chrs*, I p.90.
55. *Newbattle Reg.* p.7, *Morton Reg.*, II p.4; Raine, *North Durham* p.42.
56. S.R.O. GD 101/2; *Arbroath Liber*, p.9; for Eviot see G.W.S. Barrow, 'Hidden Record II: An unremembered Scottish family', *Scottish Record Society* (1994).
57. Matthew Paris, *Chron. Majora*, IV pp.381–2.
58. *Cal. Close Rolls* (1242–47) p.221.
59. Watt, 'Minority of Alexander III' pp.6–7.
60. *Ibid.* p.7.
61. *Chron. Fordun* II.
62. Grant G. Simpson, 'A Seal of Minority of Alexander III' in Grant and Stringer (eds), *Medieval Scotland*, pp.134–5.
63. *Ibid.* p. 135, Duncan, *The Making of the Kingdom*, p.559.
64. Barrow, *Kingdom of the Scots*, p.85 and no.11; *Chron. Fordun*, II p.289.
65. *Lindores Cart* p.41; *C.D.S.*, I no.1763.
66. E.L.G. Stones and Grant G. Simpson, *Edward I and the Throne of Scotland* (1978), II pp.204–5.
67. S.R.O. GD 175/1; *Acts Parl. Scot*, I p.245.
68. *Chron. Fordun*, II p.291.
69. *Concilia Scotiae*, e. J. Robertson (Bannatyne Club, 1866), ii pp. 241–2.
70. Young, 'The Political Role of Walter Comyn' in Stringer (ed.), *Essays on the Nobility*, p.135.
71. M. Ash, 'The Church in the Reign of Alexander III' in Norman H. Reid (ed.), *Scotland in the Reign of Alexander III*, p.37.
72. *Ibid.*
73. *Ibid.*
74. Young, 'The Political Role of Walter Comyn', p.135.
75. *Ibid.* p.136.
76. *Ibid.* pp.135–6 – the chronicle presumably meant the legitimation of Durward's wife.

77. *Ibid.* 136 and p.147 n.49.
78. *Chron. Fordun*, II p.291.
79. Young, 'The North and Anglo-Scottish Relations in the Thirteenth Century' pp.85–6.
80. *C.D.S.*, I no.2013.
81. G.W.S. Barrow, 'Some Problems in Twelfth and Thirteenth Century Scottish History – a Genealogical Approach', *The Scottish Genealogist* XXV No. 4 Dec. 1978 pp.105–7; Young, 'The Political Role of Walter Comyn', p.136.
82. Matthew Paris in Anderson, *Scottish Annals*, pp. 368, 370.
83. Young, 'The North and Anglo-Scottish Relations in the Thirteenth Century', p. 86–7.
84. *Chron. Fordun*, II p.292; Simpson, 'Kingship in Miniature' in Grant and Stringer (eds), *Medieval Scotland*, pp.134–5.
85. Matthew Paris in Anderson, *Scottish Annals* p.369.
86. Young, 'The Political Role of Walter Comyn', p.137.
87. Marinell Ash, 'The Church in the Reign of Alexander III' in Reid (ed.), *Scotland in the Reign of Alexander III*, p.41.
88. *Melrose Liber*, I no.336; *Dunfermline Reg no.84.* cf. Duncan, *Scotland, the Making of the Kingdom*, p.575.
89. Matthew Paris in Anderson, *Scottish Annals* p.369.
90. *Chron. Fordun*, II pp.292–3; *Chron. Bower* (Watt), V p.303.
91. Watt,'The Minority of Alexander III'; Young, 'The Political Role of Walter Comyn'.
92. Young, 'The Political Role of Walter Comyn', p.138.
93. *Ibid.* p.139; Chron. Melrose in Anderson, *Early Sources*, pp.575–6.
94. *Cals. Docs. Scot.* I nos. 1895, 1956, 1984–5, 2022.
95. Matthew Paris in Anderson, *Scottish Annals* pp. 371–2.
96. *Ibid.* pp. 370–1.
97. Stones, *Anglo-Scottish Relations*, pp.61–9; Chron. Melrose in Anderson, *Early Sources*, p.582.
98. *Chron. Bower* (Watt), V p.317.
99. Stones, *Anglo-Scottish Relations*, pp.61–9.
100. *Ibid.* p.67.
101. *Chron. Fordun*, II p.292.
102. Watt, 'The Minority of Alexander III', pp.15–16.
103. Young, 'The Political Role of Walter Comyn'. p.140.
104. *Ibid.*
105. *Foedera* I, I p.353.
106. *Cal. Docs. Scot.* I no.2080.
107. Young, 'The North and Anglo-Scottish Relations in the Thirteenth Century' p.87.
108. Chron. Melrose in Anderson, *Early Sources*, p.589.
109. *Foedera* I, I p.370.

110. Translation taken from G.W.S. Barrow, 'Wales and Scotland in Middle Ages', *Welsh Historical Review*, 10 (1980–81), pp.311–12.

111. Matthew Paris in Anderson, *Scottish Annals* p.376.

112. *Scone Liber*, no.108.

113. Matthew Paris supra.

114. *Chron. Fordun*, II p.289.

115. *Ibid.* p.293; Young, 'The Political Role of Walter Comyn', p.143, and p.149 no.104.

116. See n.90.

CHAPTER FOUR

A Responsible, Aristocratic Governing Community, c.1260–1286

T he compromise council of 1258, in which supporters from both Comyn and Durward groups were apparently willing to work together, is normally taken as a sign that the unsettled minority period was drawing to a close. Two events, apparently marking the decline of the Comyn party – the death of Earl Walter Comyn in 1258 and the decision of the king and aristocratic community in 1261 not to allow John Comyn to succeed to the earldom of Menteith after Comyn had seized the countess and her second husband and forced them to resign the earldom to him[1] – have been used to confirm that the days of the overmighty subject were finally over: 'Thus 1261 sees the end of our sub-plot "The Challenge of the House of Comyn".'[2] From 1261 the aristocracy have usually been seen as being firmly under royal control, allowing the Scottish kingdom to develop with royal authority extended in the west and north, and with greater political independence being gained from England. Yet such a scenario favours too much the monarchocentric views of Fordun and Bower. A view from the baronial milieu is necessary.

The fact that Alexander III's reign started with a political crisis, the minority period 1249–58, has tended to dominate the discussion of the reign in general and distort the role of nobility in particular.[3] Political crises lend themselves not only to atypical behaviour on the part of the protagonists but also to extreme interpretations by commentators both contemporary and modern. Yet while family interests came to the fore and naturally guided the actions of the nobility in Scotland during the difficult minority years, a reverence for royal authority is still unmistakable. The minority period as a whole displays a natural inclination to work through the normal channels of government despite the crisis. It is therefore unwise to make too great a distinction between the years of Alexander III's minority and those of his maturity. Those who make such a distinction have to explain why there was such a dramatic change in the nobility's role and attitude after the minority was over. The explanation has normally been (a) that the Comyns were in decline and no longer able to dominate the political scene[4] and (b) that Alexander III was able to supervise a delicate balancing operation between rival baronial factions.[5]

The notion of a balancing operation between baronial factions after 1258 is based most of all on the compromise council apparently agreed in September 1258. Yet, as has been pointed out, details of the council involving an equal number of Comyn and Durward supporters are only known from an English source: 'It is certainly possible that the text of the document of 6th November 1258 which gave recognition to a council of ten represents more what the English thought should happen in Scotland rather than what the Scots felt bound to put into effect – and this applies not only to the people mentioned, but also to the whole tone of the text in that it implies the perpetuation for some unspecified period of a system of minority government under English supervision'.[6] As for the Comyns, it has been suggested that there is no evidence of a Comyn domination in the period 1260 to 1286 and that they were, in fact, 'willing to co-operate with their seventeen-year-old king in letting him run his own show'.[7] A slightly different explanation for Comyn decline combines both reasons for the supposedly dramatic change in the attitude of the nobility – that Alexander III took the initiative by denying his patronage to disruptive barons and restricting the monopoly of power enjoyed by the Comyns.[8] He did this by encouraging the presence at the royal court of a junior branch of the Comyn family, the Comyns of Kilbride, rather than the more senior Buchan and Badenoch branches; he also promoted other 'new men' in the royal circle such as Simon Fraser, Reginald Cheyne, Thomas Randolph and Hugh Berkeley.

While the removal of baronial malcontents from the minority period and their replacement by 'new men' seems a logical way to explain a more responsible attitude on the part of the nobility between 1258 and 1286, an analysis of offices held, and royal missions accomplished in this period, presents a different picture. It is true that Alan Durward, a major participant in the politics of the minority, did not hold major office after 1258. He was nonetheless recognised as one of the leading members of the nobility in the late 1250s and early 1260s. He was, for instance, a royal messenger to England in 1259 as well as a member of the provisional regency council set up in 1261;[9] he was involved in the important royal mission to counter the Norwegian threat in 1263 and 1264. Durward, however, witnessed relatively few royal charters and was at the royal court infrequently in the 1270s.[10] When the fortunes of the Comyn faction after 1258 are reviewed, however, a surprising picture emerges. Far from being eclipsed, the Comyns dominated political and public offices, royal missions and witness lists to royal charters. There is, moreover, little evidence of an imposed balance with the Durward party.

It is striking that the same members of the Comyn party so roundly condemned in 1257 and 1258 retained the offices which they then held. The premier political office, the justiciarship of Scotia, which assumed so much more weight during the minority period, was held by Alexander Comyn, earl of Buchan, from 1258 until his death in 1289.[11] An interesting sidelight on Earl Alexander's role as justiciar was the appointment of deputies. In 1260 Freskin de Moray, David de Lochore, and John Cameron (the latter two both afterwards sheriffs of Perth) performed the office of justiciar in Earl Alexander's place.[12] It is notable that David de Lochore was prominently involved in Comyn 'party' activities between 1251 and 1258 and remained a member of the Comyn following in the 1260s and 1270s. Freskin de Moray was also in the Comyn 'party' in 1258 and members of the family were quite frequently in the Comyn circle. Thus two of the three deputies for the justiciar in 1260 were, it seems, selected from Earl Alexander's close associates.

The chief of the Badenoch branch of the family after Walter Comyn's death in 1258, his nephew John Comyn, held the justiciarship of Galloway in 1258, for a time in the 1260s and again in 1275. Other members of the Comyn following[13] who held justiciarships were Thomas de Normanville, justiciar of Lothian c.1259–60, Hugh de Berkeley, justiciar of Lothian c.1262–79, William de Soules (son of Nicholas de Soules), justiciar of Lothian c.1279–c.92, and Aymer de Maxwell, justiciar of Galloway in 1264. With regard to other important offices, William Wishart retained the post of chancellor between 1258 and 1273 and Aymer de Maxwell, named chamberlain in the 1258 treaty with the Welsh, retained the post of chamberlain until 1266. It is interesting to note that between 1251 and 1290 (with a break from 1255–57) a succession of prominent Comyn supporters held the office of chamberlain – William earl of Mar (1251–55), Aymer de Maxwell (1258–66), Reginald Cheyne (1266–78) and Thomas Randolf II. Known Comyn supporters, Gamelin and William Wishart, held the office of chancellor from c.1254 (with a break from 1255–57) until 1273.

Comyn dominance of offices of state becomes even more apparent when possession of sheriffdoms is analysed.[14] Comyn men held the sheriffdoms of Fife[15] (through the Lascelles family), Roxburgh, Dumfries, Dingwall, Forfar[16] (through the Mowat family), Peebles, Perth, Kincardine (or Mearns), Elgin[17] (through the Munfort family), Lanark, Berwick, Cromarty, Dumbarton, Wigtown and Ayr for much of Alexander III's reign. Comyn dominance was particularly marked in the sheriffdoms of Roxburgh, Dingwall, Forfar, Kincardine, Elgin, Berwick and Cromarty. Some key Comyn men held a multiplicity of offices. Alexander Comyn, as well as being justiciar of Scotia, was sheriff of Wigtown c.1263–66, sheriff of Dingwall c.1264–66, and from c.1275 he was constable of Scotland, and dominated the witness lists of Alexander III's charters; Aymer de Maxwell was chamberlain c.1259–60, justiciar of Galloway c.1264, sheriff of Roxburgh c.1249?, sheriff of Peebles c.1262 and sheriff of Dumfries 1264–66; Thomas Randolf was chamberlain c.1269–77, sheriff of Roxburgh in 1266 and sheriff of Berwick c.1264–66, and was a frequent witness to the king's charters; William de Soules, son of Nicholas de Soules (related to the Comyns through marriage), was justiciar of Lothian 1279–92/3, sheriff of Roxburgh by 1289 and before 1289–91 sheriff of Inverness,[18] while John de Soules was sheriff of Berwick by 1289; David de Graham, who had been deputy justiciar of Lothian in 1248, was sheriff of Berwick c.1264 while his son Patrick was very prominent in royal witness lists of the 1270s and 1280s and was to be sheriff of Stirling by 1289. Both Patrick de Graham and John de Soules took part in Alexander III's search for a second bride in 1284.

William earl of Mar (who had married a daughter of William Comyn earl of Buchan) was for a time chamberlain, c.1252–55, but was also sheriff of Dumbarton c.1264–66 and a prominent witness of Alexander III's charters; regular Comyn supporters, the Mowats, featured in office through William, sheriff of Cromarty c.1266, Robert, sheriff of Forfar c.1250–64 and Michael who had been justiciar of Scotia c.1251–53, while Bernard Mowat was one of the nobles who escorted Margaret, daughter of Alexander III, to Norway and was a regular witness to Alexander III's charters; two members of the

Lochore family, David and William, were respectively sheriff of Fife c.1264–75 and sheriff of Perth 1255–62; William de St Clair (or Sinclair) was sheriff of Edinburgh, Linlithgow and Haddington c.1264 and a frequent witness to royal charters in the 1270s, while perhaps a son was sheriff of Dumfries by 1290; Reginal Cheyne was chamberlain c.1267–c.1269, and sheriff of Kincardine c.1264–66; either this man or his son was sheriff of Kincardine by 1290 and both appeared regularly in royal witness lists. Hugh de Abernethy was sheriff of Roxburgh c.1264 and was seen regularly in royal witness lists in the 1260s and 1270s. Many of these officials took part in important royal missions during Alexander III's reign.

It is interesting to find similar Comyn domination of ecclesiastical offices between 1260 and 1286.[19] Again familiar names recur: Gamelin was bishop of St Andrews 1255–71; Henry Cheyne was bishop of Aberdeen 1282–1328; William Comyn of Kilconquhar was bishop of Brechin 1275–77; William Wishart (from a family prominent in the 1251–55 list of Comyn supporters) was bishop of Glasgow 1270–71 and bishop of St Andrews 1271–79, while Robert Wishart was bishop of Glasgow 1271–1316.

Analysis of offices held and presence in the royal circle indicate a clear dominance of the Comyns and noble families known to be in the Comyn following. Alexander Comyn earl of Buchan was the most regular of all witnesses to Alexander III's charters. The Badenoch branch, represented by John Comyn, both father and son, was also present in the royal circle though not as frequently. The prominence of William Comyn of Kilbride in royal witness lists of Alexander III is surely a sign of yet another member of the family coming to prominence – in addition to, rather than instead of, the two more senior branches. Absence of direct Kilbride representation in the political actions of the Comyn party from 1251 to 1258 should not be taken as a sign that there was no active support from this branch for the two more senior branches of the family. William Comyn of Kilbride's father, David, (d.1247), was clearly a member of Earl Walter's party in 1244. Charter evidence suggests that William Comyn was an active member of the Comyn party and maintained close connections with the Badenoch lines.[20] Members of William's feudal following, the Gourlay family, actively participated in the Comyn government 1251–55.

Comyn dominance in government hardly suggests a delicate balancing act between rival baronial families. Of the four members of the compromise council of 1258 who were regarded by the English source as balancing the Comyn presence – Alan Durward, Robert de Meyners (Menzies), Alexander Stewart and Gilbert de Hay – only Gilbert de Hay is known to have held office, as sheriff of Perth (1262–3). Gilbert had been in the Comyn following in 1244 but was named in the non-Comyn council of fifteen in 1255. He was married to a daughter of William Comyn earl of Buchan and it seems possible that he became reconciled to the Comyns after 1258. Robert de Menzies, who had also been in the Comyn following in 1244, appeared only occasionally in the royal circle in the 1260s. Alan Durward and especially Alexander Stewart[21] appeared more frequently at the royal court in the 1260s and 1270s, though without holding any office other than those indicated by their surnames. The Stewart family as a whole did become a more important part of the Scottish political scene.

When the other eleven names associated with the 1255 non-Comyn council are also looked at, an interesting picture emerges. Only Patrick earl of Dunbar, perhaps the leading baron of the 1255 non-Comyn council, appeared very frequently in the royal circle in the 1260s and 1270s. In fact, only Alexander Comyn earl of Buchan was a more frequent witness to Alexander III's charters in this period. Earl Patrick, however, remained without any political office or apparent responsibility. Evidence from royal witness lists hardly suggests that Earl Patrick dropped 'out of sight' or was wholly ignored[22] but it is interesting to note that he apparently became tied to the Comyn family by marriage to one of the daughters of Alexander Comyn earl of Buchan.[23] Of the other three earls, associated with the non-Comyn council of seven years – Malise earl of Strathearn, Nigel earl of Carrick and Malcolm earl of Fife – Earls Malise and Malcolm continued, albeit infrequently, to witness royal charters, and the successors to Earls Nigel and Malcolm appeared infrequently too. Of the other men named in the 1255 non-Comyn council – Robert Bruce, Walter de Moray, David Lindsay, William de Brechin and Hugh Giffard – Walter de Moray appeared occasionally at the royal court in the 1260s, Robert de Bruce rather infrequently, and another member of the Lindsay family, Walter, appeared occasionally.

Naturally there would be some ebb and flow in family fortunes in the period 1260 to 1286 but a constant factor was the political dominance of the Comyn party. Marriage alliances further sealed this dominance (see family tree).[24] Alexander Comyn's sisters had made good marriages. Elizabeth married William earl of Mar, a most prominent Comyn supporter in the 1250s and a continuing influence through the 1260s; his half-sister John had married William earl of Ross; Idonea had married Gilbert de Hay and Agnes had married Philip de Meldrum. This trend continued with five of Alexander Comyn's daughters marrying major Scottish barons: Patrick earl of Dunbar, Malise earl of Strathearn, Gilbert de Umphraville earl of Angus, William Brechin and Nicholas de Soules. Further, Alexander's son and heir, John, married Isabella, daughter of Colban earl of Fife. Marriage alliances, with four families who had been associated with the non-Comyn government of 1255, are a particularly marked feature. Alexander Comyn's place at the head of the aristocratic establishment of Scotland was secure both socially and politically. The marriages of the Badenoch line of the family further developed this network of influence. John Comyn I of Badenoch (d. c.1277) probably took as his second wife Alicia de Lindsay of Lamberton. He had a large family – five sons and four daughters. His son and heir John II the Competitor (d. 1302) married Eleanor sister of John Balliol, (the future king) probably in the 1270s; according to Wyntoun his four daughters married Richard Siward, Geoffrey de Mowbray, Alexander Macdougall lord of Argyll, and Alexander de Moray.

While the Comyns consolidated their role at the head of the Scottish aristocratic establishment after 1258, it should be noted that other families grew more prominent too. Members of the Moray family gathered political strength in the period 1260 to 1286.[25] Alexander de Moray was sheriff of Inverness after 1264 and sheriff of Ayr by 1288. Malcolm de Moray was sheriff of Perth 1257×1289 and Walter and William de Moray were witnesses to several royal charters. They seem to have been associated with the Comyns in the 1230s but their affiliation with the Comyns was less clear in the 1250s – Walter de Moray was in the non-Comyn party of the 1250s and appears to have been justiciar of Lothian 1255–57. Freskin de Moray was, however, linked to the Comyn family by marriage and was clearly in the Comyn following of 1258. Other members of the family (Walter and Malcolm) appeared as witnesses to charters of Alexander Comyn earl of Buchan in the 1260s. It appears that a daughter of John Comyn I of Badenoch married Alexander de Moray. Thus the de Morays may have risen to prominence principally because of their association with the Comyns.

Such associations played no part, however, in the continuing rise of the Stewart family. With their hereditary position as Stewart of Scotland and their vast estates derived from the first royal grants to the family in the twelfth century, the Stewarts were already a powerful family by the middle of the thirteenth century, with access to the royal council.[26] They were prominent in the non-Comyn group in 1255 and 1258. In Alexander III's reign, however, especially after c.1260, they stepped more firmly to the forefront of the political stage. Walter Stewart, a younger member of the family, became earl of Menteith in controversial circumstances c.1261, was sheriff of Ayr by 1264, sheriff of Dumbarton between 1271 and 1288 and was also prominent in royal witness lists in the 1280s. Alexander Stewart and his son James were regularly in the royal circle from the 1250s to the 1280s and James was sheriff of Ayr later in 1288 and sheriff of Dumbarton in 1289.

From a less prominent background and with no known affiliation at first (though they were linked with the Comyns by the 1290s), the Fraser family, especially in the person of Simon Fraser, emerged in the 1260s and 1270s to a position of real importance.[27] Other prominent nobles in the royal circle included John de Lamberton, sheriff of Stirling c.1265 and a regular witness to royal charters, especially in the mid-1260s. It is noticeable moreover that the Bissets, great rivals of the Comyns in the 1240s, were also prominent at the royal court in the person of William Bisset, a regular witness to royal acts in the 1270s – but by then the Bissets were no longer a threat to the Comyn position. It is perhaps appropriate to end an analysis of the baronial establishment in the period 1260 to 1286 with the names which dominated the politics of the 1290s – Balliol and Bruce. Members of the Balliol family made only occasional appearances in the Scottish king's circle; the name Bruce made very little impact at the Scottish court in the 1260s, though after gaining the earldom of Carrick in 1272 Robert Bruce began to make some impact in the later 1270s. Neither held political office or looked like disturbing the Comyn grip on the Scottish political scene. It is important to note that there was little sign before 1286 of the great conflicts of the 1290s and the War of Independence. It is misleading to look at the period from 1260 to 1286 with hindsight and concentrate on the potential rivalries rather than the actual baronial scene in Alexander III's reign. Alliance and harmony between monarchy and nobility were the main features of Alexander III's reign.

Comyns, Stewarts and Morays were the principal beneficiaries of this alliance between crown and aristocracy. They had sufficient territorial influence for their authority, wielded on behalf of the king, to be accepted in the north and the south-west, or, in the case of the Comyns, in both areas. The crown was dependent on its magnates for wielding royal power and authority in the provinces and the sharing of government between crown and aristocracy was, in the circumstances, mutually beneficial. Interdependence was the logical outcome of a situation where the Scottish king had enough material resources to reward magnates but not enough to overawe them and where the nobility did not (unlike the nobility of England) have to suffer the consequences of an aggressive and expensive foreign policy with its heavy aides, scutages and tallages. In these circumstances, it is not difficult to see why confrontation between crown and magnates was commoner in thirteenth-century England than in Scotland. The notion that there was, in Scotland, an 'inveterate hostility of great houses to the Crown and to each other[28] could hardly be further from reality in the period 1260–1286. In practice, the nobility of Scotland in this period had a real interest in preserving the integrity of the Scottish kingdom and extending the authority of a king who could give them and their followers rich rewards. This is seen in the early years of Alexander III's maturity.

The loss of Comyn control of the earldom of Menteith after 1258 has usually been seen as a sign of Comyn decline, an end to their days as overmighty subjects. This episode, however, if viewed from the baronial viewpoint, shows the realities of the relationship between crown and nobility in Alexander III's reign. When, after the death of Walter Comyn, earl of Menteith in 1258, his widow married John Russell, a large body of magnates, according to John of Fordun, 'took this in high dudgeon'.[29] They thought that she had disdained the noble lords of Scotland who wanted to wed her, in order to marry a low-born English knight. This is another episode which, like the hounding of the Bissets after the death of Patrick of Atholl in 1242, illustrates a very conservative aristocratic elite acting in unison to protect its collective status from new or low-born intruders. Nevertheless, the leading nobles of Scotland did, at the request of the king, sanction the marriage which meant that the new head of the Badenoch branch of the Comyn family, John Comyn, Earl Walter's nephew and successor, would only succeed to the lordship of Badenoch. When John Comyn responded to this decision by seizing the countess and her new husband and forcing them to resign the earldom to him, the general baronial response is an important contribution to the debate about relations between crown and aristocracy. At an assembly of king and magnates, eleven of whom were known members of the Comyn 'party', a compromise was agreed upon: Walter Stewart, on his wife's behalf (she was either a sister or cousin of Countess Isabella), should be invested with the earldom.

If narrow factional interest was all-important to the nobility, then surely a Comyn-dominated court would have made a decision in favour of John Comyn. The decision reached may have been recognised at the time as *contra justitiam*[30] and the Comyns did not drop their claim,[31] but a politically sensible solution had been achieved – political stability had been promoted 'while the king was still a minor'.[32] John Comyn's loss of the earldom of Menteith by 1260–61 was a personal setback for him in Scotland, not a setback for the Comyn family. Earl Alexander was recognised as the head of the Comyn party and as leader of the aristocratic governing community in Scotland. His experienced counsel was very evident in the early years of Alexander III's maturity – Alexander was still a young man of 17 years in 1258.

One major and very delicate political matter to be dealt with in 1258 was the relationship between Scotland and England. In 1255 the Scots had agreed to the continuation of the minority until 1262 with the terms of the agreement indicating the importance of Henry III's oversight of Scottish affairs. In 1259 Master William de Horton came to Scotland on behalf of Henry III to discuss with the Scottish king matters concerning the minority and the king of England's part in it.[33] He asked that the young king and queen should come to England to discuss the matter with Henry. The Scots were suspicious but at length agreed to discussions in England. Soon after William de Horton's departure, Earl Alexander Comyn, Master William Wishart (a member of the Comyn government of 1251–55) and Alan Durward were sent to England as messengers of state to explain the Scottish attitude and to recover the document of September 1255.[34] This episode revealed that the three most influential members of the Scottish government were Earl Alexander Comyn the justiciar, William Wishart the chancellor, and Alan Durward. It showed in practice, rather than the theory of the English document of November 1258, how a compromise government in Scotland was working.

Earl Alexander was involved in another matter relating to the preservation of the Scottish kingdom's integrity in 1260–61. This was when Alexander III, showing a little more confidence than in 1259, allowed his wife to go to England to stay with her mother during her confinement prior to the birth of the heiress to the Scottish throne.[35] The conditions on which this trip was made reveal extremely shrewd counsel of the sort which those magnates involved in the power struggles of the minority could provide. The realisation of the dangers of a minority was implicit in terms which tried to counter any possibility of Scottish government disintegrating: the queen and her offspring were to be delivered to Scotland forty days after the birth; if the queen should die, her child should be returned to Scotland; if the Scottish king should die, a body of thirteen men (in effect, a regency council of four bishops, five earls and four barons) or three or four of them would take his heir to Scotland and have responsibility for government. Obviously a lesson had been learned from 1249 by Earl Alexander and other experienced councillors as no formal plans had apparently been made before Alexander II's death.

It is significant that the council of regency was carefully thought out, comprising four bishops, five earls and four barons drawn equally from the Comyn and non-Comyn groups.[36] This formal arrangement was probably based on the informal alliance worked out in September 1258. These plans for an emergency council were to be invaluable in 1286 when the next minority crisis arose in Scotland. They were surely a sign of a responsible aristocratic governing community in which the Comyns played a key part, and Earl Alexander of Buchan, in particular, a leading part. The perpetuation of kingship and kingdom loomed large again when the succession was threatened by the deaths of Alexander's son David in 1281, his daughter Margaret in 1283 and his eldest son, the prince Alexander, in 1284. In February 1284, in a parliament at Scone, the most important magnates in Scotland (thirteen earls and twenty-five barons) bound themselves to maintain the succession of Margaret, 'Maid of Norway'.[37] Such formal and mature constitutional procedures in the period 1260–1286, together with the refusal of Alexander III to acknowledge English overlordship in 1251 and 1278 and many other lesser actions,[38] such as the precautions taken in York in 1251 to provide separate quarters for the retinues of the English and Scottish kings, the decision of Scottish king and magnates to acquire the fief of Bathgate and Ratho and to attempt to purchase from Reading abbey its dependent priory on the Isle of May, all point to a clearer sense of nationality in Scotland.

Just as the nobility in Scotland had a real interest in preserving the integrity of the kingdom, they had also a real incentive in extending the authority of its king. Alexander Comyn, earl of Buchan, played a key role as justiciar of Scotia. In Alexander III's minority, it has been seen that Alan Durward tried to heighten the status of this office. Comyn landowning power throughout Scotland undoubtedly made Alexander Comyn's authority more effective as justiciar of Scotia than Alan Durward's had been. Indeed, Alexander's authority seemed to extend beyond the boundaries of Scotia (Scotland, north of the Forth). A sign that the justiciarship of Scotia was 'being elevated' into a justiciarship of Scotland is seen in the king's licence, dated at Kilwinning in 1260, commanding the earl of Buchan 'and his (i.e. the king's) baillies of Carrick' to hold an inquest 'to inquire whether Hector son of Hector of Carrick was vested and seized "per dies at annos" in five pennyworths of the land at "Achinsauhile" (Auchensoule in Barr, Ayrshire) and how he was ejected therein'.[39] Earl Alexander is not known to have had interests in Carrick until after 1264.[40]

Earl Alexander's role as justiciar, certainly very useful to the king administratively, judicially and financially,[41] was also very important militarily. Earl Alexander played a leading part along with Alexander Stewart in the defence of the country against a Norwegian threat in the 1260s and also in the extension of royal authority in the Western Isles.[42] He can thus be seen as continuing his father Earl William's role as an instrument of royal policy – Earl William had brought a degree of royal control to northern Scotland in 1211–12 and 1229–30. In the early 1260s Alexander III began to take up his father's policy of wresting control of the Western Isles from Norway. In the 1240s Alexander II had made annexation of the Isles a fundamental part of his policy but had unexpectedly died during an expedition against Argyll in 1249. By c.1263 Alexander III was beginning to put pressure on the king of Norway. He sent an embassy to King Hakon to negotiate for the ceding of the Isles. At about the same time, the earl of Ross plundered the Isle of Skye. Such pressure produced a reaction from Norway. Whether this reaction was in the form of an invasion or merely a show of strength is not certain. What is certain, however, is Alexander Comyn's prominent role in the Scottish counter to this threat. The earl of Buchan and Alan Durward had joint responsibilities in the defence against the Norwegians.[43] There was no large pitched battle. A storm arose, many Norwegian ships were blown aground near Largs and after fighting ensued, the Norwegians were defeated. After the king of Man, son-in-law of the Norwegian king, had done homage to the Scottish king at Dumfries, Earl Alexander, together with William earl of Mar and Alan Durward, was ordered to follow up the defeat of the Norwegians by suppressing those Scots who had encouraged and supported the king of Norway in the Western Isles. Thus, perhaps three of the leading men of the realm set off with a large force in the summer of 1264,[44] slew some of the Scottish traitors, put some to flight, hanged some of the chiefs and brought back much plunder.

Though the defeat of the Norwegians could be put down largely to the unfriendliness of the elements, Earl Alexander's supervisory role in the Scottish defence was important. He was also given added responsibility for the coastal defence as both sheriff and baillie[45] of the king. In his account as baillie of Inverie (probably Inverie in Knoydart) there is direct evidence of preparations made against the Norwegian threat. Besides outlay for repairs on the royal castle and drawbridge there, Earl Alexander disbursed 104 shillings on the food of eight soldiers garrisoning that place for six months.[46] In 1265 in his account as sheriff of Wigtown, he referred to 40 marks attorned to master Peter the mason in order that he might repair the houses inside the castle of Wigtown.[47] Another account of Earl Alexander as sheriff of Wigtown in 1266 refers to the payment of envoys between the kings of Scotland and Man.[48] Earl Alexander must have been sheriff of Wigtown by 1263–4. It is worthy of note too that Earl Alexander was, by 1264–6, also baillie of Dingwall,[49] another key coastal area for defence against possible invasions.

By the Treaty of Perth of 2nd July 1266, the Western Isles and the Isle of Man were ceded to Scotland in return for a payment of 4,000 marks and an annual rent of 100 marks.[50] In the definition of the kingdom of Scotland, this was an important treaty and it is a reflection of Earl Alexander's importance in political affairs that he was the first layman to append his seal to this significant document. As justiciar of Scotia, sheriff of Wigtown, sheriff of Dingwall and baillie of Inverie, Earl Alexander played a major role, not only in the defence of Scotland but in the reorganisation of royal control in the south-west and north of the kingdom. The erection of sheriffdoms at Wigtown and Dingwall in the period c.1263 was an important extension of the general pattern of sheriffdoms made in the 1260s. That both sheriffdoms were placed under Alexander Comyn's control, apparently as hereditary offices, was important for the Comyn family as much as for the kingdom.

The territorial influence of the Buchan branch of the family in the south-west was greatly increased on the death of Roger de Quincy in 1264, through the vast inheritance won by Alexander Comyn's wife, one of the co-heiresses to the estate.[51] It is interesting to note that the custody of Earl Roger's lands went not to royal clerks but in part to a great magnate like Earl Alexander, who was also one of the interested parties. Alexander was keeper of two-thirds of Roger's Galloway lands and also held two parts of Carrick at farm. Royal favour is apparent here. Earl Alexander established himself even more closely with the king when he also acquired the office of constable c.1275, again as a result of the de Quincy inheritance.[52] The Buchan branch's new interests in the south-west, through royal office and inheritance, added to those of the Badenoch branch of the Comyn family in the region. John Comyn of Badenoch had important landed influence in Peeblesshire and Dumfriesshire,[53] and was justiciar of Galloway in 1258, probably 1262×1272 and again in 1275. John Comyn also played a military role as one of the leaders of a royal expedition against Man in 1275.[54] Comyn presence in the south-west was further emphasised by William Comyn of Kilbride's role as sheriff of Ayr c.1265. The importance attached to William's contribution to the development of royal authority in the west is perhaps gauged by his regular appearances in the royal circle especially in the 1270s.

In the north Earl Alexander was sheriff of Dingwall c.1264–6 but his role in this part of the country was even more clearly seen in 1282 when he was sent on urgent royal business to the northern isles.[55] In a letter to excuse his absence from conflicting responsibilities in England, Alexander III made it very clear to the English king that the earl's activities in the north were indispensable to both Scottish king and kingdom. The contribution of the three branches of the Comyn family to the extension of royal authority in the south-west and the north is significant, but the involvement of Comyn associates in this process adds to this contribution. Thus William earl of Mar was sheriff of Dumbarton c.1264–6, Aymer de Maxwell was sheriff of Dumfries c.1264–5 and the sheriffdom of Cromarty was founded c.1266 as another hereditary office for the Mowat family.

Any analysis of the aristocratic governing community in Scotland is incomplete without reference to the significant group of nobles who held land in both Scotland and England.[56] Most major baronial families were included within this group.[57] As has been pointed out,[58] cross-border magnates held nine out of thirteen Scottish earldoms during the thirteenth century. In this period also senior offices such as the justiciarships of Scotia and Lothian, and chamberlain, were usually occupied by nobility with land in England. Access to the larger resources of the Angevin monarchy and the greater wealth of the kingdom of

England were attractive considerations for the nobility. The realities of peace rather than the potentialities of war governed baronial attitudes for much of the thirteenth century. The relationship between the kings of Scotland and England was particularly close during Alexander III's maturity, 1260 to 1286, and this enabled magnates holding land on both sides of the border to reinforce social and economic ties by involving themselves, their families and officials in their cross-border enterprises. This seems to have been the case even when estates were separated by great distances: the chief landholding of the Comyn earls of Buchan was in northern Scotland, but the family's interests and commitments were still vigorously pursued on the other side of the border, both by attorneys[59] and by the family's personal presence on their estates.

Anglo-Scottish magnates exhibited varying degrees of attachment to the kingdoms in which their lands lay, though they all accepted the commitments which went with land ownership on both sides of the border. Even within one family, different branches developed different policies and aspirations, dependent on individual circumstances. All three branches of the Comyn family – Buchan, Badenoch and Kilbride – had substantial estates in England. The de Quincy inheritance brought the Buchan branch of the family substantial landed estates in Dorset, Leicestershire, Warwickshire, Huntingdonshire, Berkshire, Cambridgeshire, Bedford, Essex, Worcester, Cumberland and Oxfordshire.[60] Though Alexander Comyn was actively and heavily engaged in Scottish government, he showed himself to be most anxious to secure the full rights of his wife in England, the break-up of the English de Quincy lands being a protracted affair. Attorneys used by Earl Alexander between 1264 and 1279 were drawn from both his Scottish and English estates, and appear alongside each other in the records.[61] While Earl Alexander was slow to come to the king's court in person to do homage for his wife Elizabeth's property, it would not be fair to call him an absentee landlord. He was present at Shepshed, one of his chief administrative centres in the Midlands, to receive the homage of William de Brideport in 1281,[62] and his sons were involved in their father's English estates before his death in 1289.[63]

Alexander Comyn's ready acknowledgement of the commitments, both military and financial, which were owed to the king of England for his English lands was a sign of the importance of his English inheritance. In 1276 he was among 178 tenants-in-chief summoned to meet Edward I at Worcester in order to fight the Welsh. Although Earl Alexander did not serve personally, he paid the scutage of 50 marks (one third of two knights' fees).[64] Similarly, in 1282, Alexander Comyn recognised his duty to serve the king of England. In his letter to Edward I he expressed his regret at being unable to serve personally against the Welsh – on this occasion his son Roger served in his stead. This episode, interestingly, showed how dual allegiance worked in practice, for on this occasion he had been sent by the Scottish king to the north of Scotland on urgent business.

A different set of circumstances governed the activities in England of John Comyn chief of the Badenoch branch of the family. This branch, which had landed influence throughout Scotland, also held important land in Tynedale, Northumberland.[65] When John Comyn suffered a set-back in 1260–1 with the loss of the earldom of Menteith, he took advantage of the opportunities open to him for advancement in England. Although appearing at the Scottish court in the 1260s, John Comyn was conspicuous at the English court in 1262, 1264 and 1265. He served Henry III personally in 1264 at the Battle of Lewes, being captured there along with John Balliol and Robert Bruce.[66] John Comyn was handsomely rewarded for this personal service. For serving Henry III in 1264 and 1265, he received 100 marks[67]; in 1267 for 'his laudable service' John Comyn and his heirs were granted the lands of Simon de Veer, the king's enemy;[68] and later in the same year he was granted 'before all others' £300 yearly of land.[69]

In contrast to the Badenoch involvement in England was the attitude of the Kilbride branch of the family which held the lordship of East Kilbride, land in Peeblesshire and around Falkirk,[70] and in England had land in Northumberland, Norfolk, Suffolk, Essex and Hertford.[71] Unlike his father David, William of Kilbride tended to disregard his obligations to the king of England. He was frequently involved in court cases between 1259 and 1279 either to answer for his scutage or as defendant for cases involving land dealings.[72] His disregard for his obligations to the king of England was most apparent in the 1260s when not only did he fail to serve Henry III against his baronial opposition but he actually sided with Simon de Montfort against the English king. As a result, his English lands were forfeited.[73]

It is clear, however, that not only in the minority of Alexander III but also in his maturity there was a common regard for the superior weight of the English king's influence. Nobles ousted from Scotland by political ill-fortune from the 1240s onwards had found Henry III and England a suitable and often profitable refuge. The Bissets, Alan Durward, David de Lindsay, Walter de Moray and Malise earl of Strathearn all received favour from the English king, usually in return for some service.[74] Alan Durward in particular frequently appeared in English records between 1251 and 1255 when he was ousted by the Comyns from Scottish government. Although part of the Scottish political scene again between 1258 and 1264, Durward was without political office (and perhaps reward?) and gradually faded from Scottish affairs in the early 1270s. It is interesting to note, however, that he was still in receipt of favours in England between 1268 and his death in 1275.[75] When John Comyn received a setback in Scotland in 1260/61, we saw how he became more conspicuous at the English king's court and gained suitable reward.

The names Bruce and Balliol appeared only irregularly in Scottish records. Playing only brief roles in the changing governments of the minority period, they held no political office during Alexander III's maturity, but were both deeply involved in English politics in the 1250s and 1260s. Marriage to Dervorguilla, daughter of Alan of Galloway, in 1233 had ensured that the Balliols had acquired vast estates in both countries by the mid-thirteenth century, through Dervorguilla's paternal and maternal inheritance.[76] The family thus had a secure territorial base for advancement in both countries but in the 1260s were prominent only on the English political scene. By the 1270s they were amongst the top-ranking English nobility. Potential in Scotland had not yet been realised though their position there was undoubtedly strengthened further through the marriage c.mid-1270s of a sister (Eleanor) of John Balliol II (future king of Scotland) to John Comyn, lord of Badenoch (d. 1302). The Bruces, too, were more active on the English political scene, at least until the 1270s. The family held positions of responsibility such as the governorship of Carlisle Castle,[77] served in Henry III's army in 1264, were keen to promise future service,[78] and as a result were in regular receipt of the English king's patronage. The Bruces had already gained sufficient territorial power, through marriages, to have a political platform in both Scotland and England,[79] but, in practice, they were seen very little in the Scottish royal circle in the 1250s and 1260s. It was not until the marriage of the Competitor's son to the countess of Carrick in 1272 that the Bruces stepped into the elite of the Scottish nobility. From this point the family had the opportunity to realise their political potential in Scotland and the name of Robert Bruce became more familiar in Scotland.

During the 1240s and 1250s the English king had shown that he was prepared to respond to pleas for help from Scotland, with force if necessary. Thus he responded to pleas for help from Bissets, Comyns and Durwards in 1244, 1251 and 1255. In the maturity of Alexander III, his influence with the Scottish king also led to appeals for help from Scotland. Thus in 1264 Margaret, queen of Scotland, appealed to her father, Henry III, to procure the release of Richard Comyn, brother of John Comyn, who had been made a prisoner in the King's service.[80] In 1282 William Comyn of Kirkintilloch, son of John Comyn (d. 1277), pleaded with Edward I to use his influence with the king of Scotland and his son in favour of his claim to the earldom of Menteith.[81] Amicable letters were sent to Alexander III and his son, and as a result in 1285 William gained half the earldom, but not the title. In peaceful conditions the Scottish king's influence over the English king could also be seen. Even William Comyn of Kilbride, who had so flagrantly disregarded his commitments to the English king, benefited from this when in 1268 Henry III restored William's forfeited English lands *ad instanciam regis Scotiae*.[82] On the whole, Anglo-Scottish nobles undoubtedly benefited by retaining land and influence on both sides of the border. They were a force for stability between two neighbouring kingdoms. Thus Bruce, Balliol and Comyn were prominent in support of Henry III when he faced baronial opposition in England between 1258 and 1264. Similarly, John de Vesci, lord of Alnwick and Sprouston, was one of the leaders of Alexander III's expeditionary force to the Isle of Man in 1275.[83] The combination of peaceful conditions between the two kingdoms of England and Scotland and the widespread incidence of cross-border land ownership meant that identification with nation does not appear to have been an overriding concern in Alexander III's reign. The problem of suzerainty and English claims of suzerainty over Scotland had been raised in 1251 and again in 1278 at Edward I's court but it was not a central issue governing relationships between the kingdoms in the political circumstances between 1260 and 1286.

Anglo-Scottish families were an essential part of the aristocratic hierarchy in Scotland in the later years of Alexander III's reign. The essence of this aristocratic establishment is effectively captured in the list of thirteen earls and twenty-five barons who swore in 1284 to uphold the succession of Margaret of Norway to the Scottish throne.[84] This aristocratic hierarchy was a very diverse group comprising native dynasties, 'settler' families (though some families established in Scotland since the early twelfth century do not perhaps deserve this description), families whose territorial strength was almost entirely

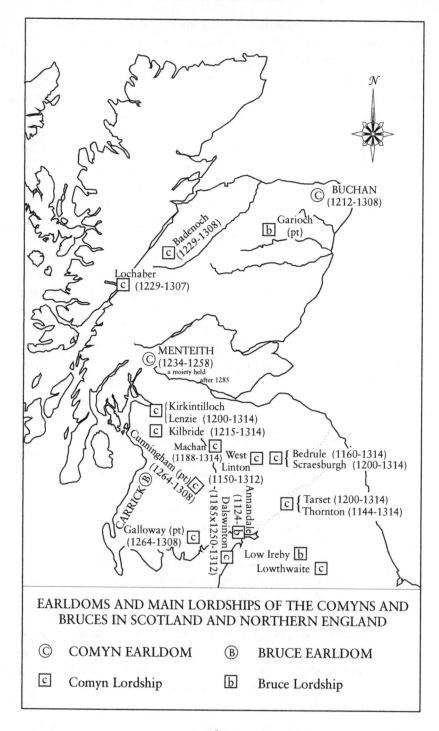

$\mathcal{N}$

ⓒ BUCHAN
(1212-1308)

Garioch
ⓑ (pt)

Badenoch
ⓒ (1229-1308)

Lochaber
ⓒ (1229-1307)

ⓒ MENTEITH
(1234-1258)
a moiety held
after 1285

ⓒ { Kirkintilloch
Lenzie (1200-1314)
ⓒ Kilbride (1215-1314)

Machan ⓒ
(1188-1314) West ⓒ ⓒ { Bedrule (1160-1314)
Linton Scraesburgh (1200-1314)
(1150-1312)

Cunningham (pt) ⓒ

CARRICK ⓑ
(1264-1308)

Annandale
(1124- ⓑ
Dalswinton
(1185x1250-1312)

ⓒ { Tarset (1200-1314)
Thornton (1144-1314)

Galloway (pt)
(1264-1308) ⓒ

Low Ireby ⓑ

ⓒ Lowthwaite ⓒ

EARLDOMS AND MAIN LORDSHIPS OF THE COMYNS AND
BRUCES IN SCOTLAND AND NORTHERN ENGLAND

ⓒ COMYN EARLDOM   ⓑ BRUCE EARLDOM

ⓒ Comyn Lordship   ⓑ Bruce Lordship

based in Scotland, and many who held lands on both sides of the border. Certain families featured strongly in the list: the Comyns, who had dominated the baronage for most of the thirteenth century, were represented by two members of the family, with the pre-eminent nobleman of the reign, Alexander Comyn earl of Buchan, constable and justiciar of Scotland, heading the list. Comyn leadership of the baronial community in Scotland in 1284 is well attested by the number of names in the list connected to the family by marriage, political association, or both – Patrick earl of Dunbar, Malise earl of Strathearn, Gilbert earl of Angus, Alexander Macdougall lord of Lorn, Balliol, Brechin, Soules, Hay, Graham, Maxwell and Cheyne. The progress of the Stewarts to the forefront of the political stage after 1260 was confirmed by their presence in the list – they had acquired an earldom and much territorial influence through valuable royal service. The Bruces and the Balliols had come to the fore, by 1284, through good marriages. The Bruces had gained an earldom and much territorial influence through marriage in 1272; their rise was not through royal service though Robert Bruce was very prominently in royal service in 1278. In that year, Robert was given the privilege of swearing fealty to the king of England in the name of and on behalf of the king of Scotland. The Balliols, who were represented on the 1284 list by two members of the family, also had come to the fore in Scotland principally through good marriages, unlike the relatively 'new' families such as the Frasers, Sinclairs and Morays who had risen mainly through royal service.

Native families were also represented in the 1284 list. Some had risen to prominence through association with the dominant families,[85] others by royal service. Alexander Ewenson Macdougall, lord of Lorn, and Alan Macruaidhri, lord of Garmoran, had been leaders of Alexander III's expedition in 1275 to suppress the Manx revolt. Angus Mor Macdonald, lord of Islay, represented a family which, like the Macdougalls, had much power in Argyll and Kintyre. It seems that in or about 1284 Alexander Macdougall was given responsibility over the west highlands and islands by Alexander III.[86] The Macdougalls, it seemed, enjoyed benefits similar to the Morays, Stewarts and Comyns in the service of the Scottish king. The marriage alliance between Macdougalls and Comyns, of course, greatly extended Comyn influence in the highlands.

Traditional accounts of self-seeking noble factions causing difficulties for the Scottish monarchy during the minority, being 'tamed' during

Alexander III's maturity, and lapsing once more into factional fighting after his death in 1286, are disproved by detailed analysis of Alexander III's reign. Traditionally, credit for the development of the Scottish kingdom between 1260 and 1286 has been given to Alexander III himself for his successful eclipse of the 'overmighty' Comyns and the careful balancing of rival baronial factions. An analysis of Alexander III's reign has pointed neither to the eclipse, partial or otherwise, of the Comyns nor to an attempt to balance baronial factions. In reality, Alexander III relied on his great magnates such as the Comyns, Stewarts and Morays who naturally became even more powerful as a result. In particular, the Comyns and their associates dominated political offices and the royal circle throughout Alexander III's maturity. The achievements of Alexander III's reign were the result of an effective, mutually beneficial alliance between crown and nobility. The authority of the king, which was accepted by the nobility even in the difficult minority period, was undoubtedly a factor for stability in Scotland between 1260 and 1286. However, the dominance of the Comyns, and their acceptance as leaders of a well-established aristocratic governing community by the nobility as a whole, was another important factor for stability. It is against this background that the rivalry between Comyns and Bruces after 1286 should be set.

NOTES
1. Theiner, *Monumenta* p.93; *Chron. Fordun* II pp.293–4.
2. Watt, 'The Minority of Alexander III', p.23.
3. Young, 'Noble Families and Political Factions in the Reign of Alexander III' in Norman H. Reid, *Scotland in the Reign of Alexander III 1249–1286* (1990), pp.1–2 and for much of what follows.
4. Duncan, *Scotland, the Making of the Kingdom*, p.589.
5. Watt, 'The Minority of Alexander III', pp. 18, 20.
6. Watt, 'The Minority of Alexander III', p.20.
7. *Ibid.*
8. Duncan, *Scotland, the Making of the Kingdom*, pp.587–9.
9. *Foedera*, I, 715; Young, 'Noble Families and Political Factions', p.8.
10. Durward did appear in the king's company as witness to an Earl Alexander Comyn charter issued at Kelly (Buchan) in 1272 (*Aberdeen Reg.* I. pp.30–4).
11. Barrow, *Kingdom of the Scots*, pp.137–8.
12. *St Andrews Liber*, p.346.
13. For lists of Comyn supporters in 1244, see *Cal. Docs. Scot.* I nos.2671–2; in 1255, *Cal. Docs. Scot.* I no.2013; in 1257 *Chron. Bower* (Watt), V p.320.
14. For the majority of sheriffdoms see *Exchequer Rolls* I pp.1–51.

15. S.R.O. G.D. 52/388; *Aberdeen Reg.* II pp.276–7; *Arbroath Liber*, pp.185–7; *Inchcolm Chrs.* pp. 25, 26, 41; *St Andrews Liber*, pp.282–3.
16. S.R.O. RH 1/2/32; *St Andrews Liber*, pp.250–3.
17. S.R.O. G.D. 101/2; RH 1/2/31; *Glasgow Reg.* I p.101.
18. William de Soules and John de Soules appear as auditors for Bruce in the 'Great Cause', 1290–1.
19. Watt, *Fasti*, pp. 2, 39, 146, 293.
20. S.R.O. Maitland Thompson Transcript Notebook, VI, p.37; *Glasgow Reg.* I p.195, *Kelso Liber* I p152.
21. Young, 'Noble Families and Political Factions', p.10.
22. Duncan, *Scotland, the Making of the Kingdom*, pp.573–4.
23. *Chron. Wyntoun* (ed. Laing), II p.310.
24. Young, 'Noble Families and Political Factions', p.11.
25. *Cal. Docs. Scot.* I nos. 10, 1987, 2013, 2121; Barrow, *Kingship and Unity*, pp.52–3; *Arbroath Liber*, pp.265–6; *Inchcolm Chrs.* pp. 25, 26, 141; S.R.O. RH 6/52.
26. Barrow and Royan, 'James Stewart' in K.J. Stringer (ed.), *Essays on the Nobility of Medieval Scotland*, pp.167–9.
27. Duncan, *Scotland, Making of the Kingdom*, p.588; Watt, *Fasti*, p.293.
28. A.M. Mackenzie, *The Kingdom of Scotland* (Edinburgh, 1948), p.113.
29. *Chron. Fordun* II p.293.
30. Theiner, *Monumenta.* 92.
31. *Cal. Docs. Scot.* IV no.1763; *Scots Peerage*, vi p.131.
32. Theiner, *Monumenta*, p.93. This suggests that the king was not fully in control of government c.1260/1.
33. Matthew Paris, *Chron. Majora*, V pp.739–40.
34. *Ibid.* p.740.
35. *Foedera*, I, p.715; *Cal. Docs. Scot.* I no.2229.
36. *Ibid.;* the Comyn members of this group were Alexander Comyn, Earl of Buchan and John Comyn I of Badenoch with their associates William earl of Mar and Hugh de Abernethy. Malise earl of Strathearn may also have been in the Comyn party – he married a daughter of Earl Alexander. Comyn influence was dominant amongst the bishops.
37. *Foedera II* p.266.
38. Matthew Paris, *Chron. Majora*, V pp.266–70; Stones, *Anglo-Scottish Relations*, pp.77–83. Duncan, *Scotland, the Making of the Kingdom*, p.587.
39. *Cal. Docs. Scot.* I no.2193.
40. *Exchequer Rolls (E.R.)*, I pp.27–8. Alexander Comyn had married Elizabeth de Quincy, co-heiress to Roger de Quincy, earl of Winchester and constable of Scotland (d.1264).
41. For the profits of the justiciarship, totalling £405.13.4d. for 1264–6 see *E.R.*, I p.18.
42. *E.R.* I pp. 18, 20, 30–1; *Chron. Fordun* II p.296. Earl Alexander was the first layman to append his seal to the Treaty of Perth in 1266.

43. *E.R.* I p.20.

44. *Ibid.* p.11.

45. Baillies 'ad extra' were administrators of portions of crown lands or sometimes of lands temporarily in crown's occupation, e.g. for strategic reasons as in 1263–4.

46. *E.R.* I p.18.

47. *Ibid.* I pp.30–1.

48. *Ibid.* p.22.

49. *Ibid.* p.19.

50. *Acts Parl Scot.* I pp. 78–9.

51. *E.R.* I pp. 31, 33; *Cal Close Rolls,* 1268–72 p.8.

52. G.G. Simpson, An Anglo-Scottish Baron of the Thirteenth Century: The Acts of Roger de Quincy, earl of Winchester and Constable of Scotland (unpublished Ph.D. thesis University of Edinburgh, 1965), pp.69–70.

53. *Melrose Liber,* pp.280–1. P.R.O., SC 18/147.

54. Annals of Furness in Anderson, *Scottish Annals,* p.382.

55. P.R.O., SC I 16/93; P.R.O., SC I 20/158.

56. The following section owes much to K.J. Stringer, *Earl David of Huntingdon* 1152–1219: A study in Anglo-Scottish History (Edinburgh, 1985), ch. 9 'Anglo-Scottish Proprietorship: A Wider View', pp.177–211.

57. The earls of Huntingdon, Strathearn, and Dunbar, and the families of Comyn, Bruce, Quincy, Forz, Balliol, Moray, Vesci, Durward and Umphraville all had interests in both kingdoms.

58. K.J. Stringer, *Earl David,* p.190.

59. *Cal. Docs. Scot.* II nos. 216, 369, 421.

60. Young, 'Noble Families and Political Factions', p.18.

61. In 1276, for example, Robert Leslie, Richard of Pocklington (in the East Riding of Yorkshire), Richard Aleyn and Matthew of Wigston (Leicestershire) were named as Earl Alexander's attorneys: *Cal Close Rolls,* 1272–9, p.429.

62. *Cal. Inq. Post Mortem,* IV p.171 no.138.

63. For Roger, see *Placita de Quo Warranto* (Rec. Commission, 1818), p.559; for John, see *Cal. Inq. Post Mortem,* II p.460, no.753 and *Cal. Docs. Scot.* II no. 421.

64. *Cal. Fine Rolls,* I p.85.

65. *Cal. Charter Rolls,* II (1257–1300) pp.40–1.

66. *Cal. Docs. Scot.* no.2678.

67. *Cal. Liberate Rolls,* V p.198.

68. *Cal. Docs. Scot.* I no.2431; *Cal. Pat Rolls* 1266–72 p.110.

69. *Ibid.* p.175.

70. *Morton Reg.* II pp.3–4; *Newbattle Reg.* pp.135–6.

71. *Book of Fees,* I p.919, II p.911, 1118; *Cal. Docs. Scot.* I nos. 1523, 1558.

72. *Ibid.* nos. 2096, 2278, 2638; II no.148. Even this widow married again without the English king's consent (*Ibid.* no.376).

73. *Cal. Close Rolls,* 1264–8 p.437.

74. *Cal. Docs. Scot.* I nos. 2120, 2121, 2156.
75. *Ibid.* nos. 1888, 1895, 1956, 1984–5, 2022, 2043, 2099; in 1260 *ibid.* nos. 2218, 2221–1; in 1268, *ibid.* nos.2492–3; in 1274, *ibid.* ii no.18.
76. Stell, 'The Balliol Family' in Stringer, *Essays on the Nobility of Medieval Scotland*, pp.155–8.
77. *Cal. Docs. Scot.* nos. 1994, 2472.
78. *Ibid.* nos.2357–9, 2429.
79. Robert Bruce the Competitor was described as 'a noble as great in England as in Scotland' in the Lanercost Chronicle (*Chron. Lanercost*, p.111); see also Barrow, *Robert Bruce*, pp.23–6 and Stringer, *Earl David*, pp.185–6, 188–9.
80. *Cal. Docs. Scot.* I no.2678.
81. *Scots Peerage*, VI pp.129–31. It is interesting that William is recorded as about to go abroad in 1281 – perhaps on the king's service? (*C.D.S.* II no.198).
82. *Cal. Close Rolls* 1264–8, p.437.
83. Annals of Furness in Anderson, *Scottish Annals*, p.382.
84. *Foedera*, II pp.266–7.
85. The Abernethys through Hugh de Abernethy were favoured by the Comyns and rose to prominence through them, though Hugh was not in the 1284 list (Barrow, *Kingship and Unit*, pp.137–8).
86. Barrow, *Kingdom of the Scots*, p.383; see Barrow, *Kingship and Unit*, p.119.

CHAPTER FIVE

Balliol, Bruce and Comyn: Guardians, Competitors and Constitutional Crisis, 1286–1292

A lexander III died suddenly, aged forty-four, on 18th March 1286, the result of a tragic accident on a dark, stormy night when he was on the way to Kinghorn to meet his new French wife (of less than six months), Yolande of Dreux.[1] Discussion of the consequences of this tragic death has been long dominated by the powerful, emotional accounts of the fourteenth- and fifteenth-century commentators, John of Fordun, Andrew of Wyntoun and Walter Bower:

> ... How worthy of tears, and how hurtful his death was to the kingdom of Scotland, is plainly shown forth by the evils of after times....
>
> ... O Scotland, truly unhappy when bereft of so great a leader and pilot; while-greater unhappiness still! he left no lawful offspring to succeed him...
>
> (John of Fordun)[2]

> ... your lyre changed to playing a lament and your pipes became the voice of the mourners, when you learnt of the sudden death of your dearly beloved king, as bitter as it was unwelcome. But if you too had recognised how many evils were hurrying to surround you on all sides, your heart, foreseeing the news to come, would have trembled violently from fear...
>
> (Walter Bower)[3]

Our gold was changyd in to lede
Chryst, borne in to Vyrgynte
Succoure Scotland and remede
That stad [is in] perplexyte
(Andrew of Wyntoun)[4]

Such dramatic language has had a deep impact on our view of the years 1286–1296. It has contributed substantially to the myth of the 'Golden Age' of Alexander III,[5] an idealised kingship which was destroyed by baronial faction after 1286 before finally being restored by the hero of the fourteenth- and fifteenth-century narratives, Robert Bruce, in 1306. Such a monarchocentric, patriotic approach does, of course, reflect the political insecurities – minorities, civil war, English interference in Scottish affairs – at the time when Fordun (in the later fourteenth century) and Wyntoun and Bower (in the fifteenth century) were writing. However, the insecurities of the fourteenth and fifteenth centuries, together with the evidence that Alexander's death was followed by a period of thirty years of political unrest and invasion from England, have tended to distort discussion of the years 1286–1292 and especially the role of the nobility in these years. As with fourteenth- and fifteenth-century commentary on Alexander III's minority,[6] there has been a tendency to emphasise the problems caused to the crown by the factiousness of the nobility. Hindsight has caused historians to seek in Alexander III's reign the roots of the baronial conflicts and alliances which were so much a feature of the 'Great Cause' of 1291–92 and after. There has been, for example, a tendency to concentrate on the Bruce–Balliol conflict and look for the roots of this conflict before 1290.[7] A more valid approach is to look for contemporary attitudes to the constitutional crisis in the years following Alexander III's death and to analyse the actions after 1286 of that responsible aristocratic governing community which had played such a key role in the development of the Scottish kingdom up to that year.

To contemporaries, the sudden, tragic loss of their king was naturally a cause for alarm. It was a political crisis in the same way as the death of Alexander II in 1249 was a crisis – a medieval kingdom needed a king and a king of sufficient age to rule. Yet the view of Fordun, Wyntoun and Bower that 1286 was a year of political catastrophe is not borne out by contemporary commentators or by the actions of the leaders of the political community. Indeed, lack of panic and a speedy, mature response to Alexander

III's sudden death are notable features in the months after 18th March. In the context of thirteenth-century Scotland, this should not be wondered at. The government of Scotland was stronger, more centralised and more stable in 1286 than it had been in its last crisis in 1249 when there had evidently been no contingency planning before Alexander II's death. In 1249 an informal regency council was set up. In 1286, at an assembly (parliament) at Scone about 28th April, the nobility first swore fealty to the heir, and took a solemn oath both to guard the land of Scotland on the heir's behalf, and keep the peace there.[8] In order to implement these promises, a provisional government was swiftly set up – the realm would be governed by six wardens or 'Guardians' comprising two earls (Alexander Comyn earl of Buchan, Duncan earl of Fife), two bishops (William Fraser of St Andrews and Robert Wishart of Glasgow) and two barons (John Comyn of Badenoch and James Stewart).[9]

The years after 1258 had seen the Comyns, controlling the main political offices and acting in cooperation with non-Comyn councillors at the royal court, become an essential instrument of royal policy. The years after 1258 had seen much political progress – both the extension of royal authority (notably in the south-west and the Western Isles) throughout Scotland and a breaking away from English domination. Earl Alexander Comyn of Buchan had played an important part in these developments. He had experience of Alexander III's minority and was still present on Alexander III's death to lend his experience and practical knowledge of this minority. It is hardly surprising that a formal, rational system of government was worked out and quickly put into practice on Alexander III's death. In composition, the provisional government of six guardians can be seen as stemming from the emergency council of regency set up in 1260–61. This comprised thirteen named bishops, earls and barons drawn from Comyn and non-Comyn supporters. Earl Alexander's experience in the planning of this council – he was justiciar of Scotia from 1258 – obviously influenced the structure of the 1286 committee of guardians. It is not surprising that Earl Alexander was one of the joint guardians in 1286.

Contemporary sources emphasise the wisdom and relative sophistication of the decisions taken in 1286:

... the greatest men of the land of Scotland provided for
themselves salutary counsel, and chose for the community
guardians of peace, both from among the nobles and the bishops;
until it should be decided by discussion who should be put into a
position of so great authority.

(Chronicle of Lanercost)[10]

If the biased commentaries of the fourteenth- and fifteenth-century
writers can be set aside, their actual descriptions of the setting up of
the committee of guardians:

> (Thare) thai delyveryed wyth hale intent
> And ordanyd Wardanys twys three
> (Chron. Wyntoun)[11]

and the composition of the committee:

... six guardians ... were chosen by the clergy and estates of the
whole kingdom of Scotland, in a parliament held at Scone... So it
was governed by six guardians: namely, William Fraser, now lord
bishop of Saint Andrews – Duncan, earl of Fife – and John (for
Alexander) Comyn, earl of Buchan, deputed from the northern
part, this side of the Forth; and Robert, bishop of Glasgow – the
lord John Comyn – and James, steward of Scotland, appointed
from the southern side of the water of the Forth...

(Chron. Fordun)[12]

give further evidence of prudent reflection rather than panic.

The description of the Guardians is interesting. The *Lanercost
Chronicle* referred to them as 'guardians of peace'. The Guardians
usually described themselves as 'appointed by common counsel' or
'elected by the community of the realm'.[13] The idea of the 'community
of the realm' thus became openly expressed in 1286 although in practice
a Scottish political community had been developing throughout the
thirteenth century and especially in its second half. The political
community was based on consensus between crown and aristocratic
establishment in an alliance of mutual benefit. The seal of the Guardians,
cut especially for their use, symbolically sums up their role, acting on
behalf of the community of the realm while at the same time acting
as delegates of the crown.[14] Professor Barrow eloquently described the
relationship between crown and community of the realm: 'The king of

Scots was one side, the community of the realm of Scotland the other side, of a single coin'. This idea is emphasised in both the design of the Guardians' seal – on one side a shield of the royal arms, on the other side the figure of St Andrew on his cross – as well as its inscriptions: 'the seal of Scotland appointed for the government of the kingdom' and 'St Andrew be leader of the compatriot Scots'.

Thus in 1286 the duties of the Guardians were clear and the business of Scottish government between 1286 and 1290 shows these duties being implemented. Most of the business in these years was fairly routine, mainly writs to the chamberlain of Scotland requesting him to pay the fees of certain knights.[15] The commission of Guardians also had to decide the rights as to certain pastureland in Panmure in October 1286.[16] Such routine and internal business gives an impression of stability and conscientious, efficient government. Two matters in which the Guardians expressed concern were not internal. On 11th November 1286, the Guardians complained to Edmund, earl of Cornwall, warden of England, that a certain Sir Andrew de Moray and his wife were aggrieved by King Edward's escheator.[17] The complaint referred to the escheator Thomas de Normanville's harsh conduct north of the Trent. In another letter of 13th May 1288, again to Edmund earl of Cornwall, the Guardians asked for the security of the advowson of the church of Knaresdale for John Wishart.[18] These actions represent an active government keenly aware of Scottish rights and the rights of Scottish men in England. The two items of business concerning Scottish rights in England represented a policy towards England which had been consistently held since 1259 – a keen desire to protect Scottish rights and move away from dependence on England after the minority of Alexander III.

The *Lanercost Chronicle's* description of the Guardians as 'guardians of peace' highlights perhaps the most important royal role to be performed by Guardians: to maintain peace and stability within the kingdom and secure freedom from external interference. A brieve issued by the Guardians (probably late in 1286) refers to army service due to the 'royal dignity' after the death of a king.[19] One of the Guardians, James Stewart, justified by reference to the public peace the decision to override Melrose abbey tenants' exemption from musters and military aid in Kyle Stewart: 'because the peace and tranquillity of the realm were disturbed after King Alexander's death and the state was threatened by conflict'.[20] In 1287 'the peace and tranquillity of the realm of Scotland' was again an issue when Malise earl of Strathearn had to raise men in his earldom from among the tenants of Inchaffray abbey.[21] These two instances bear witness to the potential threat to national order indicated in the Guardians' brieve in late 1286 and early 1287.

Thus evidence from the Guardians' activities between 1286 and 1290 would suggest on the one hand a mature and stable government. Of the seventeen recorded acts between 1286 and 1289, no fewer than thirteen were issued at Edinburgh, and one each at Linlithgow, Stirling and Perth, giving the clear impression of centralised government. Yet there were also clear signs of internal unrest in 1286 and 1287 and much discussion has centred on the nature of this unrest. In view of the 'Great Cause' of 1291–92, much of this debate has been directed at the apparently burgeoning rivalry between the two great protagonists in the 'Great Cause', the Balliols and the Bruces.

When Alexander III died in March 1286, there was uncertainty rather than a crisis over the succession. Yolande, Alexander III's queen, was believed to be pregnant.[22] Failing the birth of a living child as heir, the 'Maid of Norway', Alexander III's granddaughter, acknowledged as rightful heir by the magnates of Scotland in February 1284, and less than three years of age when Alexander III died, would succeed to the Scottish throne. A very long minority period seemed inevitable and there were a number of noble families, including principally the Comyns but also the Bruces, who had had experience of the last minority, that of Alexander III between 1249 and 1258. The Guardians elected in 1286 had key positions of power in Scotland – and would hold that power for a long time. It is in this light rather than in the context of a Balliol versus Bruce rivalry for the Scottish throne that the period 1286 to 1290 should be judged. In the parliament of late April 1286, Bower reported a 'bitter pleading regarding the right of succession to the kingdom'.[23] It seems probable[24] that the aged Robert Bruce (d.1295) first put forward the claim in the parliament which met at Scone on 2nd April that a female could not succeed and that when the parliament re-adjourned about 28th April – perhaps to allow John Balliol to attend from England – Balliol took the opportunity to contest Bruce's claim and the 'bitter pleading' resulted. This incident has tended to be interpreted in the light of the 'Great Cause' of 1291–92, i.e. that Bruce and Balliol were in fact denying Margaret the 'Maid of Norway's' right to inherit in 1286 and were putting forward their own claims to the throne in that year. However, both Bruce and Balliol had attached their names to the 1284 entail by which the magnates agreed to support the succession of Margaret. The

1286 pleading was probably to establish the next heir, to either Yolande's child or Margaret, clearly a necessary procedure – as necessary as it had been in 1284 – in a time of high infant mortality. The insecurity of the succession dictated that the position of heir presumptive was a serious issue and likely to cause 'bitter pleading'.

It is important to note that Guardians had been elected at the same late April parliament (1286) of the 'bitter pleading' as 'guardians of the peace ... until it should be decided by discussion who should be put into a position of so great authority'.[25] They were in a key position to implement the succession and control the discussion over the heir presumptive in 1286. It can be shown that the setting-up, and composition, of the committee of Guardians reveal both maturity and sophistication in Scottish government. It has also been claimed that the six Guardians chosen represented 'a nice compromise between rival factions' or 'were probably elected to provide a balance in the government between those supporting each of the two main factions in the country at that time, the Bruces and the Balliols ...'[26] Thus the two Comyns, Alexander Comyn earl of Buchan, and John Comyn lord of Badenoch, together with the bishop of St Andrews, William Fraser, were deemed to represent the Balliol interests and James Stewart, linked to the Bruces by marriage,[27] and Robert Wishart, bishop of Glasgow, an ally of Stewart, represented the Bruce interest. The loyalties of Duncan earl of Fife were less certain – though it is known that he was the enemy of a close Comyn associate, Hugh de Abernethy, and that he had an unenviably poor contemporary reputation.[28] The composition of the Guardianship reflected the political situation in 1286 rather than in the 1291/92 legal battle. The reality was Comyn leadership of the aristocratic elite rather than rivalry between Bruce and Balliol factions. If the committee had been set up to balance aspirations of Balliols and Bruces as heirs presumptive, it failed. The Bruces evidently felt that the Guardians would not effectively represent their interests as they soon resorted to strong-arm tactics. They launched attacks in south-west Scotland on the Balliol lordship at Buittle and also the royal castles of Wigtown and Dumfries.[29] Such attacks can be seen as evidence of the Bruce–Balliol rivalry of 1291–92. Yet they reveal more than an attack on the Balliols – they reveal an attack on the Comyn position in the south-west as the Comyns had been hereditary sheriffs of Wigtown since c.1263–4, and more especially they show clear resistance to Comyn leadership of the political community of the realm.

It is hardly surprising that the Guardians sent out embassies to

Edward I in the summer of 1286[30] – Edward was in France from 13th May 1286 and did not return to England until 1289. The first embassy in May 1286 was led by Bishop Fraser, the second, in August, consisted of William Comyn, bishop of Brechin, Sir Geoffrey de Mowbray, lord of Dalmeny (and related to the Comyns by marriage), and the abbot of Jedburgh.[31] The composition of these embassies shows a distinctly Comyn-led government in Scotland. The purpose of these embassies is not clear though Bower reports how speedily (and therefore how urgently) the second embassy rushed to meet the English king north of Bordeaux. Bower reported that this embassy was to 'appeal for his [Edward's] advice and patronage over the state of the kingdom of Scotland and of the lands of Penrith',[32] and it is probable that there was at this stage a general request for counsel from a friendly neighbour. The Comyn-led guardianship must have been aware from their own experience of Alexander III's minority that the English king could be the bringer of much-needed stability when the political situation within Scotland was unstable. In 1286, however, it seemed that Gascony was at the top of Edward I's political priorities[33] (as indicated by his continuing presence there until 1289) and that Scotland was of relatively little consequence. It is not known whether a possible marriage alliance involving the Maid of Norway was mooted as early as 1286.

Further evidence of Bruce's disregard for the Guardians' authority occurs in September 1286 when he made a bond with associates at Turnberry[34] (the chief castle of the earldom of Carrick). This Turnberry pact, which involved Robert Bruce, lord of Annandale, his son Robert Bruce, earl of Carrick, James Stewart (the Guardian), his brother, John Stewart of Jedburgh, Walter Stewart earl of Menteith and his sons, Patrick earl of Dunbar, Angus Macdonald lord of Islay and his son, was an agreement to support Richard de Burgh, earl of Ulster, and Thomas de Clare against their enemies. The pact involved saving oaths of allegiance to the English king and whoever should be king in Scotland 'by reason of the blood of the lord Alexander, king of Scotland according to the ancient customs hitherto approved and used in the Kingdom of Scotland'.[35] This oath has been interpreted as an indication of a deliberate bid by the Bruces for the Scottish throne. This is perhaps reading too much into the oath. Yet Robert Bruce had apparently been recognised by 'ancient custom' as heir to Alexander II in 1238[36] and the vague oath taken at Turnberry did leave open a possible Bruce claim, given the uncertainty of the succession in September 1286 when either the Maid of Norway or a child of Queen Yolande could be heir. More importantly, the fact that such a pact of family and factional, if not national, intent (and with an uncertain military objective) could take place and that a member of the committee of Guardians was involved, was certainly an 'ugly defiance of the "community of the realm" '.[37] In these unsettled circumstances after Alexander III's death, it is hardly surprising that, in August 1286, the Guardians were seeking advice, perhaps aid, from Edward I and that in late 1286 the Guardians were issuing a brieve asking for the host to be on twenty-four hours' alert.

The Guardians, perhaps by the threat of this national military action, managed to maintain the peace in Scotland. It is interesting to note that James Stewart, despite showing himself to support the Bruces in the Turnberry pact, tended to put his duties as guardian before the interests of his allies, the Bruces. The disorder in Scotland in the two years after Alexander III's death seems to have been initiated by the Bruces. There is little evidence to indicate *mutual* rivalry, a civil war, between Bruces and Balliols before or during 1286: 'there is no evidence to show that the Balliols had similar, conflicting aims or that the Bruces had ever seriously impinged on Balliol consciousness before 1286'.[38] Similarly, after the Scottish parliament of late April 1286, when Balliol appears to have been present to oppose the claim of Robert Bruce to be heir presumptive, there is no evidence of the Balliols actively pursuing factional interests. Perhaps the Balliols felt secure about possible future claims *because* of the dominance of the Comyns, their relatives, in the regency government. Bruce actions in 1286 seem to have been aimed principally against Comyn dominance of the Guardianship and Scottish government which would indeed threaten any future family claim to the Scottish crown.

The extent of the threat posed by Bruce between 1286 and 1288 and the nature of Scottish government between 1286 and 1290 are well revealed in the royal accounts of 1288–90.[39] Actions were taken at the Guardians' command to secure the castles at Dumfries, Ayr and Stirling. The existence of war or the danger of war is made the grounds for claiming additional sums for the defence, custody and watching of the castles of Dumfries, Ayr, Edinburgh and Jedburgh. The accounts of the sheriffdoms of Dumfries, Wigtown and Edinburgh refer to lands uncultivated for two years because of war or remission for tenants 'lest they leave the land and leave the king's land uncultivated'.[40] It is perhaps not surprising that most of the disruption occurred in the south-west.

This is clearly shown in the accounts of the sheriffs of Ayr, Dumfries and Wigtown and also by the account of the justiciar of Galloway.[41] In 1288 William Sinclair as justiciar of Galloway returned, as his 'lucra' for a year, only £9-1s-8d. However, the impact of the war or the fear of war was felt outside of the south-west of Scotland. The accounts of the sheriffdom of Edinburgh refer to extra watches needed at the castle because of the danger of war and to the fear engendered in the king's tenants. The accounts of the sheriffdom of Stirling detail the building work undertaken at Stirling castle.

The account of John Comyn of Buchan as sheriff of Wigtown refers specifically to the earl of Carrick, i.e. Robert Bruce, as the instigator of war after the death of the king.[42] Evidence of the government's activities, revealed in the 1288–90 accounts perhaps demonstrate, why Robert Bruce resorted to such strong-arm tactics. They reveal an experienced Comyn-led government coping efficiently in a crisis. They reveal continuity in government from that of Alexander III's reign with most of the same families continuing in their public offices. Thus members of the Comyn family continued to hold the sheriffdoms of Wigtown and Banff through the Buchan branch of the family. The Sinclairs (St Clairs) continued to hold the sheriffdoms of Edinburgh and Linlithgow in the period 1286–89 with William Sinclair (who had been made, by 1279, guardian of Alexander, heir to the Scottish throne) holding the sheriffdom of Dumfries as well as the sheriffdom of Edinburgh in the period before 1290. William Sinclair was also justiciar of Galloway by 1287. Another family long associated with the Comyns, the Cheynes, held the sheriffdoms of Elgin and Kincardine in the period prior to 1290, while the Mowats continued to control Cromarty and the Meldrum family held the sheriffdom of Aberdeen. The Moray family, generally supporters of the Comyn family in the thirteenth century, held the sheriffdom of Ayr through Andrew de Moray by 1288 and the sheriffdom of Perth through Malcolm de Moray up to 1288. The sheriffdom of Perth was then in the hands of Nicholas de Hay who was certainly in the Comyn party in 1291. A Comyn supporter from the Graham family, Patrick de Graham, held the sheriffdom of Stirling by 1289. Comyn supporters, the Lochore family, held the sheriffdom of Fife by 1289 and David de Bethun, from the earl of Buchan's following, held the sheriffdom of Forfar by 1290.

In comparison with this very extensive Comyn representation in public offices between 1286 and 1290, known members of the Bruce following in the Great Cause, 1291–92, were relatively poorly represented in public office after 1286. The Stewarts, prominent allies of Bruce, held the sheriffdom of Dumbarton through Walter Stewart earl of Menteith – he held this sheriffdom between 1271 and 1288, being succeeded by Duncan earl of Fife, a less certain Bruce follower, by 1289. James Stewart, the Guardian, held this sheriffdom after Duncan's death in 1289, also the sheriffdom of Ayr (by late 1288). Another family in support of the Bruce candidature in 1291, the de Soules, held the sheriffdom of Berwick through John de Soules and the sheriffdoms of Roxburgh and Inverness through William de Soules prior to 1289. William de Soules was also justiciar of Lothian from 1279 to his death c.1292/3. Yet the Soules were, in fact, related to the Comyns through marriage and their political supporters from the 1250s to c.1291. They should not be seen as unequivocal Bruce supporters.

To add to the Comyn dominance of Scottish government in the period 1286 to 1290, it should be noted that Alexander de Balliol, a member of the family which was related to the Comyns by marriage, held the post of chamberlain between 1286 and 1289. Comyns and their supporters also continued to form a powerful group dominating the church hierarchy and participating in Scottish government. William Comyn of Kilconquhar was bishop of Brechin from 1275.[43] He had been an envoy for Alexander III in 1275 and was employed on another embassy on behalf of the Scottish government in 1286. Henry Cheyne, a member of a family who were regular supporters of the Comyns, was bishop of Aberdeen from 1282 to 1328.[44] Members of the Fraser family were prominent supporters of the Comyns in the late thirteenth century. William Fraser, bishop of the pre-eminent bishopric in Scotland, St Andrews, 1279–1297,[45], was a Guardian in 1286 and led an urgent embassy of the Scottish government to visit Edward I in northern France in May 1286. Two other members of the Fraser family, Andrew and Simon, appeared in the Comyn/Balliol party in the Great Cause 1291/92.

The reaction of the Comyn-led regency government to the Bruce attacks on Balliol and royal castles and property especially in the south-west was to strengthen Comyn military power there. The Buchan branch of the Comyn family had acquired large areas of land in the south-west when Alexander Comyn's wife Elizabeth inherited a third of the vast estates of the Anglo-Scottish magnate, Roger de Quincy, on her father's death in 1264. Thus Alexander Comyn, earl of Buchan, acquired estates in Galloway and Dumfries as well as in Lothian and Fife. The Buchan branch of the Comyns were also hereditary sheriffs of Wigtown from 1263, playing a key role in the extension of royal authority in the south-west. In 1288 Earl Alexander's son John, the future earl of Buchan, took extra responsibility in response to the Bruce threat. He became keeper of the king's castle and lands in Kirkcudbright as well as having responsibility for the sheriffdom of Wigtown.[46] He also intromitted with the land of Sypland.[47] The Badenoch branch of the Comyn family also took extra responsibility during the disturbances after 1286. John Comyn of Badenoch strengthened his family's presence in southern Scotland, especially Roxburghshire, by becoming bailie of Jedburgh in 1288, being responsible for garrisoning of the castle and for the farm of the manor of Jedburgh.[48] The Guardians also placed Malise earl of Strathearn, a Comyn supporter, in charge of the sheriffdom of Auchterarder with responsibility for the farm of the burgh of Auchterarder. Duncan earl of Fife was given responsibility for the farm of the manor of Dull.

One of the interesting features about the documentation deriving from the Guardians' administration is the number of brieves issued to pay fees between 1286 and 1290.[49] Was the issue of writs for the payment of fees more than a sign of the efficiency of the Guardians' administration? Was it a sign of the Guardians using all the administrative armoury at their disposal, as well as military might, to defend their regime and keep contented those working in the interests of that regime from justiciars, sheriffs and knights to clerks and masons? It is noticeable that key officials such as Thomas de Carnoto (de Chartres) the chancellor received fees and gifts,[50] and that justiciars such as William Sinclair[51] received their fees for service despite the lack of 'lucra' deriving from the office because of the disruption in Galloway due to the war.

The Comyn-led Scottish government between 1286 and 1290 succeeded, with some difficulty, in resisting pressure from the Bruces who feared the consequences of their exclusion from political power. This pressure, not only aimed against Balliol interests but at the stability of the Scottish government itself, was most obvious in the south-west, but the fear of a more extensive war was present in other areas of Scotland. The Comyns as leaders of the political community of the realm were defenders of the rights of the successor to Alexander III whether that successor was the Maid of Norway or the child of Queen Yolande and they would undoubtedly champion the rights of their relatives, the Balliols, to the position of heir presumptive. In these circumstances, and understandably, the enmity of Bruces and Comyns came into the open for the first time between 1286 and 1289. It was the start of a fierce rivalry that was to continue until the Battle of Bannockburn in 1314 decisively tilted the balance in favour of the Bruces.

It is interesting to note that the partisan Bruce source, John Barbour, in his epic biography of the hero-king Robert Bruce omits all mention of the child-queen Margaret. This could be taken to imply a lack of recognition by the Bruces of the Maid of Norway's claim to the throne in 1286. However, by 1289 it seems that Robert Bruce had ended his defiance of the Guardians as he was appointed on 3rd October, along with the bishops of St Andrews and Glasgow and John Comyn of Badenoch, to treat with the Norwegian envoys concerning the Maid of Norway and her return.[52] After two years of strife and fear of strife, as recorded in the royal accounts audited in March 1289, it seemed everyone agreed that the Maid of Norway was the rightful 'queen', a style which is most frequently found in documents of 1289–1290.[53]

Yet the political situation in Scotland was far from stable in 1289. There was need for the Maid of Norway to be brought back to Scotland and formally inaugurated as queen; there was also the need for outside help which could be guaranteed by a marriage treaty involving the young queen. The precedent of English mediation during the difficult minority of Alexander III and the marriage alliance involving the young Alexander III and Margaret daughter of Henry III, discussed as early as 1244 but not implemented until 1251, would have been clear to the more experienced Scottish counsellors such as Alexander Comyn earl of Buchan. The dangers of a more powerful neighbour taking advantage of Scotland's internal difficulties would also have been appreciated – the issue of England's overlordship of Scotland had been raised in 1251 and 1278 and a considerable degree of oversight had been exercised in practice between 1251 and 1258. It is known that the Guardians had sent envoys to Edward I in France in 1286 to ask for the English king's counsel. It is not known, however, whether the prospect of a marriage involving the Maid of Norway was raised then, in August 1286 (at that time Queen Yolande's pregnancy may still have clouded the issue of succession). Correspondence from Alexander III to Edward I in 1284 had certainly hinted at the desirability of a future marriage alliance involving the Maid.[54] What passed between Edward I and the Scottish envoys in August 1286 must remain conjecture but it is unlikely, given past precedent, that Edward I would have missed the opportunity to ask for recognition of English overlordship in return for aid. It is clear that Edward I did not give the Scottish government aid between 1286 and 1288 and was content to devote his time and energies to greater priorities in France. It is also probable, of course, that the Scottish envoys had said that they had no authority to discuss such a matter.

The situation changed in 1289. A Scottish embassy led by the Guardian, Bishop William Fraser, made its way to Edward I in Gascony early in 1289, apparently at Edward's request.[55] Again the business of this meeting is uncertain but there is direct evidence of Edward's involvement in negotiations concerning the Maid and a future marriage by 1st May 1289.[56] In the autumn, by which time Edward I had returned from France, negotiations between the English, Scots and Norwegians had begun in earnest.

The political situation in Scotland, however, had significantly deteriorated by the autumn of 1289. Alexander Comyn, earl of Buchan, leader of the Comyn 'party' and the most experienced political leader in Scotland – he had been involved in Scottish politics for almost fifty years – died probably shortly after 10th July 1289.[57] He had been a mainstay of Scottish government, a pillar of the monarchy, and a great contributor to an increasingly mature Scottish political community. Equally damaging to political stability was the murder of another Guardian, the young Duncan earl of Fife, outside Brechin 'with the advice and consent of [Hugh] de Abernethy'.[58] Hugh de Abernethy was a leading associate of the Comyns. Despite the bad contemporary reputation of Earl Duncan 'enmities provoked by his deeds had been deservedly roused against him'[59] and the fact that the murderers and their accomplices were swiftly dealt with by Andrew de Moray,[60] acting as the new justiciar of Scotia rather than as a new Guardian, the impression given to those outside Scotland was probably that faction was breaking out once more. That this was a concern to Edward (and probably to the Norwegian king) is obvious in terms by which the Scottish envoys were called to meet the Norwegian envoys in the presence of Edward I to discuss the Maid's return and no doubt hammer out a preliminary treaty of marriage. There is reference to the English awareness of the need for peace in Scotland and also the unspecified need to reform or alter the realm of Scotland.[61] The choice of Scottish envoys itself is interesting. There were three Guardians plus Robert Bruce, lord of Annandale. Was the composition of this group an attempt to show a united front, indicating that strife was over between Comyns and Bruces in Scotland in much the same way as Alexander Comyn earl of Buchan had worked alongside Alan Durward in the early 1260s? Did Edward I himself have some influence on Bruce's presence in the embassy? The involvement of Bruce in Scottish government for the first time under the Guardians deserves more attention than it has received.

The Treaty of Salisbury, 9th November 1289,[62] presented the agreements of the Scottish, Norwegian and English envoys. It was agreed that the young Queen was to reach Scotland or England before 1st November 1290 and that she would come free of any marriage contract. Edward was to be assured that the Scottish kingdom was in a safe and peaceful condition. He himself made it clear that the government of the Guardians should be obeyed. The political stability of Scotland was a key factor to establish before the Maid would be sent to Scotland. Edward I, who had established a reputation as a mediator in Europe,[63] would have the role of arbiter if the Scots and Norwegians were in dispute. Although the Guardians had given their envoys instructions to preserve 'the liberty and honour of the realm of Scotland' in the negotiations, the Treaty of Salisbury had conceded the right of Edward to intervene in Scotland.

The terms of the Treaty would be ratified by the community of the realm of Scotland on 12th March 1290 at the border – in fact the meeting, another stage in the negotiations, took place at Birgham, with the Treaty of Birgham not being signed until 18th July 1290.[64] The Salisbury agreement did not mention a marriage agreement between Margaret and Edward I's son, Edward, though it appears that Edward I was certain that such a marriage would take place as he had already petitioned the pope in 1289. The bull granting the necessary dispensation for the marriage was issued on 6th November 1289, so it seems that negotiations must have started earlier in 1289.[65] The anxiety of the Guardians to secure a marriage treaty and to gain favour with Edward in order to bring greater stability to their government is shown in their correspondence with Edward in March 1290.[66] They declared both their appreciation for what Edward and his predecessors had done for Scotland and their agreement to the proposed marriage subject to certain conditions. The difficulty of both gaining favour with and giving concessions to Edward *and* preserving the liberties of the kingdom of Scotland was well demonstrated between February and August 1290. On 20th February Edward granted to Anthony Bek, bishop of Durham, the custody of the lands and tenements in Cumberland and Northumberland which had formerly been held by the king of Scotland.[67] On 4th June, the custody of the Isle of Man, clearly a part of the Scottish kingdom, was given to Walter de Hunterscumbe.[68] Later in the month, the bishop was given a commission to receive the men of the Isles of Scotland to the peace of Edward I.[69] Edward was already, it seems, taking the opportunity to interfere in Scottish affairs. The approach of the Scots for his help since 1286 no doubt encouraged this attitude. It may also account for the aggressiveness of the sheriff of Northumberland on the border – he even rode into Scotland to survey the de Vesci lands in Sprouston.[70] Yet here the Guardians reacted against such an invasion of Scottish liberties by ordering William de Soules, justiciar of Lothian and sheriff of Roxburgh, to arrest the sheriff of Northumberland and bring him before the Guardians to answer for his actions.[71]

The Treaty of Birgham, which was eventually signed in July 1290, was a marriage treaty uniting the heir of England with the heiress of Scotland. The terms of the treaty represent an attempt by the Scottish political community to define the conditions by which they agreed to the marriage. These were basically that Scotland would retain its independence and would keep intact its own rights, laws, liberties and customs. No parliaments would be held outside Scotland to deal with matters concerning the kingdom. Yet although the treaty sought to preserve Scotland from external interference, as with the arrangements made in 1260–61 for the confinement of the Scottish queen in England, certain concessions were made: 'We reserve to our aforesaid lord, and to any other person, such right, concerning matters on the border or elsewhere, as may have belonged to them prior to the date of this present grant, or which could rightfully belong to them in the future' and 'by reason of this present treaty nothing shall be added to, nor taken away from, the right of either realm'.[72]

The English tendency to interfere in Scottish affairs, seen before Birgham, continued thereafter. In August, Edward ratified Birgham at the Treaty of Northampton but most significantly asked the Guardians to recognise Anthony Bek, bishop of Durham, as the lieutenant in Scotland of his son Edward and of his future wife Margaret.[73] Bek had been Edward's chief agent in border affairs since the 1280s and his appointment as bishop of Durham in 1283 consolidated that role. His appointment as lieutenant in Scotland for his son further extended the royal administrative role in northern and Scottish affairs which he was developing from February 1290. His empowerment in June 1290 to admit to the king's peace the men of the Isles of Scotland 'who were in war and discord' was another sign of Edward's fear of Scottish political instability. Bek's appointment as Edward's lieutenant in Scotland was an extension of this – the Guardians were instructed by Edward to defer to Bek in matters 'which are required for the governance and peaceful state of the realm'. The notion of the need to reform the Scottish realm, present in English correspondence prior to the Treaty of Salisbury in 1289, is firmly stated in August 1290.[74] Bek had to 'reform and set to rights the aforesaid realm in conjunction with the remaining Guardians, by the counsel of the prelates and magnates'. Edward's actions show – despite the promises made at Birgham that Scotland's independence would be safeguarded – that Scotland could only be politically stable, especially after the loss of Alexander Comyn earl of Buchan's experience, with *his* oversight. He even felt that the castles of Scotland should be put under his control. This attitude and the need to have representation in Scotland is similar to the policy – almost hysterically paternal at times – of Henry III in the minority of Alexander III.

The precedent of Henry III's oversight over Scottish affairs between 1251 and 1258 (an oversight which was stopped in 1258 principally by the English king's preoccupation with the baronial reform movement in England) plus the practice of appeals to Edward I from Scotland and the Scottish nobility prior to 1289 no doubt encouraged Edward to pursue an increasingly interventionist approach to Scotland. The attitude of the Comyns, who still dominated the Scottish political scene after the death of their leader Earl Alexander of Buchan, demonstrates the reality of relationships between the Scottish nobility and the English monarchy. For much of the thirteenth century, the Comyns as a group and as individuals looked to the English king as an authority, even in Scottish affairs. This was particularly evident in the minority of Alexander III when in turn the Comyns and the non-Comyn political groupings in Scotland appealed for Henry III's intervention in Scottish affairs.[75] It was only when Henry refused requests for help from the Comyns in 1256 that they 'seized the young Scottish king and assumed control of Scottish government by force' in 1257. In more peaceful conditions in Scotland, the Comyns – especially the Buchan and Badenoch branches – acknowledged their military obligations to the English king in the 1260s and 1270s.[76] Perhaps more significant, however, was the readiness of the Comyns who, despite their great landholding in England, were more firmly attached to the Scottish kingdom by landholding and royal service than were the Bruces, to look to the English king to influence their landed position in Scotland. Thus in 1282, William Comyn of Kirkintilloch, son of John Comyn of Badenoch, pleaded with Edward

I to use his influence with the king of Scotland and his son in favour of his claim to the earldom of Menteith.[77] A writ was attached ordering amicable letters to the king of England and his son, and as a result in 1285 William of Kirkintilloch gained half of the earldom of Menteith but not the title. The period 1250 to 1290 showed that the king of England could, given his political priorities at the time, exercise much influence in peaceful as well as politically disturbed conditions. This was both recognised and accepted by the Comyns who were leaders of the Scottish political community in this period.

However, by 1290 there was a much more self-conscious awareness in Scotland of national independence, and the Comyns as the pillars of the Scottish monarchy had contributed significantly to this. The Treaty of Birgham was the clearest expression of this desire for a kingdom 'separate and free, ecclesiastically, feudally and judicially self-sufficient, its offices filled by Scotsmen, its heirs in wardship free of disparagement, its business dealt with in parliament within Scotland, and its taxation for its own customary needs only'.[78] The treaty, described as 'the high-water mark of the common endeavour by Guardians and community',[79] is a testament to the achievement of the Comyns as leaders of the political community in thirteenth-century Scotland and protectors of the liberties of the kingdom. The treaty and its safeguards for Scotland's independence had grown out of the experience of Alexander III's minority and the long and successful alliance between Alexander III and the aristocratic elite in Scotland. It should be remembered, however, that this alliance had been allowed to develop (and a quite sophisticated government machinery with it) because Henry III was unable to build on his 'overlordship' of Scotland because of his own political difficulties in England after 1258.

Political circumstances were different in 1290, however. The Guardians' denial of Edward I's request for custody over Scottish castles,[80] and their arrest of the sheriff of Northumberland for interference in Scottish affairs were practical expressions of the ideas contained in the Treaty of Birgham. It is impossible to conjecture how successful the Guardians would have been in denying Edward I and Anthony Bek extensive rights of oversight in Scottish affairs on behalf of Edward's son and his wife. The Comyns had been remarkably successful in denying real influence to Henry III's representatives in Scotland between 1251 and 1255. The aristocratic governing community had made a treaty safeguarding the rights of the kingdom but Edward I had already shown after Birgham, for example in his appointment of Bek as his lieutenant in Scotland, that he was prepared to go beyond the terms of Birgham. The death of the young 'Queen' Margaret in Orkney late in September 1290[81] as she made her way to Scotland meant that a political crisis turned into a much more serious political problem. There was no agreed successor as the dispute over the position of heir presumptive in 1286 had shown. There was an even greater need for outside assistance to help the leaders of the Scottish political community to control the inevitable pressure from the Bruces in 1290.

John Comyn, leader of the Comyn party and secular leader of the political community in Scotland, had already worked with Edward I. On 8th August 1290 he had been involved, with Anthony Bek, Robert Wishart bishop of Glasgow and two English representatives as part of an Anglo-Scottish commission set up to negotiate the marriage with the Maid.[82] Comyn was also given responsibility for informing Edward I about the arrival of the 'Maid' in Orkney and in 1290 received partial payment of £100 out of £200 of the king's gift.[83] Comyn's ally, the experienced bishop of St Andrews, William Fraser, who had been involved in numerous embassies to Edward I since 1286, seems to have taken the initiative when, on 6th October 1290, he wrote to Edward I informing him how rumours of Margaret's death had brought political instability to Scotland and asking for his intervention to prevent war.[84] He pointed out that Robert Bruce the elder, and his supporters, the earls of Mar and Atholl, had come to Perth and were gathering a large armed force. His letter added the recommendation: 'If Sir John Balliol comes to your presence we advise you to take care so to treat with him that in any event your honour and advantage be preserved ... Let your excellency deign, if you please, to approach towards the Marches for the consolation of the Scottish people and to save the shedding of blood, and set over them for king him who of right ought to have the succession, if so be that he will follow your counsel'. Such an appeal, from perhaps the most experienced leader of the Scottish political community, should be seen as another attempt by the governing elite in Scotland to secure the support which they had requested in 1286. They wanted political stability – this involved assistance in securing the royal succession and resisting the strong-arm tactics of the Bruces. It was clear that the dominant Comyn party would back the claims of John Balliol who was John Comyn's brother-in-law. Some contact had already been made between the Comyn party and the English by November 1290 when

Anthony Bek, Edward I's influential adviser, came to an agreement with John Balliol.[85] On 16th November 1290, at Gateshead, Balliol issued a charter as 'heir of the kingdom of Scotland' granting Bek the manors of Wark in Northumberland and Penrith in Cumberland together with all the other lands held by King Alexander in Cumberland. The overseeing role of Edward I was already in evidence as the grant was conditional on the English king's ratification. If he did not ratify it, Balliol would give Bek an annual rent of five hundred marks in Scotland. Balliol, and no doubt the Comyns, were aware of the importance of winning Bek and the English king over to their side, quickly finding a king and thereby maintaining political security in Scotland as well as their own power.

Bruce was also aware of the need for English support in 1290 and 1291, and these years seem to replicate the struggle between Comyns and Durwards to gain English support in the 1250s during another political crisis, the minority of Alexander III. In the winter of 1290–91 the elder Bruce had asked Edward I to support him as the choice of 'the Seven Earls'.[86] He had tried to destroy by force the stranglehold which the Comyns had on political power in 1286 but the years 1286 to 1288 had shown that he had an insufficiently broad power-base. By ingeniously using the ancient constitutional concept of 'the Seven Earls', the document asserted that Robert Bruce's claim was backed within Scotland by the whole body of the earls and that this body had a right in elections. The 'Appeal', which is weakened by the fact that only two earls (those of Fife and Mar) are named, asserted a wider political base for Bruce and argued that John Comyn and William Fraser bishop of St Andrews did not represent the 'whole community of the realm' but were acting by 'private authority'. Bruce thus tried to take the high moral ground:

> .... we, Robert Bruce lord of Annandale ... the legitimate and true heir designate to the rule of the realm of Scotland have put forward a claim concerning the right which we have in the realm of Scotland, and are urgently pursuing our right, as we are bound to do...

> ... you [i.e. Comyn and Bishop Fraser] with some persons of the realm of Scotland supporting you and falling in with your wishes intend and propose to make John Balliol king in the realm of Scotland and to confer on him the rights and honours which go with the rule of the kingdom to our prejudice and the hindrance of our right...

... you, William bishop of St Andrews and John Comyn ... have
substituted others, by your own authority, as your subordinate
guardians, for which substitution no authority or power was
given by the nobles and magnates and community of the realm of
Scotland; and these your subordinate keepers ... have gone to the
land of Moray ... and have there destroyed and robbed lands and
villages...

Then Robert Bruce made an appeal for Edward I's help:

In the name of the seven earls and their adherents I seek urgently
the help of the king of England.

There is evidence even before the Maid of Norway's death that
Edward was developing an interventionist policy towards Scotland.
His central role in the negotiations for a marriage between his son and
the young heiress of Scotland gave him some authority to oversee and
ensure some stability in Scottish affairs. The death of Margaret altered
the paternal role which Edward could legitimately have played, a role
which Henry III had performed in the 1250s to much acclaim in later
Scottish record. The urgent appeals from the two rival political forces
in Scotland, the ruling group led by the Comyns on the one hand and
the Bruces on the other, gave Edward every reason to believe that his
intervention was welcome and that he could take the opportunity to
insist on his recognition as lord superior of Scotland. Edward's actions
in the early months of 1291 show that he was prepared to intervene
decisively. That English claims for overlordship were central to his
policy is shown by his search through the chronicles of English religious
houses for theoretical evidence for his claims.[87] He also showed that
he was willing to place financial and military resources behind such
a claim[88] – he prepared for an English shipping blockade of Scotland
as well as sending 10,000 marks to Newcastle and summoning both
feudal magnates and the shire levies of northern England to gather at
Norham on 2nd June 1291. In May 1291 Edward declared the reason for
his coming to Norham:[89] 'by virtue of the overlordship which belongs
to him he may do justice to everyone, and, after all disturbances have
been quelled, may restore settled peace to the kingdom of Scotland'.
His family interest is mentioned – 'Our lord the king has observed
the peace of the realm of Scotland to be disturbed by the deaths of
King Alexander and of his children, who were kinsfolk of our lord the

king (by which deaths he is greatly distressed)' – but he clearly asks for recognition of his overlordship in order that this matter may be brought to a satisfactory conclusion. The fact that military resources were being prepared by the English king suggests that Edward felt there would be some opposition to his claim. The Treaty of Birgham less than a year earlier represented a firm commitment by the political community of Scotland to an independent kingdom.

The request of Scottish representatives at Norham for time to ponder Edward's claim to overlordship was in keeping with the views expressed at Birgham, as was their eventual reply:[90] 'of any such right or demand made or used by yourself or your ancestors they know nothing ... they have no power to reply in the absence of the lord [i.e. the king of Scots] to whom such a demand should be addressed and who could reply to it ... Meanwhile they can only refer to the oath they took after the death of the king [Alexander III] saving your faith and theirs and (? to the treaty) confirmed in your presence at Northampton'. This reply, given 'in the name of the community of the realm of Scotland', was rejected by Edward who cleverly outflanked the leaders of the political community of the realm[91] by asking the claimants to the Scottish throne – one of them must be king and have the right to reply – to reply. In early June all the claimants (the thirteen 'Competitors') agreed that Edward was the rightful overlord and that they would abide by his judgement on the succession. Further, they agreed that the English king should have possession of the land and especially the royal castles. Control of the Scottish government by the political community of the realm was gradually being forfeited in unusual and difficult circumstances – it was surely the responsibility of the Guardians, if anyone, to relinquish the kingdom and its castles.

Despite such important concessions, the spirit behind the Treaty of Birgham was still present. Edward I did not quite achieve the full unequivocal recognition of his claims that he required.[92] An admission by the 'Competitors', who could not be regarded as a representative body in Scotland, could not have the same authority as the Guardians and the political community of the realm. On 6th June Edward promised that he would maintain the customary laws and liberties of the kingdom until a decision about the rightful king was made. On 12th June, he agreed that this decision would be made within Scotland and he also promised to restore both kingdom and castles to the rightful king within two months of the decision being made. He also promised that, on the death of any Scottish king leaving an heir whose rights were incontrovertible, the English king would demand the rights of homage and sovereign worship only, not rights of custody, marriage or possession of the kingdom. According to Bower,[93] Robert Wishart bishop of Glasgow and one of the Guardians rejected Edward's claim to suzerainty, and some, perhaps all, of the castle commanders refused at first to hand over their castles to Edward on the grounds that they had been entrusted with their custody by Alexander III or the Guardians, not by the English king.[94]

However, while signs of resistance to full English overlordship and concessions won from the English king show the natural reactions of a mature Scottish government at the end of the thirteenth century, the Guardians as leaders of the Scottish political community had compromised the independence of their kingdom in June 1291. They had not only agreed to surrender Scottish royal castles, on 11th June they had even resigned their very authority to be reappointed by the English king. They were no longer 'elected by the community' but 'appointed by the most serene prince, the Lord Edward'.[95] The composition of the Guardians was changed too with an English baron Brian fitz Alan, lord of Bedale, added to their number.[96] On 13th June at Upsettlington, opposite Norham, the Guardians and other magnates swore fealty individually to Edward. These leading nobles included the four Scottish Guardians (including John Comyn of Badenoch), two other members of the Comyn family (John Comyn earl of Buchan and William Comyn of Kirkintilloch), John Balliol and two members of the Bruce family (Robert Bruce of Annandale and Robert Bruce, earl of Carrick).[97] There then followed a general swearing of fealty to Edward at Perth, Ayr, Inverness and Galloway. In his capacity as Guardian, John Comyn of Badenoch together with Brian fitz Alan and the bishop of St Andrews organised the general swearing of fealty at Perth.[98]

A court was appointed to decide which of the thirteen claimants or 'Competitors' had the best right to the Scottish throne and this met for the first time in August 1291 – the lawsuit which came to be called the 'Great Cause' in the eighteenth century[99] had begun. Of the thirteen candidates, it was clear at the time that the two most serious candidates were John Balliol and Robert Bruce. The drama of both the legal confrontation between Balliol and Bruce and the events following it has generated both legends and misconceptions. Subsequent Bruce propaganda, for instance, gave rise to a long-lasting tradition that Balliol was a puppet nominated by Edward I to the Scottish kingship in defiance of a national belief that Bruce had the better claim. Certainly Balliol hardly seems to have been as active in pursuing his interests in Scotland as Robert Bruce had been between 1286 and 1290. He countered the Bruce claim in 1286 but did not get involved in faction-forming activities afterwards: 'John Balliol appears to have been somewhat detached from the political storm that was gathering on his behalf north of the border'.[100] The attitude of the Bruces following the death of Alexander III in 1286, attacking both Balliol interests and those of the leaders of the political community, the Comyns, would suggest that the Bruces saw Balliol as a puppet of the dominant Comyns. The letter of Bishop Fraser to Edward in October 1290 also represents a recommendation from this dominant Comyn party of their candidate, Balliol, to Edward I. If John Balliol was a puppet, he was a puppet of his relatives, the Comyns.

It has been argued that 'Edward ... does not seem to have had a decided preference for Balliol or Bruce',[101] and that he was 'less concerned about the individual competitors than about ensuring the peace of Scotland during the vacancy of the throne and an authoritative admission by the Scots of his feudal overlordship over the Scottish kingdom'.[102] It was in the interests of both the leaders of the political community in Scotland and Edward I to secure an early decision and it seems most unlikely that Edward I was not advised by his agent for Scottish affairs about both the legal and political situation in Scotland. It has been pointed out that an English mission, led by Anthony Bek, came to Scotland in January 1291.[103] Anthony Bek, as bishop of Durham, must have known John Balliol through his lordships of Barnard Castle in Co. Durham and Bywell in Northumberland. It is interesting to note that John Balliol already referred to himself as 'heir of Scotland' in a charter of 16th November 1290, granting Bek lands under the Scottish king's jurisdiction either in northern England or Scotland. Edward I and Anthony Bek would have been well aware of the Comyns as the leaders of the aristocratic community in Scotland after 1286. The Comyns, especially John Comyn of Badenoch, had worked on the English king's behalf to inform him of the Maid's arrival in Scotland. There is no indication that Edward I sought to use John Balliol as a puppet. It is probable, however, that he hoped for the success of Balliol as the candidate of the ruling aristocratic party in Scotland which had wider support and a better chance of producing stability in Scotland.

The way that auditors were organised to decide between the rival candidates also leads one to move away from the narrow depiction of 'Balliol versus Bruce' confrontation. Bruce was allowed to nominate forty auditors and Balliol and Comyn together another forty, while all other candidates were to nominate through Balliol, Comyn and Bruce. Edward I himself nominated twenty-four auditors. The Comyns, leaders of the political community, were clearly a central political force in the 'Great Cause'. The 'Great Cause' was another stage of the Bruce challenge to the Comyn-controlled political community. This becomes more obvious when the list of forty auditors for Balliol and Comyn is analysed.[104] It represents above all the Comyn following rather than a Balliol following. The names of Comyn relatives figure prominently – John Comyn earl of Buchan, Gilbert de Umphraville earl of Angus, Malise earl of Strathearn, Alexander of Argyll, Andrew de Moray and Geoffrey de Mowbray. The representatives of the families of Fraser, Graham, Lascelles, Hay, Cheyne, Sinclair, Maxwell, Wemyss and Scot were particularly associated with the Comyns. What is more, the nominees of Balliol and Comyn represent the Scottish government of the day[105] – the offices of Guardian, justiciar of Scotia and Galloway, sheriff of Ayr, Banff, Auchterarder, Edinburgh, Linlithgow, Dumfries, Kincardine, Elgin, Perth, Fife and Aberdeen, and representatives who appeared on Scottish embassies make this list of auditors appear to be the 'government-approved' list and John Balliol the official government candidate. In comparison, the list of Bruce auditors reflects much less political weight – there is one Guardian in the list, one justiciar (of Lothian), representatives of the sheriffdoms of Ayr, Berwick, Roxburgh, Dumbarton and Inverness, and a number of representatives who appeared on Scottish embassies. It is noticeable that the Bruces' auditors represent, predominantly, strength in the south-west and south whereas the Balliol/Comyn list of auditors represent a much more wide-ranging strength. This, of course, reflects the Comyns' wide-ranging interests and influence in both northern and southern Scotland. It is also worth noticing that the Balliol/Comyn list had a much higher ecclesiastical representation.

The legal process revealed the superior strength by the principles of primogeniture of the Balliol cause which claimed seniority of line against the Bruces' claim of nearness of degree. Whereas Balliol's submission was short and centred on two arguments, the arguments of Bruce were 'many and varied'.[106] Once the Bruces lost the initial argument on the issue of seniority versus nearness of degree, Bruce's lawyers changed their argument on the indivisibility of the kingdom, claiming that Bruce should be allowed a third share. On 14th June 1292 Robert Bruce made an agreement with Count Florence, another claimant, which provided help for each other, if one became king, against the remaining claimants. The root of Count Florence's claim, which has probably been underestimated in the 'Great Cause',[107] was based on his allegation that David, earl of Huntingdon, the common ancestor of Balliol, Bruce and Hastings, had resigned his right to the Scottish kingdom. Evidence of this resignation, if it had been produced, would have seriously damaged Balliol's claim and given Bruce, in co-operation with Count Florence, an important entry to power. Count Florence had a serious claim to worry Balliol and this is clear from Florence's complaint against Balliol's 'favourers and maintainers'. Count Florence accused the prior of Pluscarden, perhaps a supporter of Balliol's candidature, of retaining an inspeximus of the resignation.

Behind the legal arguments, there were clearly intense political manoeuvrings. The influence of the Comyns, using all their power as the dominant political group to support the candidature of their relative, John Balliol, whose success would both maintain and even increase Comyn ascendancy, must be set beside the ambitions of the Bruces who were determined to stake their claim to power and were prepared to take advantage of every opportunity to turn this claim into reality. Bruce opposition had been apparent since 1286. Even before the Maid's death in September 1290, Bruce had tried to increase his territorial power in the north, where the Comyn political power was virtually unchallenged, by trying to gain complete control of the Garioch.[108] This, of course, was another attack on Balliol interests as Balliol, Bruce and Hastings inherited equal shares of Earl David's large Scottish lordship there. Bruce came to an agreement with Nicholas Biggar for Biggar to bring a case before the king's court to claim Balliol and Hastings lands in the Garioch. Such a scheme, if it had been successful, would have greatly increased Bruce's influence in northern Scotland and strengthened the northern alliance which he enjoyed with his neighbour, the earl of Mar.

Bruce had used force and legal means to strengthen his political position. In the winter of 1290–91, Bruce had also presented himself as the rightful heir, as the choice of the 'Seven Earls'. In the 'Great Cause', he first of all based his claim as sole heir to an indivisible kingdom, then changed it to a claim as co-heir of a divisible barony. He also made an agreement with Count Florence of Holland and hoped to benefit 'as an ally and conditional beneficiary'.[109] During the 'Great Cause' he also put forward a case that he was the designated successor of Alexander II in 1238. It is also apparent that, like his rivals in Scotland, Bruce had appealed to Edward I for support.

The final judgement, on 17th November 1292, went, as expected, in favour of John Balliol who was eventually enthroned on St Andrew's Day 1292. This decision was clearly in the interests of the Comyns, Balliol's relatives and the most powerful political force in Scotland at the time of the 'Great Cause'. The fact that Balliol was the official 'ruling party' candidate is emphasised by the Comyns' conduct of his own claims through John Comyn of Badenoch, the Competitor. The Comyn claim was based on descent from Donald Ban, king of Scots after the death of his brother Malcolm III in 1093. He did not press his claim, saying specifically in his petition that he did not want to compete against, and therefore prejudice, the claims of John Balliol, his brother-in-law.[110] It was still important, however, for the Comyns to put forward, and therefore preserve, a claim for the future: '... if the main line of the Balliols died out, his own descendants by Eleanor Balliol would have a double claim to the throne, and it was important that the Comyn side of it be put on record now. Distant descent, like illegitimate descent, was not a sound reason for failing to put in a claim.' In a similar way, Bruce the Competitor, as soon as the court decided against him and for Balliol on the issue of seniority versus nearness of degree, on 5th and 6th November, resigned his claim on 7th November to his son and heir and in turn to his heirs.[111]

The 'Great Cause' was a victory for Comyn power in Scotland over the pretensions of the Bruces. It was an important phase in the escalation of their rivalry but certainly not an end to it. The Comyns were the dominant political force in Scotland between 1286 and 1292. They represented and led the political community of the realm which they had helped to establish in conjunction with Alexander III. The Bruces sought to break the Comyn grip on territorial and political power in Scotland. The Bruce propaganda of the fourteenth and fifteenth centuries suggests Robert Bruce, the king, rescued Scotland from years of faction fighting among self-interested baronial groups after 1286. In practice, the period 1286 to 1292 was disturbed chiefly by the Bruce family's military, legal and territorial challenge to the Comyn leadership of the political community of the realm. The Comyns were the power behind the Balliol kingship in 1292 but would clearly have to

The Guardians' Seal (S.R.O. Laing Seal Casts i 17, i 18) (diameter 3 inches). The provisional government of six guardians, formed shortly after the death of Alexander II in 1286, acted on behalf of the community of the realm while at the same time acting as delegates of the crown. The seal of the Guardians, cut especially for their use, symbolically sums up this role. One side of the seal (Laing i 18) (top) bears a shield of the royal arms with the lion rampant and the inscription 'the seal of Scotland appointed for the government of the kingdom'. The other side (Laing i 17) (bottom) bears the figure of St. Andrew on his cross with the inscription 'St. Andrew the leader of the compatriot Scots'. These symbols more accurately reflect the role of the Comyns, dominant in the Guardianship and pillars of monarchy in thirteenth-century Scotland, than the writings of Fordun and Bower in the fourteenth and fifteenth centuries. *By permission of the Keeper of the Records of Scotland.*

Deer Abbey was founded in 1219 by William Comyn, earl of Buchan, who was buried in the abbey when he died in 1233. The abbey became the religious centre of the Comyn earldom in the very heart of Buchan and its scant, round-arched remains are one of the few remaining signs of Comyn lordship in Buchan after Bruce's 'herschip' (harrying) of Buchan in 1308. Deer, as an austere Cistercian monastery, did not require elaborate architecture but it is apparent that in 1267 it was more than usually spartan. In that year, the resigning abbot, Adam of Smailholm, described it as a 'hovel'. *Crown Copyright: Historic Scotland.*

Inchmahome Priory. Walter Comyn became earl of Menteith c. 1234 and soon marked his elevated status by founding an abbey. He founded the Augustinian priory of Inchmahome in 1238 on the largest of the three islands in Lake Menteith. The splendidly sited Inchmahome is the finest visible symbol of Comyn ecclesiastical lordship in Scotland and, as Earl Walter was regarded as the leading baron in Scotland in 1237, a fitting monument to his status. It is worth noting that Earl Walter's political dominance in the 1250s was generally supported by the Church. *Crown Copyright: Historic Scotland.*

Ruthven Castle, regarded as the head of the Badenoch lordship, held a strategic position, commanding the northern end of two passes over the Mounth, the Drumochter and Minigaig passes. The site, now unfortunately covered by the eighteenth-century Ruthven Barracks, is on a prominent hill artificially scarped and rising from the flat floor of the Spey valley. Ruthven Castle was probably started in the time of Walter Comyn, first lord of Badenoch (d. 1258), but most development took place under Walter's nephew and heir John Comyn I of Badenoch (d. 1277), noted for his military prowess as well as castle-building at Tarset (Tynedale) in 1267 and Blair Atholl in 1269. *Crown Copyright: Royal Commission on the Ancient and Historical Monuments of Scotland.*

Blair Atholl. The medieval castle site (top left) at Blair Atholl, like that at Ruthven, is covered by later buildings. Unlike Ruthven, however, the precise date of castle-building at Blair Atholl is known. It is recorded that John Comyn I, lord of Badenoch, built the castle in 1269, thus upsetting his neighbour, the earl of Atholl. The Blair Atholl site controlled the southern end of the Drumochter and Minigaig passes just as Ruthven commanded the northern end. It seems that Blair Atholl, along with Ruthven, was part of a precise Comyn castle-building strategy developing in the second half of the thirteenth century. *Crown Copyright: Royal Commission on the Ancient and Historical Monuments of Scotland.*

Seal of Alexander Comyn, earl of Buchan, 1244-1289 (diameter 2 inches). The top photograph represents the reverse of the seal. It features a shield bearing arms: three garbs. This is within a finely curved rounded and pointed quatrefoil panel with trefoils between annulets in the spandrils; the background has vine branches. The legend (in capitals) is: SIGILLUM: ALEXANDRI: COMMIN: COMITIS: DE: BUCHAN. The bottom photograph represents the obverse of the seal. It features a knight on horseback in chain mail, short surcoat, conical-topped helmet with a fan crest, a long sword in the right hand, the left holding the reins, with a shield bearing arms suspended from the neck. The galloping horse has a fan crest and long caparisons with arms. The arms are three garbs, two and one. The legend (in capitals) is S' - ALEXANDRI: COMMIN: DE: BUCHAN. *By permission of the Court of the Lord Lyon.*

Balvenie Castle. Alexander Comyn, earl of Buchan (d.1289), acquired Balvenie (Mortlach) in highland Banffshire between 1264 and 1282. Located only twenty miles from Badenoch's eastern boundary, it formed a strategic bridge between the Comyn bases of Buchan and Badenoch. Balvenie featured in Edward I's invasion in 1303 and in Robert Bruce's movement against the Comyns' northern power bases in 1307 and 1308. Situated on a promontory high over the River Fiddich, Balvenie relied for its strength on massive defensive walls (25 ft high and 7 ft thick) and a great outer ditch which enclosed the castle on three sides. *Crown Copyright: Historic Scotland.*

The Comyn Charter. The charter (dated c.1270 x 1289, possibly c. 1270) is a grant by Alexander Comyn, earl of Buchan, to Fergus son of John de Fothes of the estate of Fothes (Fiddes, Newburgh). Newburgh was the urban foundation of the Comyns in Buchan. The strength of the Comyn 'party' is revealed in the witness list. First witness was Earl Alexander's younger brother, William; second witness, Alexander's eldest son and heir, John; third witness, Philip de Feodarg (Meldrum) who married Alexander's sister, Agnes; fourth witness, Robert de Walchop, a regular witness to Earl Alexander's charters; and fifth witness Jacob de Lascelles, from a family with feudal connections to the earl. *By permission of the Keeper of the Records of Scotland.*

The Comyns of Buchan acquired *Cruggleton Castle* in Galloway after 1264 through the de Quincy inheritance of Earl Alexander's wife, Elizabeth. Although only a single arch now survives on its cliff-top site, a stone castle survived until the sixteenth century. In 1292 Edward I gave John Comyn earl of Buchan permission to export sufficient lead from the Isle of Man to cover eight towers at Cruggleton. Archaeological evidence has suggested castle-strengthening phases, in the 1260s and 1270s, which is in line with Comyn castle-building elsewhere in Scotland. *Crown Copyright: Royal Commission on the Ancient and Historical Monuments of Scotland.*

Left: *John Comyn, son of Alexander Comyn earl of Buchan* (S.R.O. Laing Seal Cast i 1213). John Comyn succeeded to the earldom on Alexander's death in 1289. The seal cast (left) is from the original brass matrix in the possession of Sir William Gordon Cumming Gordon of Altyre and Gordonstown. It was found on the site of the monastery of Tungland in Galloway in 1788. The seal is one inch in diameter, and features a shield of arms: three garbs, two and one. The legend is S' IOH'IS COMYN FIL' - COMIT' D' - BOTHA. Right: *Alexander Comyn of Buchan, brother of John Comyn earl of Buchan* (Alexander died c. 1308) (S.R.O. Laing Seal Cast i, 223). Alexander Comyn of Buchan was the member of the family most associated with Edward I's attempt to impose English control over the administration of northern Scotland. The seal (right) (7/8 inch in diameter) depicts a shield of arms: three garbs. The shield is on the breast of an eagle displayed. At the sides of the head of the eagle are three small balls. *By permission of the Keeper of the Records of Scotland.*

Inverlochy Castle. Inverlochy, the chief castle of the Comyns in Lochaber, commanded the entrance to the Great Glen, securing its southern sea outlet, and the scarcely less important overland route to the Spey. Its strategic position explains its importance in the 1297 revolt of the Comyns' allies, the Macdougalls, against Edward I's agents in the area. In Scotland, Inverlochy is a rare example (though not a very advanced one) of the quadrangular castle with high curtain walls fortified by round towers (not uncommon in England and Wales: cf. Harlech 1283). At Inverlochy, one tower (Comyn's tower) is larger than the rest and was apparently planned as a keep with residential accommodation. *Crown Copyright: Royal Commission on the Ancient and Historical Monuments of Scotland.*

Seal of John Comyn II, lord of Badenoch, the Competitor (S.R.O. Laing Seal Cast i 222 date 1292). The seal is one inch in diameter. It depicts a knight on horseback in a hauberk of mail, short surcoat, a flat-topped helmet, a sword in his right hand, and shield of arms suspended from his neck. The arms are three garbs, two and one. Above the helmet is a crescent enclosing a star. The legend reads: S' SECRETI IOH'IS CVMIN. By permission of the Keeper of the Records of Scotland.

Lochindorb Castle was strategically situated in the heart of Moray on a loch two miles long and three miles wide, between Forres and Grantown, and fully occupied its island site one acre in extent. The importance of the castle is attested by John Comyn II of Badenoch's death there c.1302 and by Edward I's use of Lochindorb in 1303 as a base to accept the formal submission of northern areas. The castle, which was certainly in existence by 1279, was entered from the east where there is a landing place but it is noteworthy that there are no special arrangements to strengthen the defence of the entrance doorway. Top: *Crown Copyright: Historic Scotland.* Bottom: *Crown Copyright: Royal Commission on the Ancient and Historical Monuments of Scotland.*

contend with continuing Bruce ambitions as well as the newly established English overlordship over Scotland in the years that followed.

NOTES

1. *Chron. Lanercost* (trans. Herbert Maxwell, 1913), pp.39–42.
2. *Chron. Fordun* II pp.304–5.
3. *Chron. Bower* (Watt), V p.427.
4. *Chron. Wyntoun* (Laing), II p.266.
5. For discussion of the 'Golden Age' see Norman H. Reid, 'Alexander III: the Historiography of a Myth' in Reid, *Scotland in the Reign of Alexander III*, pp.181–208.
6. Young, 'Noble Families and Political Factions', pp.1–2.
7. For full discussion see G. Stell, 'The Balliol Family and the Great Cause of 1291–2' in Stringer (ed.), *Essays on the Nobility*, pp.150–51.
8. G.W.S. Barrow, 'A Kingdom in Crisis: Scotland and the Maid of Norway', *S.H.R.* LXIX, 2, no.188 Oct. 11990, p.126.
9. *Chron. Fordun* II p.305.
10. *Chron. Lanercost* p.43.
11. *Chron. Wyntoun* (Laing), II p.275.
12. *Chron. Fordun* II p.305.
13. Barrow, *Robert Bruce*, p.17.
14. *Ibid.* p.xi.
15. Grant G. Simpson, *Handlist of the Acts of Alexander III, the Guardians, and John* (1960), pp.44–5.
16. J. Stevenson, *Documents illustrative of the History of Scotland* (1870), I p.25.
17. *Ibid.* I pp.26–7.
18. *Ibid.* I pp.49–50.
19. A.A.M. Duncan (ed.), *Formulary E Scottish Letters and Brieves* 1286–1424 (University of Glasgow, Occasional Papers, 1976.) no 89.
20. *Melrose Liber no.* 396 as cited in Barrow, *Robert Bruce*, p.17.
21. *Ibid.* p.17.
22. A.A.M. Duncan, 'The community of the realm of Scotland and Robert Bruce, a review', *S.H.R.* XLV (1966), pp.189–90.
23. *Ibid.* p.186; *Chron. Bower* (Watt), VI p.8.
24. Duncan, 'The community of the realm', *S.H.R.* pp.185–6.
25. *Chron. Lanercost* p.43.
26. N. Reid, 'The Kingless Kingdom: the Scottish guardianships of 1286–1306', *S.H.R.* LXI, 2 no.172, Oct. 1982 p.106; Geoffrey Barrow and Ann Royan, 'James Fifth Stewart of Scotland, 1260(?)–1309' in Stringer (ed.), *Essays on the Nobility of Medieval Scotland*, p.170.
27. Barrow, *Robert Bruce*, pp.15–16.
28. *Ibid, Chron. Lanercost* p.59.
29. G. Stell, 'The Balliol Family and the Great Cause', p.151.

30. Duncan, 'The community of the realm of Scotland', p.187.
31. *Chron. Bower* (Watt), VI p.9.
32. *Ibid.*
33. M. Prestwich, 'Edward I and the Maid of Norway', *S.H.R.* LXIX, 2, No.188, Oct. 1990, pp.163–4.
34. Barrow, *Robert Bruce*, p.18; Stevenson, *Documents*, I pp.22–3.
35. Duncan, 'The community of the realm of Scotland and Robert Bruce', p.186.
36. E.L.G. Stones and G.G. Simpson (eds), *Edward I and the throone of Scotland* (1978), p.170; Stones, *Anglo-Scottish Relations*, p.99.
37. Barrow, *Robert Bruce*, p.18.
38. Stell, 'The Balliol Family and the Great Cause', p.151.
39. *Exchequer Rolls* I pp.35–51.
40. *Exchequer Rolls* I p.41, pp. 35, 39.
41. *Exchequer Rolls* I pp.36–7.
42. *Exchequer Rolls* I p.39.
43. D.E.R. Watt, *Fasti Ecclesiae Scoticanae Medii Aevi* (1969) (2nd draft), p.39.
44. *Ibid.* p.2.
45. *Ibid.* p.293.
46. *Exchequer Rolls* I. p.39.
47. *Ibid.* I p.36.
48. *Ibid.* I p.43.
49. Simpson, *Handlist of the Acts of Alexander III, the Guardians and John*, pp.44–5.
50. *Exchequer Rolls* pp. 35, 42, 46.
51. *Ibid.* p.36.
52. Stevenson, *Documents*, I p.106.
53. N. Reid, 'Margaret "Maid of Norway" and Scottish Queenship', *Reading Medieval Studies*, VIII (1982) p.80.
54. E.L.G. Stones, *Anglo-Scottish Relations*, pp.85–6; see M. Prestwich, 'Edward I and the Maid of Norway', pp.166–7.
55. Stevenson, *Documents*, I pp.79–80.
56. Prestwich, 'Edward I and the Maid of Norway', p.166.
57. Stevenson, *Documents*, I pp.95–6.
58. *Chron. Fordun* II p.313.
59. *Chron. Lanercost* p.59.
60. *Chron. Fordun* II p.314.
61. Stevenson, *Documents*, I p.106.
62. *Ibid.* pp.105–11.
63. Prestwich, 'Edward I and the Maid of Norway', p.169.
64. For translation see G.W.S. Barrow, 'A Kingdom in Crisis: Scotland and the Maid of Norway', *S.H.R.* LXIX 2, No.188, Oct. 1990, pp.137–41.
65. *Ibid.* pp.165–6. The dispensation was required because the couple shared

a common ancestor in Edward's grandfather who was Margaret's great-grandfather.

66. *Acts of the Parliament of Scotland*, I pp.441–2.

67. Stevenson, *Documents*, pp.156–7.

68. *Ibid.* p.122.

69. *Ibid.* pp.161–2.

70. *Ibid.* pp. 115–16, 126.

71. *Ibid.* p.126.

72. Barrow, 'A Kingdom in Crisis', pp. 137, 141.

73. Barrow, *Robert Bruce*, p.29.

74. *Ibid.*

75. See ch. 3, pp.51ff.

76. For relationships between all three branches of the Comyn family and the English in the thirteenth century see Young, 'Noble Families and Political Factions', Reid (ed) *Scotland in the Reign of Alexander III*, pp.17–20.

77. *Cal. Docs. Scot.* II no.1763, *Scots Peerage*, VI pp.129–31; see also William Comyn of Kilbride's claim in the English courts for what was owed him and his wife from the manor of 'Athelgalthwyn', in Scotland (*Cal. Docs. Scot.* II no.2302).

78. A.A.M. Duncan, *The Nation of Scots and the Declaration of Arbroath* (Historical Association, 11970), p.11.

79. Barrow, *Robert Bruce*, p.28.

80. R. Nicholson, *Scotland: the Later Middle Ages* (1974), p.34.

81. *Cal. Docs. Scot.* II no.459.

82. *Foedera*, I (2) 737.

83. *Cal. Docs. Scot.* II nos. 463, 477.

84. *National Manuscripts of Scotland*, I no.LXX.

85. Stevenson, *Documents*, I pp.203–4.

86. Stones, *Anglo-Scottish Relations*, pp.89–101.

87. E.L.G. Stones and G.G. Simpson (eds), *Edward I and the throne of Scotland*, I pp. 137–62, 224 ff.

88. R. Nicholson, *Scotland: the Later Middle Ages*, p.36; for details see Stevenson, *Documents*, I pp. 202–3, 204–13.

89. Stones, *Anglo-Scottish Relations*, p.103.

90. *Ibid.* pp.107–11.

91. M. Prestwich, *Edward I*, pp.364–5; R. Nicholson, *Scotland: the Later Middle Ages*, p.27; Barrow, *Robert Bruce*, p.33.

92. *Ibid.* p.33.

93. *Chron. Bower* (Watt), VI p.29.

94. Stones and Simpson, *Edward I and the throne of Scotland*, II pp.100–101.

95. Barrow, *Robert Bruce*, p.35.

96. *Ibid.*

97. Stones and Simpson, *Edward I and the throne of Scotland*, II p.104.

98. Barrow, *Robert Bruce*, p.38.

99. M. Lynch, *Scotland, a New History* (1992), p.111.
100. G. Stell, 'The Balliols and the Great Cause', p.151.
101. F.M. Powicke, *The Thirteenth Century* (1962), p.607.
102. Barrow, *Robert Bruce*, p.30.
103. *Ibid.* pp.30–31.
104. Stones and Simpson, *Edward I and the throne of Scotland*, II pp.82–3 (for nominees of Bruce), pp.84–5 (for nominees of Balliol and Comyn).
105. See *Exchequer Rolls* I pp.35–51 (for sheriffs); also Barrow, 'The Justiciar' in *Kingdom of the Scots*, pp.137–9.
106. Barrow, *Robert Bruce*, p.41 and following.
107. Grant G. Simpson, 'The claim of Florence, count of Holland to the Scottish throne, 1291–2', *S.H.R.* XXVI p.115.
108. Barrow, *Robert Bruce*, pp.43–4.
109. Grant G. Simpson, 'The claim of Florence, count of Holland', p.116.
110. Stones and Simpson, *Edward I and the throne of Scotland*, I p.15, II p.138.
111. Stones, *Anglo-Scottish Relations*, p.17; Stones and Simpson, *Edward I and the throne of Scotland*, II p.228.

CHAPTER SIX

The Comyns and the Kingship
of John Balliol, 1292–1296

The period from 1286 to 1296, the eve of the Anglo-Scottish wars, has suffered more than most periods of Scottish medieval history from the problems of hindsight and the influence of pro-Bruce propaganda. The summary of these years by Walter Bower illustrates this point:

> King John intruded through the guile and power of the king of England, was king for less than four years, in very great servitude and bondage to the king of England; before this the kingdom was so to speak headless for seven years after the death of the peace-making King Alexander III, *and abnormal in the time of this disastrous King John*.[1]

Yet, as has been seen by the years 1286 to 1292, such a view misrepresents the political reality of a Scottish government, under the accepted leadership of the Comyns, continuing to govern quite efficiently and effectively despite very difficult political circumstances and despite attempts by the Bruces to challenge and weaken Comyn authority. Emphasis on the legal confrontation, the 'Great Cause', between Bruce and Balliol has distracted us from the real political battle between an experienced, Comyn-controlled government and the challenge of the Bruces.

In a similar way, discussion of John Balliol's kingship after 1292 has been dominated by the 'powerful legend of Balliol the ineffective puppet'[2] of Edward I, the picture created by pro-Bruce Scottish writers of the fourteenth and fifteenth centuries. To Fordun, Balliol submitted to 'thraldom'.[3] Barbour almost wrote him out of Scottish history: 'He was king bot a litill quhile';[4] while Bower, as we saw, considered the Scottish kingdom 'abnormal in the time of this disastrous King John'.[5] None of these views does justice to the period 1292 to 1296. It is recognised by modern historians that an attempt needs to be made to get behind the legend. It has been acknowledged that the history of this important period has been distorted: 'it is understandable, though misleading, that the history of Scotland has usually been written from the point of view of the Bruces (who were ultimately successful) rather than that of the Balliols (who were ultimately unsuccessful).'[6] Yet a perspective from the Comyn family, leaders of the political community in Scotland, is surely as vital an ingredient for discussion of the period 1292 to 1296 as it was for the years 1286 to 1292. The reign of King John should be seen as a further stage in the struggle for power within Scotland between the Comyn-led aristocratic community who held power and the Bruces who did not. The reign should also be set in the context of an established political community in Scotland, with a new king, *having* to react to the new position of Edward I as overlord of Scotland.

It was obvious before the enthronement of John Balliol as king of Scotland on St Andrew's Day in November 1292 that the Scottish government would continue to be opposed by the Bruces. On 7th November 1292 Robert Bruce, the Competitor, realising that his claim to the Scottish throne was going to be unsuccessful, resigned it to his son Robert Bruce earl of Carrick, thus preserving the claim for his family: 'we give and grant, of our free will, to our son and his heirs, full and free power to sue for the realm, and to prosecute in his own name the right which pertains to him in this matter'.[7] On 9th November, this Robert Bruce surrendered the earldom of Carrick to his son and heir, Robert (aged eighteen), the future king. In addition, the two elder Bruces refused to do homage to King John Balliol[8] and thus more obviously kept open the family claim to the Scottish throne. An aggressive attitude to Bruce rights over land and animosity to an influential Comyn relative and supporter, Geoffrey de Mowbray, is demonstrated by a dispute between Robert Bruce the elder and Geoffrey de Mowbray on 3rd November 1292 in Cumberland.[9] Robert Bruce the elder's influence is clear from the *Lanercost Chronicle*'s description given after his death at Lochmaben in 1295: 'a noble baron of England as well as Scotland . . . He was of handsome appearance, a gifted speaker, remarkable for his influence . . .'[10]

Despite refusing homage to John Balliol, the Bruces seem to have maintained their powerful position in south-west Scotland. With the backing of Bruce allies, James Stewart and the earl of Mar, Robert Bruce, the future king, was confirmed as earl of Carrick at the Stirling parliament of August 1293.[11] His father meanwhile sought new alliances outside Scotand in 1293 when, with permission from Edward I, he went to Norway to give his daughter, Isabella, in marriage to King Eric of Norway.[12] The Bruce power-base in the south-west of Scotland gave the Bruces continuing influence here. In 1294 the Balliol kingship was embarrassed by the appointment of a Bruce candidate, Master Thomas Dalton of Kirkcudbright, as bishop of Galloway.[13] John Balliol had objected to this as lord of Galloway in a letter addressed to the archbishop of York from Buittle, the chief Balliol base in Galloway. The lords of Galloway had always regarded themselves as patrons of the see but eventually John Balliol backed down on the issue. Bruce strength in the south-west was confirmed but Bruce pretensions to wider political power in Scotland would depend on outside support.

Clearly the Bruces formed the most powerful opposition to the Balliol kingship after 1292 but they were not the only group either to resent Comyn power or to look to the king of England for help.[14] By early 1293, Angus Macdonald had also failed to do homage to King John[15] and it was his heir Alexander Macdonald of Islay who made an appeal to Edward I's jurisdiction. The Macdonalds felt that in their long-running dispute with the Macdougalls in the outlying isles they were unlikely to receive support from the Comyns who were as closely related by marriage to the Macdougalls as to the Balliols. In Fife, Macduff, a younger son of Malcolm earl of Fife, complained to Edward I that he had not received justice in King John's court concerning his inheritance of the lands of Creich and Rires. Macduff was brother of Duncan earl of Fife who had been murdered in 1289 at the behest of Hugh de Abernethy, a prominent Comyn supporter. According to Bower,[16] Macduff complained that Balliol 'showed too much favour to the other side', an indication that there was continuing friction in Fife between the family of the earls of Fife and the Comyn-favoured Abernethy family.

Much attention has been given to the issue of appeals to England and especially that of Macduff because it was this appeal which brought John Balliol to the king's court in England[17] and foreshadowed the outbreak of war between England and Scotland in 1296. In comparison, relatively little attention has been given to the nature and personnel of Scottish government between 1292 and 1296. There is much evidence to indicate continuity of both personnel and policy in Scottish government between 1286 and 1296. The dominance of Scottish government by the Comyn party continued from Alexander III's reign through the Guardianship of 1286 to 1292 and into Balliol's kingship. This was perfectly natural as Balliol was the candidate of the dominant governing elite, the Comyns and their supporters. Judging from their appearance in the royal circle, the leading secular figures in the Balliol administration were John Comyn earl of Buchan, John Comyn II lord of Badenoch, Alexander de Balliol, Geoffrey de Mowbray and Patrick de Graham. These men seemed to be the inner core of advisers most frequently in attendance at the royal court and at the centre of government.[18]

John Comyn of Badenoch was the brother-in-law of King John Balliol. His cousin, John Comyn earl of Buchan, who was over thirty at the time of his father's death c.1289,[19] was clearly a very prominent figure in the Balliol administration. He was constable of Scotland by 1292–3, and perhaps earlier. This office was inherited by the Comyns of Buchan from Roger de Quincy earl of Winchester (d.1264) through Roger's daughter, Elizabeth, wife of Alexander Comyn earl of Buchan. The Comyn earls of Buchan were, in practice, almost hereditary holders, since the early thirteenth century, of the chief political and administrative office in Scotland, the justiciarship of Scotia.[20] John Comyn earl of Buchan is not known to have gained that office before 1299 when he apparently took over from another Comyn supporter, Andrew de Moray (who seems to have remained in office until 1296). In practice, however, Moray's infrequent appearances at the royal court between 1292 and 1296 would indicate that John Comyn earl of Buchan had the influence which went with the office of justiciar of Scotia, though without the title. Geoffrey de Mowbray, a relative of the Comyns by marriage, was also a very prominent adviser to the Balliol kingship. This was recognised in 1294 when he became justiciar of Lothian following on from William de Soules who died c.1289/93.[21] Alexander de Balliol, who had held the key post of chamberlain since 1286, continued in this office under his relative John Balliol and was an important member of Balliol's government. Patrick Graham, from a family who had consistently supported the Comyns since the 1250s, was regularly in attendance at the royal court from 1292 to 1296. He had been sheriff of Stirling from at least 1289 to late 1292 but had been succeeded in that office by another Comyn supporter, Andrew Fraser, by 1293. Patrick Graham was more centrally involved in Scottish government, being involved in royal business at Norham,

Newcastle, London, Lindores, Dunfermline and Stirling between 1292 and 1295.

Also prominent in the royal circle at this time, though not appearing quite so frequently, were William Fraser, bishop of St Andrews (it is noticeable that three other members of the Fraser family, Andrew, Richard and Simon, also make appearances), and Robert bishop of Glasgow, experienced members of the Guardianship. Members of the Umphraville family – related by marriage to Comyns and Balliols – were also important in Scottish government at the time in the persons of Gilbert earl of Angus, and Ingram. Still important in Scottish royal circles after 1292 were John de Soules and William Sinclair who had been respectively sheriffs of Berwick and Edinburgh. It seems very probable that they continued in these important public offices after 1292. Although there is only fragmentary evidence of office holders at central, regional or local levels in the period 1292 to 1296, the names of those present in the royal circle would suggest a high degree of continuity after 1292 which in turn reflected the high degree of continuity in government after 1286. There was an experienced Scottish political community advising John Balliol in 1292, and the dominance of the Comyns and their supporters is very apparent.

Naturally the reign of John Balliol saw a further consolidation of the power of the Comyn family and their supporters. Before 1296 King John had given John Comyn, earl of Buchan, all the lands of his thanage of Formartine and 'Dereley' (probably Belhelvie) except the burgh and castle of Fyvie.[22] In return Earl John surrendered his hereditary claims on the lordship of Galloway. The earl of Buchan had strengthened his position in the north by not only rounding off his earldom but by extending it considerably to the south. The thanages of Formartine and Belhelvie were together worth over two hundred and fifty marks per year. The strengthening of Balliol rights in the south-west and Comyn landed power in the north was a boost to the Balliol/Comyn government in Scotland. By the end of Alexander III's reign, Earl John's father, Alexander, had also gained the thanage of Conveth (Inverkeithny, Banffshire), farming it for 80 marks a year.[23] Earl John received a further benefit in this royal thanage from King John who relieved him of £48 (annually), part of the 80 marks annual payment to the king.[24]

The strengthening of Comyn power[25] meant a strengthening of royal power in the Scotland of 1292. There is sparse evidence of Comyn *acta* in the period 1292–96 to show how their landed power was used to strengthen their own support. Yet one charter (April 1296) by Earl John to Nicholas de la Hay, who had recently also received favour from King John, is revealing.[26] It showed the earl of Buchan having already infeft his kinsman, Nicholas de la Hay, lord of Errol, in lands in his tenement of Heriot (Midlothian), adding to that grant with land to the south of Heriot. The charter, which was granted at Sweetheart Abbey, encapsulates in a remarkable way the earl of Buchan's pervasive influence and interests in the north of Scotland, the south-west and Midlothian. The names of the grantee and witnesses to this act – Nicholas de la Hay, a kinsman, Alexander Comyn, the granter's brother, Reginald Cheyne, William de Meldrum, William de Mowat, David de Bethun and William de Galloway, the granter's chamberlain – represent, too, support of long standing through Comyn family members, families related to the Comyns by marriage (Hay and Meldrum) and other families with long-held Comyn connections (Cheyne, Bethun and Mowat). Another charter (c.1295) of the Badenoch branch of the Comyn family by John Comyn to John his son[27] of land in Tynedale to the value of 400 marks yearly serves to show the continuing influence and importance of the Northumberland lands of the family.

It is hardly surprising, given the consolidation of the power of the Comyns and their supporters in Scottish government after 1292, that there was continuity in policy as well as personnel. King John was clearly very dependent on the experience of the Comyns in government. It is most probable that the treatise 'The Scottish King's Household'[28] which outlined the organisation of the Scottish royal household and government was composed for the benefit of the new king. The Comyn party, because of their experience, actually held the reins of power. As the Bruces in the south-west and the Macdonalds in the Hebrides refused to acknowledge Balliol's kingship by rendering homage, it is hardly surprising that the evidence of royal *acta*, brieves and Scottish parliaments shows particular concern with strengthening royal authority against internal opposition.[29] Comyn experience of government in alliance with Alexander III from 1260, and their dominant role in the Guardianship from 1286 to 1292, together with continuity in government personnel, must surely be given credit for the 'sensible constructive thinking ... done in government circles'[30] and the 'good grasp of political and strategic realities'. From 1260 to 1286 Alexander III had ruled in alliance with the political community of the realm, led by the Comyns. From 1286 until 1292 the Scottish kingdom was ruled by this political community of the realm on behalf of the rightful heir to the kingdom. From 1292 to 1296, the alliance between monarch and political community of the realm was renewed though the inexperience of Balliol meant that the political community remained the dominant partner, in practice governing both with and on behalf of the Scottish king.

An early problem for the Balliol kingship to deal with in the winter of 1292/93 was opposition in the north and northern isles. Rivalry between the Macdougalls and the Macdonalds in the western Highlands and Isles had been developing in the second half of the thirteenth century. Edward I had cause to make Alexander Macdougall of Argyll, lord of Lorn, and Angus Macdonald with his eldest son Alexander swear in his presence on 7th July 1292 to keep the peace in the isles 'and outer lands of Scotland'. It seems that already by December 1292, and perhaps much earlier, Alexander Macdougall, related to the Comyns by marriage, had been given wide-ranging powers over Kintyre, Argyll and Lewis,[31] perhaps similar to the temporary wardship which the Comyns had enjoyed in Moray in 1211–12 and 1229. The crown was hampered in the west by having little land of its own, apart from Lorn, and therefore was in need of a strong local agent to assert its authority – a consistent theme in Scottish royal policy in the thirteenth century. The Macdougalls, as close allies of the Comyns, were ideal candidates for such a position. In a brieve dated 24th February at Dundee, Alexander Macdougall of Argyll and his baillies of Lochawe were given responsibility for bringing Angus Macdonald, lord of Islay, and two Argyllmen before King John to do homage.[32] John Balliol was in need of the Comyns and their supporters in the north 'as the foreign "isles" and their chieftains were quite opposed and disobedient to King John'.[33] It is interesting to note the attempt by Robert Bruce to gain support in the north for his claim to the throne. In 1292 (October?) William earl of Sutherland attested that 'he has made an oath to Sir Robert de Brus lord of Annandale to assist him with all advice and power to prosecute his claim to the throne of Scotland'.[34]

The first parliament of Balliol's kingship in February 1293 sought a more permanent solution to the problem of royal authority in the north. An ordinance in this parliament sought the establishment of three new sheriffdoms in Lorn, Skye and Kintyre.[35] The sheriffdom of Lorn, which would be administered by Alexander Macdougall, lord of Lorn, as sheriff, no doubt from his impressive castle of Dunstaffnage, consisted of Argyllshire except for Kintyre. The sheriffdom of Skye, under the authority of William earl of Ross as sheriff, would consist of Lewis, Uist, Barra, Skye and the Small Isles with Wester Ross and Kintail. The sheriffdom of Kintyre, comprising Bute, the Cumbraes, Kintyre and probably Arran, would be under the authority of James Stewart, lord of Bute and Cumbraes. It is noticeable that two of the three sheriffdoms were to be in the hands of close Comyn associates, Alexander Macdougall and William earl of Ross. The earl of Ross was, in fact, empowered by King John to make war on 'the foreign "isles" and their chieftains ... opposed and disobedient to King John ... wherein he spent £1000 and more of his own but took Louwhelan and the other chieftains and brought them to King John's will'.[36] The earl of Ross was rewarded by King John for his efforts with the lease of the lands of Dingwall and Ferintosh in fee farm at the same rent as in King Alexander's time.

It is possible to see Edward I's influence in the erection of the three sheriffdoms after the Statute of Rhuddlan in 1284 had similarly set up the new shires of Anglesey, Caernarvon and Merioneth.[37] Yet the plans for the western Highlands were even more in keeping with the consistent expansion of Scottish royal authority through alliance between the crown and the nobility, its agents for control in the localities, throughout the thirteenth century. The Comyns and their associates had played a significant role in putting this policy into effect in the north and in the south-west between 1220 and 1290. The Stewarts had also played a key role, especially in the second half of the thirteenth century, in extending royal authority in the south-west, and the 1293 ordinance envisaged a further extension of the Stewart role in this area. It is probable that James Stewart retained office as sheriff of both Dumbarton and Ayr after 1292. The ordinance of 1293 represented, above all, continuity in policy and personnel.

Evidence from the four parliaments which met between 1293 and 1294 suggests that the Scottish government had a firm resolve to secure the authority of the crown.[38] In the August 1293 Parliament roll there is evidence of two nobles surrendering land to which the king was the real heir. Royal rights were zealously guarded. Tenants-in-chief who had entered land without the king's permission in the period after 1286 were summoned to show their right. The August 1293 parliament began an enquiry into the fate of royal lands and there is evidence of a brieve appointing commissioners to enquire into encroachments on crown lands. The letter of summons to a parliament of 1293 also gives the promise of a better dispensation of justice as it provided for the public summons before king and council 'of everyone with a complaint ... to show the injuries and trespasses done to them by whatsoever ill doers ... and to receive from them what justice demands'.[39] It has been argued that this provision could have come either 'from below, from widespread discontent with misdeeds by local administrators of 1286–93 or ... from above from a desire to establish King John's authority over his servants and subjects by holding them to account'.[40] The weight of evidence suggests, perhaps, that the re-establishment of royal authority was a more probable motive for such a provision after a period of great political difficulty – indeed near civil war in some parts of the country – since 1286.

The legend of John Balliol as a puppet of Edward I and the stigmatisation of his reign, in retrospect, as 'the reign of Toom Tabard'[41] following the ritual humiliation which Edward inflicted on Balliol at Montrose in July 1296, has distracted us from a key issue: what was the relationship between the Comyn-dominated Scottish government and Edward I between 1292 and 1296? There is certainly evidence of strong English influence at the very outset of John Balliol's reign. The ceremony of enthronement itself was performed by two English magnates, Anthony Bek and John de St John, the latter deputising for the young earl of Fife and fulfilling the earl's traditional role at Scottish enthronements.[42] On 26th December 1292 Balliol did homage to Edward I in most unambiguous terms, recognising that Edward was his sovereign lord and that his homage was in respect of the entire kingdom of Scotland.[43] John Balliol's first chancellor was a Yorkshireman, Master Thomas de Hunsingore.[44] There is evidence of English chancery usage in the term 'king of Scotland' in John Balliol's documents. The king's seal had the description 'by God's grace king of Scots' compared to the usage of John's predecessors 'king of the Scots under God's governance'. The appointment of a first treasurer in Scotland in December 1293 was another example of the infiltration of English practice.

Early in the adjudication proceedings in Scotland, on 12th June 1291, Edward I had promised to restore the Scottish kingdom to the rightful claimant within two months of the final judgement. He also promised to maintain the laws and customs of Scotland.[45] The handing over of the Scottish kingdom to the new ruler did take place soon after the judgement but the actual government of the country from this point was complicated by the fact that Edward I had ruled Scotland directly between June 1291 and November 1292 and there were still important financial and judicial matters from this period that had to be settled.[46] Edward I felt that he had the right to direct intervention in these and other matters. Prior to November 1292, for instance, he had held the earldom of Fife through his agent Walter of Cambo. He continued to intervene in Fife after Balliol's enthronement[47] and in 1294 granted a weekly market at Crail to Isabella de Vescy. In the winter of 1295–96, he also acted in Galloway.[48]

Edward I and his chief adviser for Scotland, Anthony Bek, bishop of Durham, had worked with the leaders of the political community in Scotland, the Comyns, throughout the difficult years after 1286. It is probable that Edward supported Balliol's candidature because it had the backing of the most powerful party in Scotland as well as that of Bek. Edward I had controlled Scotland in 1291 and 1292. The Comyns, as well as other royal castle holders, surrendered castles in June 1291. As far as the Comyns were concerned this involved Wigtown (in Galloway), Kirkcudbright, Banff and Aberdeen (held by John Comyn earl of Buchan before 13th June 1291); Jedburgh and Clunie (held by John of Badenoch); and Dingwall (held by Earl John's brother Alexander).[49] Yet despite this symbolic act of overlordship, in practice Edward I continued to rely on the Comyns. In 1292 Edward as overlord gave to 'our dear and faithful'[50] John Comyn, earl of Buchan, custody of the forests of Durris, Cowie and Aberdeen. On 27th June 1292 he gave Earl John permission to export lead from the Calf of Man 'for eight towers in the castle of Cruggleton'.[51] In 1291–2 Earl John was acting as baillie for Banff and Wigtown, and John Comyn for Jedburgh, Dull – he had responsibility for the Abthania of Dull and Stormont – Kilbride and Brideburgh (Barburgh).[52] On 8th December 1292 and 7th January 1293 Edward I wrote to King John demanding that he permit his two baillies to collect the 'farms' and returns for these areas.[53]

In England, too, the Comyns and other members of the Comyn government prior to June 1291 were shown favour. In August 1291 Edward I gave to Alexander de Balliol, chamberlain to the Comyn-led government after 1286, and Isabella his wife a weekly market at the manor of Chilham in Kent and an annual fair there for eighty days.[54] In 1293 a debt of 50 marks owed by the late Alexander Comyn earl of Buchan was discharged.[55] In June 1293 Earl John Comyn was granted a weekly market on Tuesday at his manor of Whitwick in Leicestershire and a yearly fair for four days.[56] Edward I had shown favour to the Comyns of Badenoch before 1291. In August 1290 Edward I sought to fulfil his father's grant of £200 to John Comyn's father by allocating John Comyn II this amount from the fines of Cumberland and Northumberland.[57] In 1292/3 John Comyn II and his son were acquitted from the common summons in justice eyres in Tynedale.[58] In 1293, 'of his special favour', Edward I pardoned John Comyn £20 in which he was amerced before Walter de Cambo and other justices lately itinerant in the Liberty of Tynedale.[59] An indication of Edward I's desire to work with, and through, the Comyns in Scotland was the marriage (by? 1293) of John Comyn, head of the senior Badenoch branch of the Comyn family, to Joan de Valence, daughter of William earl of Pembroke and cousin of the English king.[60] William de Valence's influence with Edward I was seen when he asked permission for his son-in-law to send attorneys in all pleas before justices in eyre in Tynedale.[61] Marriages had played an important role in the rise to power of the Comyn family in Scotland. Marriages linking the main branch of the family to the Balliols in the 1270s and to the English royal house in the 1290s played a crucial role in the family's political fortunes from the 1290s to 1314.

It is clear that in late 1292 Edward I felt he could control both Balliol and the Comyns and define his overlordship to suit his own wishes. He made full use of his overlordship and his direct rule of Scotland from June 1291 to December 1292 to assert feudal control over Balliol and the Comyn earls of Buchan. It is interesting to note that on 28th November 1292, two days before John Balliol's enthronement, he ordered an extent to be made of the lands in Scotland both of the late Dervorguilla de Balliol, mother of John Balliol,[62] and the late Alexander Comyn earl of Buchan, father of Earl John,[63] and established that relief should be paid to him. On 20th December 1292 Edward I wrote to the barons of the exchequer and ordered them to produce a report on the debts of John Balliol King of Scotland: 'They are to inquire how much he owes the king, both personally and through his ancestors and for what reasons; also which debts are clear and which are not. They are to let John have respite of these debts in the meantime.'[64] On 8th May 1293 Edward, 'of his special favour', pardoned King John £3000 of the £3289 14s 1d 'due for his relief of his late

mother Devorguilla de Balliol's lands in Scotland, the remainder
to be paid in instalments £40 yearly'.[65] On 5th June 1291 Edward
respited the payment of relief due by John Comyn earl of Buchan.
In 1293 there was recognisance by Earl John 'for the payment of
the sum due for the relief of his lands in Scotland'. The sum
owed was 1,417 marks.[66] A schedule of payments, to William de
Valence earl of Pembroke, was agreed, from 29th August 1293 to
13th May 1295. On 22nd April 1294 Edward gave permission to
pay his relief £120 (presumably his relief for his English lands)
by moieties.[67] As for John Comyn of Badenoch, arrears of £1563
14s 6d were owed, presumably for the 'fermes' from his baillies
of Jedburgh, Dull, Kilbride and Barburgh.[68] On 6th January 1293
King Edward 'by our special grace' remitted John Comyn these
debts.[69] Edward I also showed himself keen to enforce all marriage
rights over Anglo-Scottish landowners. In 1289 he had asserted his
right to the marriage of Euphemia, widow of William Comyn of
Kilbride, who married a Comyn associate, Andrew de Moray, without
licence.[70] In May 1295, Christiana, widow of the late Robert Brus,
lord of Annandale, took an oath not to marry without the king's
permission.[71]

Edward I felt he had the means to control both the king and the
main political leaders in Scotland and thus define his overlordship
to his own requirements. Henry III had used both his superior
power and Anglo-Scottish magnates to the full to establish some
control over Scotland between 1244 and 1258. The question of
English overlordship over Scotland was an important background
issue in 1244, 1251 and 1255, but Henry III's own political troubles in England in 1258 and Alexander III's maturity and ability
from this time prevented the matter from being actively pursued
from the English side. Similar, though more serious, constitutional
problems to those of 1249 beset Scotland in 1286; they worsened
in 1290. However, the Scottish kingdom and the Scottish political
community were rather more mature and sophisticated in 1290
than they had been in the 1240s and 1250s. The Comyns were
not the leaders of a self-interested faction; they were leaders of
the political community of the realm and strongly defended the
rights and liberties of the Scottish realm which had, after all, given
the family its status in Scottish society. More than any noble family
in Scotland, the Comyns represented the political community of the

realm in the Treaty of Brigham in 1290 and won a full and clear recognition for

> the rights, laws and liberties and customs of the realm of
> Scotland to be preserved in every respect and in all time coming
> throughout the said realm and its borders, completely and without
> being impaired ... We promise, in the place and name of our lord
> the king and his heirs, that the realm of Scotland shall remain
> separated and divided and free in itself, without subjugation to
> the realm of England, by its rightful boundaries and marches, as it
> has been preserved down to the present ... No-one of the realm
> of Scotland by reason of any contract entered into or any offence
> committed in that realm or in any case, shall be obliged to answer
> for this outwith the same realm, contrary to the laws and customs
> of the same realm, as has been reasonably observed down to the
> present.[72]

The Comyns, in particular, must have been dismayed by the interventionist approach adopted by Edward I from the very beginning of John Balliol's kingship. In fact as soon as judgement had been made in favour of Balliol's claim to the Scottish throne, there was apparently a warning that if he did not rule justly, Edward would have to intervene.[73] It was only one week after John Balliol's enthronement, on 7th December 1292, that Roger Bartholomew, a Berwick burgess, complained to Edward about three adverse judgements of the Guardians.[74] Edward I's rapid response – compensation payments were made by 6th January 1293 – indicated his desire to demonstrate his right to hear appeals.[75] This in turn brought a response from the leaders of the political community of the realm. John Comyn earl of Buchan, Bishop William Fraser, Patrick Graham and Thomas Randulf,[76] leading advisers of the Balliol government, lodged a petition, on behalf of their king, objecting to Edward I taking appeals outside Scotland and asking that the English king should keep the promises made in the Treaty of Birgham. The English reply highlighted the weakness of the position of the Scottish leaders after June 1291 when they had abdicated their power as Guardians of the Scottish realm to be reappointed by Edward I, given up castles to Edward's authority and recognised, through the Competitors, Edward's right to overlordship. They were simply relying on the promises made to them in the Treaty of Birgham. Edward I's reply to the Scottish complaint was unambiguous:[77] he had the right to review their decisions as the Guardians were, after

June 1291, responsible to him alone as their overlord; any promises made by Edward in the interregnum were for that time alone and were no longer binding. Already in December 1292 Edward was expressing the forcible viewpoint that he could hear whatever pleas might be brought to him; that he could, if necessary, summon the Scottish king himself; and that, as far as appeals were concerned, he would not be bound by any previous promises or concessions which he had made. On 2nd January 1293 Edward forced an important concession from King John who 'solemnly freed Edward from all obligations and promises which the English king might have entered into with the Guardians and responsible men of the Scottish realm, declaring null and void any written evidence of such promises and explicitly annulling the Treaty of Birgham'.[78] There seems to have been some resistance from the Scottish political community to this uncompromising stance from Edward. On 4th January 1293 Edward I promised, if the King of Scotland left an undisputed heir to the Scottish throne in the future, that he would demand no rights in Scotland except those of homage and overlordship.[79]

The way Edward I handled appeals to the King of England for justice in Scottish cases was proof of his harsh definition of his overlordship over Scotland from the very outset of John Balliol's reign. The issue of appeals after 1292 has perhaps been given too much weight as the cause of such a rapid deterioration in Anglo-Scottish relations. Appeals to the king of England to use his superior political and military weight or influence in Scottish affairs had not been so unusual in the period after 1240. The question of Henry III intervening in Scottish affairs as overlord on behalf of Walter Bisset had been an issue in the mind of the chronicler, Matthew Paris, when he recorded the Bissets' plea for help from Henry in 1242 and Henry's subsequent march to the border in 1244.[80] Appeals to Henry III from political groups anxious for his support were consistent features during the minority of Alexander III when the Comyn and non-Comyn groupings appealed for Henry's support in 1251 and 1255 and throughout the period 1255–1258. It is a matter of conjecture whether Henry III *only* acted out of concerned parental interest in these years as the question of overlordship was certainly raised in 1251. The issue of English overlordship was once again raised in 1278. Even in the period of good social relationships between the royal families of Scotland and England between 1260 and 1286, there was recognition of the English king's superior power and influence. This was called upon by William Comyn, lord of Kirkintilloch, in his attempt to gain the earldom of Menteith in the 1280s.[81]

An appeal to the English king (though perhaps not formal appeals to the courts in England) was generally accepted when Scottish political difficulties began in 1286. However, what had developed since 1240 was a greater self-consciousness about national independence and the political rights of the governing community of the Scottish realm. The Treaty of Birgham has been seen as, besides a marriage treaty, a charter of baronial rights;[82] in fact, it was more a statement of the rights of the political community in Scotland. On the English side, the threat and occasional practice of English interference in Scottish affairs was replaced by a steadily more determined opportunism by Edward I and his advisers hoping to take advantage of the constitutional dilemma following the Maid of Norway's death in 1290. This change in attitude was rather more important than the issue of appeals, which was, in any case, one of several issues through which Edward I sought to define his overlordship over Scotland.

It is notable that appeals to Edward I came mainly from malcontents in Scotland[83] with either political or economic grievances. Complaints from the Macdonalds, Simon of Restalrig and from Macduff of Fife represented the opportunism of those not in favour with the leaders of the Scottish government. Simon of Restalrig's complaint was levelled at a prominent member of the Comyn-led government, Patrick Graham; the Macdonalds had long been in dispute with Comyns' relatives, the Macdougalls; and in Fife the family of the earls of Fife showed continuing resentment towards Comyn supporters, the Abernethys. Most attention has been given to the case of Macduff of Fife as it was on this matter that King John finally answered in an English court. On 8th May 1293 King John was summoned before the King's Bench to answer for his failure to do justice in the case of John Mazun, a Bordeaux wine merchant who was owed money by Alexander III. Mazun died, however, and the lawsuit became void. The Macduff appeal was scheduled to come before the Bench on 24th May. At first Balliol refused to answer or send attorneys to defend his judgement, but according to the rules Edward and his council had set out for such occasions, the king of Scotland had to attend in person and this he did at the Michaelmas parliament of 1293.[84]

The report of what took place at this Michaelmas parliament revealed the essence of the problem facing the political community of the Scottish realm – lack of a strong figurehead. It is probable that Balliol had been rehearsed in his answer by his more experienced counsellors: 'the king of Scotland says that he is king of the realm of Scotland and dare not make answer at the suit of Macduff without the advice of the "probi homines" [responsible men] of his realm'.[85] Balliol also added that he would not accept an adjournment as this would be seen as recognition of English jurisdiction. This was the official reply of the political community of the realm. It has been pointed out that 'so far he had been well briefed, and ... the same minds were at work here as in the Treaty of Birgham and the protestations of 1291 and 1292'.[86] In fact this initial defiance by John Balliol represented approximately fifty years of mature constitutional development in Scotland. It was unfortunate for the political community of the realm, however, that they had such an inexperienced figurehead. Under severe pressure from Edward, who judged Balliol to be in his mercy for contempt of court and threatened him with the forfeiture of his three chief castles and towns (probably Edinburgh, Roxburgh and Berwick), Balliol abandoned all resistance, once more acknowledged Edward's overlordship in abject terms and also asked for an adjournment.'[87]

In June 1294 war broke out between England and France and as a result on 29th June, Edward summoned John Balliol and ten Scottish earls and sixteen barons to perform personal feudal service against the French.[88] A little earlier, according to a letter from Edward I to John Balliol dated 20th April 1294, John Balliol, 'learning of Edward's intended foreign expedition had asked to be told what part Edward wishes him to play in it. Edward thanks him for his friendship.'[89] According to the *Guisborough Chronicle*,[90] John Balliol and the Scots with him at a Westminster parliament in mid-June, before the summons, had promised the English king aid, saying that they would be ready to muster given sufficient warning. When the feudal summons came, Balliol, undoubtedly under pressure from his baronial advisers, made excuses but as the Welsh rose in September shortly after (a revolt which continued until March), this particular test of England's overlordship was not examined.

The issue of a demand for feudal service in 1294 should, like the issue of appeals to the English king, be set in the context of the radically different political relationship imposed on Scotland by Edward in 1291. Most of the leading nobility in Scotland, including Balliols, Comyns and Bruces, had acknowledged their feudal obligations to the kings of England as English landowners. Throughout the thirteenth century it was clearly in their interests to keep the advantages of cross-border landownership, the privileges of having two patrons, by recognising their obligations to the English king. Earl Alexander Comyn, most experienced adviser to Alexander III, was anxious to secure the property of his wife, Elizabeth, daughter and co-heiress of Roger de Quincy, earl of Winchester.[91] Following Earl Roger's death on 25th May 1264 the break-up of his vast English estates was a slow and complex process. It was not until 22nd May 1277 that the division was finally made and there was still an echo of the dispute in 1279.[92] It was certainly in Earl Alexander's interests to acknowledge his commitments to the English king arising from his inheritance. In 1276 he was among 178 tenants-in-chief summoned to meet the king at Worcester and fight against the Welsh. Though he did not serve personally, he paid scutage of 50 marks (one-third of two knights' fees).[93] Having been summoned again in 1282, Alexander emphasised in his letter to King Edward his regret at being unable to serve personally against the Welsh and sent his son Roger in his stead.[94] In a letter of 1st July 1282 Alexander III wrote to Edward I to excuse the temporary absence of Alexander Comyn, earl of Buchan (given his full titles, Constable and Justiciar of Scotland), whom he had despatched on important business to the remote parts of the Scottish islands.[95] It was clear from the correspondence of both Earl Alexander and King Alexander that Earl Alexander's duty was to the Scottish king and kingdom first. This sense of political and national duty – 'we cannot leave this road [to the Isles] by our honour' – coming before personal, feudal duty was once more the issue for the Comyns in 1294.

The Kilbride branch of the Comyn family, too, had been keen to secure inherited lands in England from the marriage of David Comyn to Isabel, lady of East Kilbride c.1215. Between 1215 and 1247[96] cases abound in English courts of actions concerning this newly acquired inheritance. It is hardly surprising, therefore, that David Comyn recognised and accepted his feudal obligations to the English king. In 1242 he was summoned by Henry III to fight on his behalf against the King of France. As with Earl Alexander, David Comyn did not serve personally but gave the king 20 marks (reduced to 10 marks on the petition of the bishop of Glasgow).[97] It is interesting that another Comyn, John Comyn earl of Angus, was killed in France in 1242,[98] perhaps serving in the English army on behalf of David or another member of the family with military obligations to the English king at this time.

Feudal obligations were one reason for members of the Scottish nobility to accept military service to the English king. Personal service was particularly appreciated by the English king, especially when the English nobility, and notably the northern nobility, were increasingly reluctant to engage in military service overseas. Alan Durward's fortunes in Scotland were revived in 1255 after he served Henry III in Gascony in 1253/4 while in exile from the Comyn-controlled Scottish government during the minority of Alexander III. Earl Alexander Comyn's brother, Fergus, was also in the English king's service in 1253/4[99] and presumably represented Comyn interests to Henry III while he was acting, or trying to act, as 'overlord' of Scotland on behalf of his son-in-law. The Badenoch branch of the family, through John Comyn I of Badenoch, also performed personal military service for Henry III in 1264 along with Robert Bruce and John Balliol.[100] John Comyn was in the English king's household in 1262, 1264 and 1265, alongside members of the Bruce and Balliol families, and served Henry III against Simon de Montfort in 1264 at the battle of Lewes. John Comyn's personal service to the English king in the 1260s was perhaps related to his disappointment at not inheriting the earldom of Menteith from his uncle, Walter Comyn, after the Scottish king and his court decided against his claim in 1261/2. John Comyn was well rewarded for his personal service in England.[101]

Henry III was in special need of the support of the Scottish king and Anglo-Scottish barons in the period 1258–1265 against Simon de Montfort and the baronial opposition party. Edward I had similar urgent need of support from Scotland against the French in 1294. It should, however, be noted that in 1264 Bruce, Balliol and Comyn *'at the Scots' king's bidding* had come to King Henry's rescue'.[102] In 1294 Edward I summoned the king of Scots as well as his magnates to serve him in France. Thus in matters of military service as well as appeals, there was 'superior direct lordship' with a vengeance. Not since 1159, when King Malcolm IV had joined Henry II's expedition to Toulouse, had a king of Scotland performed overseas military service for a king of England.[103] Again, Edward's over-eagerness to define his overlordship over Scotland failed to take into account the political and constitutional maturity of the Scottish kingdom since the minority of Alexander III. The English king failed to appreciate that the Scottish nobility in government, chiefly the Comyns and their supporters, now represented the political community of the realm and this came before other responsibilities. In this respect duty to the Scottish realm came before responsibility to the English king as it had for Earl Alexander in 1282.

It was inevitable that the Scottish political community in 1294 would react to Edward's direct overlordship. The revolt in Wales (itself partly due to Edward's demand for the Welsh to fight for him against the French) between September 1294 and March 1295 must have encouraged them to assert independent action. There is no evidence of an attempted alliance with the Welsh as there had been between the Comyns and the Welsh princes in 1258.[104] There had, however, been a move towards freeing the Scots 'from any oaths exacted from them under duress' when the Scots gained this absolution from the pope before December 1294[105]. Between March and May of 1295 an alliance with the French had been negotiated, whether by Scottish or French initiative is not known.

By 5th July 1295 King John addressed letters to Philip IV appointing four persons to negotiate in France regarding John Balliol's son, Edward, and a relative of Philip.[106] The four were the experienced William Fraser bishop of St Andrews, Matthew Crambeth bishop of Dunkeld, John de Soules and Ingeram de Umphraville, and the treaty with France followed on 23rd October 1295.

The Scottish political community of the realm was therefore prepared to seek outside help to preserve the independence of the Scottish kingdom. At the same parliament, government was taken out of the hands of John Balliol and given to a Council of Twelve. According to the *Lanercost Chronicle*,[107] 'the magnates, prelates and other nobles of the kingdom of Scotland, having assembled, a solemn parliament was held at Stirling where by common assent it was decreed that their king could do no act by himself, and that he should have twelve peers, after the manner of the French, and these they then and there elected and constituted'. John Balliol was the candidate of the dominant Comyn 'party', in practice a figurehead for the experienced and increasingly mature Scottish government. John Balliol's inexperience and political naiveté must have become more and more obvious from the outset of his reign when he was no match for Edward I's forcefulness. He had shown himself vacillating and weak in his relationship with the king of England and in regard to the greatest internal threat to the Scottish government, the Bruces. In the summer of 1294 King John failed to prevent Master Thomas Dalton of Kirkcudbright, Robert Bruce the elder's candidate, from becoming bishop of Galloway.[108] Balliol's favours to Anthony Bek, Edward I's chief adviser on Scottish affairs, must also have caused concern, the last of three grants coming at Stirling only two days before the four Scottish envoys were sent to negotiate with the king of France.[109]

The Scottish government had itself made mistakes which handed the initiative to Edward I. The Guardians gave up their authority to Edward I to be reappointed by him and also gave up Scottish castles to him. Having refused at first to recognise Edward's overlordship, they eventually had to follow the logic of recognition of this overlordship by the Competitors. Again, they must have known that John Balliol would bow to pressure from Edward I when he went to Westminster to answer to the English king with regard to the appeals, even though senior advisers had clearly rehearsed his initial replies.[110] Experienced attorneys would have maintained the dignity of Scottish monarchy rather better. Yet despite mistakes, at least the Scottish political community represented a clear policy.

The Council of Twelve, chosen to replace Balliol as head of Scottish government, was likened by contemporary English sources to the Twelve Peers of France.[111] Yet, in fact it was a return to the Guardianship of 1286 which was in turn a development from the special emergency council set up to safeguard the interests of the Scottish kingdom when Queen Margaret came to England to give birth to her first child in 1262. The Council of Twelve also reflected English experience when a baronial council displaced Henry III from government in 1258. The Scottish Council of Twelve was composed of four bishops, four earls and four barons (doubling the number of the 1286 Guardianship, which was of similar symmetry). It is not certain who were the twelve members of the 1295 council, although it is reasonable to assume that the most prominent names involved in the ratification treaty for the French alliance (23rd February 1296) comprised the twelve.[112] The four bishops were probably William Fraser of St Andrews, Robert Wishart of Glasgow, Matthew Crambeth of Dunkeld and Henry Cheyne of Aberdeen; the four earls were probably John Comyn earl of Buchan, Donald earl of Mar, Malise earl of Strathearn, and John de Strathbogie, earl of Atholl; the four barons were probably John Comyn of Badenoch, James Stewart, Alexander de Balliol and Geoffrey de Mowbray. The Council thus represented continuity of personnel from the Scottish governments after 1286. It represented the reality that the political community of the realm in Scotland was still dominated by the Comyn family, relatives and associates. The 1295 takeover of power could be termed a political revolution but it was not a revolution in the conventional sense of dramatic change – there was no change of personnel or policy; there was no deposition of either the king or the king's council. It represented a pragmatic desire to reflect and present the wishes of the political community of the realm more effectively than their king was capable of doing.

Tensions between the English and Scottish governments became more obvious in the autumn of 1295, although it is difficult to ascertain whether news of the French alliance or the judicial argument relating to the Macduff appeal was the most important contributory factor.[113] The Macduff case was postponed until a parliament held at Bury St Edmunds after Michaelmas 1295. Macduff attended to pursue his case but the Scots leaders had learned from their previous mistake in allowing their king to appear in person and sent the abbot of Arbroath who excused his king and complained about harsh English treatment of the Scots. A further delay in the case was made when all parties involved were asked to meet at Newcastle-upon-Tyne on 1st March 1296. It seems, however, that already by October 1295 Edward was preparing for action against opposition in Scotland. On 16th October Edward issued orders to English sheriffs that all the lands and goods of King John and all those Scotsmen 'who remain in Scotland'[114] should be taken into the English king's hands. At the same time, Edward demanded that the border castles and towns of Berwick, Roxburgh and Jedburgh should be handed over till the end of the French war. Letters patent from Edward c.12th October authorised John bishop of Carlisle and the abbot of Newminster or one of them to receive these castles and towns from the Scottish king 'for the security of Edward, his realm and his other lands'.[115] On 6th October Edward committed 'to his liege' Robert Bruce lord of Annandale, who had done homage to the English king earlier in the year, the keeping of the castle of Carlisle.[116] It seemed that even some who had hitherto been supporters of the Scottish government, including Richard Siward, were prepared to offer support for the English king in order to retain their English lands[117] though he was on the Scottish side again by 23rd February 1296 when he appended his seal to the ratification of the Scottish treaty with France.

The true test of loyalty to King John and the Scottish government came when a summons to the host went out to assemble on 22th March outside Selkirk. Robert Bruce had already committed himself to Edward I and, according to the *Guisborough Chronicle*,[118] he was one of many nobles who remained faithful to the English king. As well as Robert Bruce the elder and Robert Bruce the younger, Patrick earl of Dunbar and the Comyn relative, Gilbert de Umphraville earl of Angus, testified, on 25th March, that they had done homage to Edward:[119] 'we are, and always have been, faithful to, and subject to the will of the most noble prince and our well-beloved lord, Edward ... we will serve him well and loyally against all men'. As a result, according to the *Chronicle of Lanercost*, the Scottish magnates 'pronounced forfeiture of his paternal heritage upon Robert de Brus the younger, who had fled to England, because he would not do homage to them. Also they forfeited his son in the earldom of Carrick, wherein he had been infeft, because he adhered to his father'.[120] The Bruce lordship was passed to the care of John Comyn, earl of Buchan.[121] It was perhaps no coincidence, given the rivalry between the Comyns who held political power in Scotland and the Bruces who did not, that the earl of Buchan set out with a military force on 26th March to attack Carlisle where Robert Bruce senior was in charge of the garrison. It seemed that Edward I was already trying to govern Galloway directly as 'overlord of Scotland'.[122] On 6th March he sent letters patent to 'the good men and the whole community of Galloway' at the request of Thomas of Galloway in order to grant them all their liberties and customs. He had summoned the feudal host to meet at Newcastle on 1st March.

Nationalist gestures preceded outright warfare – the Scottish government ordered English clergy to be ejected from their benefices while in England the lands of those Scots who remained in Scotland were to be seized and, further in April 1296, Scotsmen in England were to be arrested. On 5th April 1296 John Balliol formally renounced his homage to Edward in a defiant letter which certainly reflected the views of the political community of the realm better than his own actions. 'You yourself and others of your realm ... have caused harm beyond measure to the liberties of ourselves and of our kingdom ... for instance by summoning us outside our realm at the mere beck and call of anybody, as your whim dictated, and by harassing us unjustifiably ... now you have come to the frontiers of our realm in warlike array, with a vast concourse of soldiers ... to disinherit us and the inhabitants of our realm ... we desire to assert ourselves against you, for our own defence and that of our realm, to whose defence and safekeeping we are constrained by the bond of an oath; and so by the present letter we renounce the fealty and homage which we have done to you...'[123]

These words of defiance, together with the attack (on 26th March) on the Bruce-controlled Carlisle by John Comyn earl of Buchan, six other earls of Scotland and John Comyn the younger, the Guardian's son, reflect the attitudes of a Comyn-led political establishment in Scotland. They reveal opposition, on the one hand, to Edward I's infringement of the Treaty of Birgham. They also show resistance to the continuing ambitions of the Bruces to attain political power in Scotland, apparently to be achieved in 1296 through alliance with Edward I. The Comyns undoubtedly feared the possibility of such an alliance, which would undoubtedly break their political grip on Scotland. There were thus several reasons for the Comyns to defend their position by force. The war which broke out in 1296 was, in effect, the war of the Comyns.

NOTES

1. *Chron. Bower* (Watt), VI pp.51–2. (my italics)
2. Barrow, *Robert Bruce*, p.55.
3. *Chron. Fordun* II p.315.
4. W.M. Mackenzie (ed.), *The Bruce* by John Barbour (1909), p.6.
5. See note 1 above.
6. R. Nicholson, *Scotland: the Later Middle Ages*, p.44.
7. Stones, *Anglo-Scottish Relations*, p.117.
8. H. Maxwell (trans.), *Scalacronica by Sir Thomas Gray* (1907) p.12. It seems unlikely that the youngest Robert Bruce, the future king, would have been confirmed as earl of Carrick in August 1293 without doing homage for the earldom (*Acts. Parl. Scot.* I p.449.
9. *Cal. Docs. Scot.* II no.645.
10. *Chron. Lanercost* p.111.
11. *Acts. Parl. Scot.* I p.449; Barrow, *Robert Bruce*, p.66; see n.8 above.
12. *Cal. Docs. Scot.* II nos. 635, 675.
13. Barrow, *Robert Bruce*, p.66.
14. *Ibid.* pp.57–9 for discussion of appeals to England.
15. *Acts. Parl. Scot.* I p.448; *Cal. Docs. Scot.* II nos.621–3.
16. *Chron. Bower* (Watt), VI p.41.
17. See n.15.
18. For references to King John's 'acta' and those involved in royal government (cited in the following paragraphs) see Grant G. Simpson, *Handlist of the Acts of Alexander III, the Guardians and John*, pp.56–63.
19. *Calendar Inquisitions Post Mortem* (1904) Vol. II p.460 no.753; *Cal. Doc. Scot.* II no.421.
20. G.W.S. Barrow, 'The Justiciar' in *Kingdom of the Scots* (London, 1973), pp.137–8.
21. *Ibid.*

22. *Cal. Docs. Scot.* II no.1541; Young, 'Buchan in the 13th century' in *Medieval Scotland*, pp.184–5.
23. F.W. Maitland, *Memoranda de Parliamento*, 1305 (Rolls Series 1895), p.191.
24. *Cal. Docs. Scot.* II no.1541.
25. John Comyn the father and his son John the younger also benefited, with land, from Balliol patronage. King John also knighted John the younger (F. Palgrave, *Documents and Records Illustrating the History of Scotland* (1837), Vol. I p.287).
26. S.R.O. GD 175/Doc. 24.
27. P.R.O. E.40/4766.
28. R. Nicholson, *Scotland: the Later Middle Ages*, p.44.
29. A.A.M. Duncan, 'The early parliaments of Scotland', *S.H.R.* (1966), pp.40–46; R. Nicholson, *Scotland: the Later Middle Ages*, pp.44–5.
30. Barrow, *Robert Bruce*, pp.55–6.
31. *Ibid.* p.56; Duncan, *Formulary E: Scottish Letters and Brieves*, pp.22–3 no.46, p.32 no.67.
32. *Acts. Parl. Scot.* I p.448.
33. *Cal. Docs. Scot.* II no.1631.
34. *Cal. Docs. Scot.* II n.643.
35. *Acts. Parl. Scot.* I pp.447–8.
36. *Cal. Docs. Scot.* II no.1631. Louwhelan was a bastard son of Alan MacRuairi, lord of Garmoran.
37. Barrow, *Robert Bruce*, p.56.
38. Duncan, 'The early parliaments of Scotland', pp.40–46; Duncan, *Formulary E: Scottish Letters and Brieves*, p.7 no.9, p.12 no.20.
39. Duncan, 'The early parliaments of Scotland', p.46.
40. *Ibid.*
41. Grant G. Simpson, 'Why was John Balliol called "Toom Tabard"?', *S.H.R.* XLVII (1968), pp.196–9.
42. M. Prestwich, *Edward*, p.370.
43. Stones, *Anglo-Scottish Relations*, pp.127–9.
44. Barrow, *Robert Bruce*, p.50.
45. M. Prestwich, *Edward I*, p.369.
46. R. Nicholson, *Scotland: the Later Middle Ages*, p.46.
47. *Cal. Docs. Scot.* II nos. 701, 704, 708.
48. *Ibid.* II no.728.
49. Stones and Simpson, *Edward I and the throne of Scotland,* II p.101.
50. *Rotuli Scotiae*, pp. 10a, 12b.
51. Stevenson, *Documents*, I pp.329–30.
52. *Exchequer Rolls* I pp. 39, 49; Stevenson, *Documents*, I pp. 247–8, 275, 312; *Rotuli Scotiae*, I pp. 12b, 17a.
53. *Rot. Scot.* I p.12b.
54. *Cal. Docs. Scot.* II no.509.

55. *Ibid.* II no.667.
56. *Ibid.* II no.672.
57. *Ibid.* II no.447.
58. *Ibid.* II no.663.
59. *Ibid.* II no.682.
60. P.R.O. SC1 31/37 where the date is given as Nov.–Dec. 1292; also *Cal. Docs. Scot.* II no.724 dated ?1295.
61. *Ibid.*
62. *Rotuli Scotiae* I p.12b.
63. *Ibid.*
64. *Cal. Docs. Scot.* V no.119.
65. *Ibid.* II no.670, also 671.
66. Stevenson, *Documents*, I p.393.
67. *Cal. Docs. Scot.* II no.698.
68. *Rot. Sco.* I p.12b.
69. *Ibid.* p.17a.
70. *Cal. Docs. Scot.* II no.376 – this further linked the Moray family to the Comyns, see above p. 72.
71. *Cal. Docs. Scot.* II. no 709.
72. Barrow, 'A Kingdom in Crisis', *S.H.R.* (1990), pp.137–9.
73. Stones and Simpson, *Edward I and the throne of Scotland*, II pp.248–9.
74. Barrow, *Robert Bruce*, pp.51–2; M. Prestwich, *Edward I*, p.370.
75. Barrow, *Robert Bruce*, p.52.
76. *Foedera*, I p.785.
77. *Ibid.*
78. Barrow, *Robert Bruce*, p.52.
79. *Cal. Docs. Scot.* V no.126.
80. Barrow, *Robert Bruce*, pp.336–7 note 1.
81. *Cal. Docs. Scot.* II no.1763; *Scots Peerage*, VI p.129.
82. A.A.M. Duncan, *The Nation of Scots and the Declaration of Arbroath*, p.11.
83. Barrow, *Robert Bruce*, pp.57–8.
84. *Ibid*, p.59.
85. Stones, *Anglo-Scottish Relations*, p.131.
86. Barrow, *Robert Bruce*, p.59.
87. *Ibid.*
88. *Ibid.* p.62.
89. *Cal. Docs. Scot.* V no.129.
90. cited in M. Prestwich, *Edward I*, p.372.
91. *Cal. Close Rolls* (1272–9), p.236.
92. *Ibid.* p.553.
93. *Cal. Fine Rolls* I p.85.
94. P.R.O. S.C.I 16/93.
95. P.R.O. S.C.I 21/158; *Cal. Docs. Scot.* II no.215.

96. *Cal. Docs. Scot.* I nos. 632, 1172, 1183, 1251, 1313, 1341, 1391, 1394, 1416, 1463, 1480.
97. *Cal. Close Rolls* (1237–42) p.528; *Cal. Docs. Scot.* I no.1578.
98. Chron. Melrose in Anderson (ed.), *Early Sources of Scottish History*, p.530, perhaps he was serving in David Comyn's stead.
99. *Cal. Liberate Rolls* V p.5.
100. *Cal. Close Rolls* (1261–4) pp. 381–2. John Comyn's brother Richard joined him in the English king's service. *Cal. Docs. Scot.* I no.2155.
101. *Cal. Patent Rolls* (1266–72) pp. 175, 535. N.B. William Comyn of Kilbride was disinherited of his English lands for being a partisan of Simon de Montfort (*Cal. Close Rolls*, 1264–8, p.437).
102. *Chron. Fordun* II p.297. (my italics)
103. Barrow, *Robert Bruce*, p.62.
104. See above, pp.57–8.
105. Barrow, *Bruce*, p.63.
106. *Acts. Parl. Scot.* I p.453.
107. *Chron. Lanercost* p. 115.
108. Barrow, *Bruce*, p.66.
109. *Cal. Docs. Scot.* II nos. 691, 872.
110. Stones, *Anglo-Scottish Relations*, p.131.
111. Barrow, *Bruce*, pp.63–5.
112. *Acts. Parl. Scot.* p.453.
113. Prestwich, *Edward I*, pp.372–3.
114. *Cal. Docs. Scot.* II no.718.
115. *Ibid.* V no.135. NB no.136 directly relates this request to the war with France.
116. *Ibid.* II no.716.
117. *Ibid.* no.723.
118. *Chron. Guisborough* p.270.
119. Stones, *Anglo-Scottish Relations*, p.137.
120. *Chron. Lanercost* pp.115–16.
121. *Chron. Guisborough* p.270.
122. *Cal. Docs. Scot.* II no.728.
123. Stones, *Anglo-Scottish Relations*, pp.141–3.

CHAPTER SEVEN

War and the Challenge to the Comyns, 1296–1304

T he Comyns led Scotland into war in 1296 yet relatively little attention has been paid to the military strengths of the family and their allies during the Scottish Wars.[1] By the end of the thirteenth century, the Comyns had control of a network of major castles, and therefore main lines of communication across Scotland (see Map 00). Between 1296 and 1314 Edward I and the Bruces had to pay close attention to these symbols of Comyn lordship if they hoped to exercise effective power in Scotland.

In particular, Comyn power in northern Scotland by 1296 was virtually vice-regal, stretching from Inverlochy castle in the west to Slains castle in the east.[2] The Comyns had acquired the earldom of Buchan c.1212 and the lordship of Badenoch (with Lochaber) by c.1230 with the support of the Scottish monarchy in order to strengthen royal authority in the north. The hereditary lordship of Badenoch (with Lochaber) was especially created for the Comyns as a military and political response to the revolt in Moray against the Scottish crown. It was vital to the security of the area that Comyn castles controlled the vitally important passes from the north and west Highlands into the basin of the Tay.[3] The key castles of the Comyns of Badenoch and Lochaber – Ruthven, Lochindorb, Blair Atholl and Inverlochy (there is no evidence to prove that Castle Roy was a Comyn site) – were all strategically sited. It is probable that a castle-building programme was begun under Walter Comyn earl of Menteith and first lord of Badenoch (and Lochaber) in the 1230s and 1240s. Earl Walter was known to have been involved in building activity elsewhere in the period, at the Augustinian priory of Inchmahome (in 1238) and at

Tarset castle in Northumberland (before 1244).[4] Ruthven, regarded as the caput of Badenoch, was a probable early motte site although now largely covered by the eighteenth-century Ruthven barracks. The barracks stand on a prominent hill, artificially scarped, rising from the flat floor of the Spey valley. Ruthven commanded the northern end of two passes over the Mounth, Drumochter and Minigaig.

John Comyn I built a castle at Blair Atholl in 1269[5] and this controlled the southern end of the Drumochter and Minigaig passes. It seems probable that Ruthven was already well established by this date[6] and that the building of Blair Atholl was part of a developing Comyn castle-building strategy as the Drumochter Pass was the most obvious route between Perth and Inverness. Lochindorb castle, not in Badenoch but integrally related to it, was strategically situated in the heart of Moray on a loch two miles long and three miles wide, between Forres and Grantown, and fully occupied its island site one acre in extent.[7] With Inverlochy castle, the Comyns commanded the entrance to the Great Glen, securing its southern sea outlet,[8] and the scarcely less important overland route to the Spey by way of Glen Spean.

Comyn strategic control over northern Scotland was greatly enhanced by the castles of the Comyn earls of Buchan (see Map 2). As a coastal earldom, it is not surprising that Buchan was defended by an impressive group of well-sited castles along its coastline.[9] On the north coast, Dundarg, standing within the ramparts of an Iron Age promontory fort, was impressively sited on a rock of red sandstone looking northwards over the outer reaches of the Moray Firth. East of Dundarg, on the corner of Buchan, was Cairnbulg (its original name was Philorth), standing on a fairly prominent mound which was probably a motte. Close by the castle, the water of Philorth undoubtedly proved valuable both as a defence to the castle from the west and for supplying water to flood the moat which evidently surrounded the mound on which the castle stands. Further down the coast was another probable motte site, Rattray, important strategically in Buchan as it commanded what is thought to have been the port of Buchan. Further south (near Collieston) was Slains castle where documentary evidence has shown there was a castle in 1261.[10]

A known inland castle of Buchan was at Kingedward in the north-west of Buchan.[11] This was an important Comyn stronghold with a prominent site on a bold precipitous rock protected by the Kingedward burn on the south and on the north-west angle by a deep ditch which severed the neck of the peninsula. Other important inland Comyn centres in Buchan were Kelly (now Haddo) and Ellon,[12] though there is no direct evidence to prove that there were castles at these sites in the thirteenth century. The castles of Buchan were not only important as strategic military centres. Study of Buchan in the fourteenth century after the fall of the Comyns has shown that the castles at Kingedward, Rattray, Slains, Dundarg and Cairnbulg all acted as administrative centres for running five local subdivisions within the earldom of Buchan.[13]

There are few visible remains of the thirteenth-century Comyn castles in Buchan due to the destruction of these symbols of Comyn lordship by King Robert Bruce in his famous 'herschip' of Buchan in 1308.[14] It is probable, however, that the Comyn foundation of the Cistercian abbey of Deer in 1219 was complemented by visible signs of more secular lordship in the Comyn castles at around the same time. Though lacking in visible evidence, the Comyn castle sites in Buchan as a grouping provide an impressively positioned and strategic network of military strength. Comyn control of strategic castles in northern Scotland was further enhanced by the acquisition of Balvenie castle (Banffshire) by Alexander Comyn earl of Buchan between 1264 and 1282.[15] Balvenie (Mortlach) was located only twenty miles from Badenoch's eastern boundary and therefore was an invaluable link between the castles of the lordship of Badenoch (including Lochaber) and those of the earldom of Buchan.[16] Perched on a promontory high above the River Fiddich, Balvenie castle commanded the mouths of Glen Rinnes and Glenfiddich, the passes to Huntly, Keith and Cullen and the route to Elgin.[17] It was therefore a key Comyn castle for their strategic control of northern Scotland.

The acquisition of Balvenie after 1264 seems to have been part of a concentrated programme of castle building and strengthening by the Comyns of Buchan and Badenoch between 1260 and 1280. John Comyn I of Badenoch, head of this senior branch of the family from 1258 to c.1277,[18] seems to have been chiefly responsible. He was certainly behind the building of Blair Atholl in 1269 and in 1267 was given permission by Henry III to fortify his manor house at Tarset in Tynedale. Chronicles for the period 1242 to 1269 testify to his involvement and prowess in military affairs, Bower referring to him as 'a keen fighter and a most outstanding participator in all knightly encounters'.[19] He fought for Henry III against his baronial opponents in 1264 and 1265 and was also involved in a Scottish military expedition to Man in 1275.[20] A combination of documentary and architectural evidence points to building work at Lochindorb and Inverlochy between 1260 and 1280.[21] The Comyns of Badenoch were thus responsible for castle building at Lochindorb, Inverlochy, Blair Atholl, and presumably Ruthven also in northern Scotland, in the period between 1260 and 1280, with building taking place at Tarset in Tynedale in this period also.

Evidence from the Buchan branch of the family also suggests that the period after 1260 saw a parallel burst of building activity. Little visible evidence is available in Buchan but it is probable that ecclesiastical patronage – the foundation of two almshouses in Buchan in 1261 and 1272[22] – was matched by a castle-strengthening programme at Slains, Kingedward, Cairnbulg, Dundarg and Rattray. Documentary and architectural evidence from the Buchan-held castle of Balvenie, acquired in the period c.1264×1282, also suggests building activity after 1260. The Comyns of Buchan were also responsible, following their share of the de Quincy inheritance in 1264, for Cruggleton castle in Galloway where archaeological evidence has suggested building phases in the 1260s and 1280s.[23]

Both political and financial circumstances helped to dictate the optimum time for castle building as far as the nobility was concerned. It was unlikely that much building activity would take place during times of political crisis such as the minority of Alexander III from 1249 to 1258. The extensive architectural patronage of the Comyns, especially in castle building, would require large financial resources. All three branches of the family were extensive landowners in Scotland as well as in England. Rather more information about the financial value of this landholding is available for the Comyns of Buchan. The de Quincy inheritance in 1264 undoubtedly increased this branch's financial wealth in Scotland and England. The value of Comyns' de Quincy lands in Scotland can be estimated at c.£150 per year;[24] as for the English lands from the inheritance, the important Leicester lands of Whitwick were worth £100 a year while another important Leicester manor, Shepshed, was worth £34 a year.[25] Yet this was considerably less than the income from the earldom of Buchan. In 1293 Earl John Comyn was asked for a relief of 1,417 marks to succeed to his overall Buchan inheritance in Scotland.[26] In 1311 the widow of Alexander Comyn of Buchan asked the English king, in consideration for the loss of her lands, for £500 yearly for her support.[27] Rather less financial information is available for the extensive landholding of the Comyns of Badenoch in northern and southern Scotland though a similar value can perhaps be assumed. In England, the Tynedale lands of this branch were worth 500 marks per year[28] and the family were well rewarded for John Comyn I's personal service in Henry III's army in 1264 and1265. He had a yearly fee of £50 and was also granted land to the yearly value of £300 in England.[29] Despite meagre records, the Comyns appear to have had considerable financial resources if not quite on a par with the well-known wealth of the 'rich and powerful' Balliols.[30]

The most substantial remains representing Comyn power in northern Scotland are at the castles of Lochindorb (Badenoch), Inverlochy (Lochaber) and Balvenie (Banffshire). The importance of Lochindorb to the Comyns of Badenoch is attested by John Comyn II's death there c.1302. On an island site, Lochindorb consists of a large quadrilateral curtained enclosure, its walls seven feet thick and twenty feet high, with each angle strengthened by a round tower of relatively slight projection.[31] Only one of the towers survives in reasonable condition though all were standing in 1793. Archaeological evidence seems to confirm buildings of the second half of the thirteenth century. Inverlochy, the chief castle of the Comyns in Lochaber, has been dated on archaeological grounds to c.1270–1280, which again confirms documentary evidence. In Scotland, Inverlochy is a rare example of the quadrangular castle[32] (90 feet by 101 feet) with high curtain walls, fortified with round towers (a type not uncommon in England and Wales: cf. Kidwelly 1275, Flint 1277 and Harlech 1283). Inverlochy is perhaps not an advanced version of this type as its corner towers do not control the curtain walls. Nevertheless the towers project boldly (more boldly than at Lochindorb) from each corner with one tower, the donjon (Comyn's Tower), being larger than the others. This was apparently planned as a keep with residential accommodation. Beyond the curtain wall, which, with the towers, stands to a height of 30 feet, is a wide ditch and outer bank. The ditch is closely defined round three sides, the fourth side confronting the River Lochy which fed the ditch. There is thus defence in depth at Inverlochy.

Similar features are seen at Balvenie.[33] One of the most noteworthy features is the wide (averaging 40 feet) flat-bottomed ditch, 12 feet deep in places, which enclosed the castle on three sides. The earliest plan, a large quadrangular court (158 feet by 131 feet) enclosed by high walls (over 25 feet in places and 7 feet thick) with towers (now gone) at the west and north corners with another tower probably at the east where there is now a large round tower of sixteenth-century date, has been dated to the close of the thirteenth century, which suggests most of the work was done after the Comyns acquired the site (sometime after 1264). Apart from the ditch, another feature is a stretch of wall walk on the battlements of the thirteenth-century defensive wall to enable the garrison to protect their castle walls. Balvenie clearly relied for its strength on the great outer ditch and its massive defensive walls.

The impressive visible remains at Balvenie, Lochindorb and Inverlochy should be set in the broader context of Comyn castle sites elsewhere in the north, at Ruthven and Blair Atholl as well as those in Buchan. The individual defensive features seen at Balvenie, Lochindorb and Inverlochy are probably less important than the strategic position and control of key lines of communication which Comyn castles in northern Scotland represented in 1296. Without control over northern Scotland, no authority could be secure in Scotland.

The 'herschip' of Buchan by Robert Bruce in 1308 is generally recognised as having destroyed much visible thirteenth-century evidence for Comyn power in the north of Scotland. Yet we must also remember Bruce's need to destroy or dismantle symbols of Comyn power in the south. In southern and central Scotland there is even less visible evidence of Comyn castles, yet the combined landed interests of the Buchan, Badenoch and Kilbride branches of the family gave them a significant presence further south and this too was marked by visible symbols of their power. The Comyns of Badenoch, by the end of the thirteenth century, held land in Perthshire (Findogask and Ochtertyre), and the lordships of Kirkintilloch and Lenzie (Dunbartonshire), as well as land at Machan (Clyde valley), land in Nithsdale (Dalswinton was certainly in Comyn possession before 1250) and the lordships of Bedrule and Scraesburgh in Roxburghshire. Kirkintilloch, caput of the lordship of Lenzie, had a castle and burgh associated with it by the early thirteenth century. The Comyns seem to have taken over a Roman site as the location for their castle. This was located strategically at the junction of the rivers Luggie and Kelvin. The earliest Comyn castle at this site seems to have been a typical late twelfth-century motte, rectangular in shape, measuring 30 metres by 17 metres and with a broad, deep ditch on its south and east sides.[34] Details of how Kirkintilloch developed as a castle during the thirteenth century are lacking, though in the eighteenth century it apparently had a 'double rampart of hewn stone, strongly cemented with lime'.[35] References to the castle in the records of the 1290s and early 1300s indicate its importance and strategic significance in the Scottish wars. In 1304 there is a reference to its garrison comprising one esquire, eleven other men at arms, six *officiarii*, twenty crossbowmen and thirty-eight archers.[36]

Another early Comyn castle, in the same region, proved to be important in the 1290s. This was at Kilbride, the main residence of the Comyn lords of East Kilbride. When Ure visited the present Mains castle in the late eighteenth century, he mentioned the ruins of an older castle seventy yards north of that late fifteenth- or early sixteenth-century tower.[37] It was surrounded by a fosse which was much larger than that around the tower. Further south the Comyns of Badenoch had several castles – Dalswinton in Nithsdale, and Bedrule and Scraesburgh in Roxburghshire. The castle at Dalswinton commanded Nithsdale and appears, like Kirkintilloch, to have been built on a Roman site, that of a large Agricolan fort. Nothing remains of the castle, but an eighteenth-century account reported that parts of the walls were standing in 1792 and that they were '12, and in places, 14 feet thick … The Nith formerly came close to the castle and there was a pool "called Comyn's pool".[38] This brief record gives the impression of a substantial fortification which confirms documentary evidence for Dalswinton's role as a key southern base for the Comyns of Badenoch in the Scottish wars.

The Comyns held Bedrule in Roxburghshire from c.1160. There is evidence of a motte which was superseded by a castle of enceinte.[39] Although the enclosure is not complete, the discernible features and layout suggest a late thirteenth-century date, further evidence of a Comyn castle-building programme after c.1260. The court at Bedrule was approximately 200 feet from north-west to south-east and 130 feet wide. There seems to have been a gatehouse on the north-west projecting from the curtain wall and facing the Rule Water, with a circular tower on the south and two intermediate circular towers on the west and south-west, and it can be assumed that there were two further towers on the north-west side. Edward I visited this castle in 1298. The Comyns of Badenoch also had a castle at Scraesburgh, alias Hunthill, in Roxburghshire, where there is evidence of an earthwork. The Comyns held the lordship of Scraesburgh by 1296[40] although they may have held it by c.1200. Like many earthworks in Roxburghshire, Scraesburgh was a low-lying structure which was 'evidently designed for habitation and presumably contained wooden buildings'. The site had a commanding view to the east and south-east across the Pleasants Burn and the valley of the Oxnam Water though it was easily approached from all directions and therefore not a good defensive site. In this situation the defences themselves had to provide the chief strength. The oval earthwork, measuring 215 feet from east to west by 180 feet from north to south, consisted of a single massive rampart with an external ditch.

The Comyn earls of Buchan also held land south of their main base though they did not have the physical presence there which the senior Badenoch branch displayed at Kirkintilloch, Dalswinton, Bedrule and Scraesburgh. The de Quincy inheritance in 1264, however, greatly added to the landholding of the Comyns of Buchan, giving them important new lands, especially in Galloway but also in Cunningham, Lauderdale and Midlothian. Thus after 1264 the Comyns of Buchan inherited the castle of Cruggleton, which may originally have been the site of a fort of the lords of Galloway. Cruggleton was well situated on a clifftop.[41] A stone castle was still standing in the sixteenth century, although only a single arch now survives. Excavations at the promontory fortification have shown that a stone-built phase occurred in the later thirteenth century. According to Truckell, there was a castle phase in the 1260s (possibly a Comyn phase if it occurred after 1264) as well as further strengthening in the 1280s (certainly a Comyn phase). Although there are few remains, Comyn castles in central and southern Scotland – Kirkintilloch, Dalswinton, Kilbride, Bedrule, Scraesburgh and Cruggleton – were significant in both the politics and warfare of the late thirteenth and early fourteenth centuries.

The military, political and administrative strength of the Comyns' own network of castles was strengthened through their appointment as sheriffs and keepers (see Map 1).[42] Thus they had control of a number of key royal castles. The strength of the Comyns of Buchan in the north was further emphasised by their role as hereditary sheriffs of Banff and Dingwall from the 1260s. Their power in the south-west (Galloway) was strengthened by their role, also from the 1260s, as hereditary sheriffs of Wigtown. In the troubled years after Alexander III's death, John Comyn, earl of Buchan after 1289, was given added responsibility at Kirkcudbright where he acted as keeper from 1288 to 1292 and at Aberdeen where he was sheriff in 1291. In fact, Earl John was in control of the castles of Aberdeen, Banff, Kirkcudbright and Wigtown in June 1291. The power of the Comyns of Badenoch in both northern and southern Scotland was also emphasised by the responsibility that John Comyn II of Badenoch

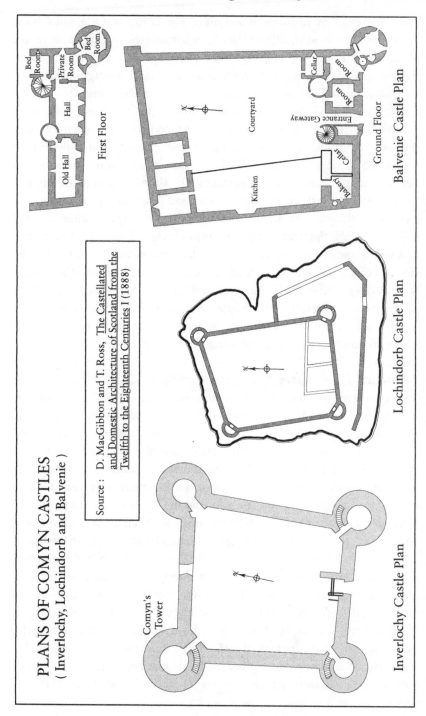

PLANS OF COMYN CASTLES
(Inverlochy, Lochindorb and Balvenie)

Source : D. MacGibbon and T. Ross, The Castellated and Domestic Architecture of Scotland from the Twelfth to the Eighteenth Centuries I (1888)

Balvenie Castle Plan

First Floor

Bed Room
Private Room
Bed Room
Hall
Old Hall

Ground Floor

Cellar
Room
Room
Courtyard
Entrance Gateway
Cellar
Bakery
Kitchen

Lochindorb Castle Plan

Inverlochy Castle Plan

Comyn's Tower

held between 1291 and 1293, as keeper of the castles of Dull and Clunie in Stormont (close to Blair Atholl), Kilbride (the main castle of the Comyns of Kilbride), Jedburgh and Roxburgh (close to the Comyn castles of Bedrule and Scraesburgh) as well as Bridburgh (Barburgh) in Dumfriesshire (close to the Comyn castle of Dalswinton).[43]

Just as the Comyns' political position in Scotland, as pillars of the monarchy after 1260, was enhanced by the support of a network of allies, many of them related to the Comyns through marriage, so their military hold on this power was bolstered by the castles of these allies. The Comyns' already formidable control over northern and north-eastern Scotland was further strengthened by their alliance with the Macdougalls of Argyll which added key castles in the west such as Dunstaffnage, Dunollie, Duart and Innis Chonnell in Loch Awe to the Comyn power.[44] Similarly, the Balliol castle of Buittle added to Comyn strength in the south-west. Comyn allies held many sheriffdoms in 1290, including those of Dumfries, Stirling, Edinburgh, Perth, Forfar, Fife, Kincardine, Elgin and Cromarty, and this added further to Comyn control of royal castles and the important lines of communication from them.

Edward I must have been very conscious of this Comyn power and the family's capacity to control these key lines of communication. As overlord of Scotland after June 1291, Edward continued to acknowledge the Comyns and their supporters as sheriffs and custodians of the major royal castles. In the first years of John Balliol's kingship, 1292–1296, Edward showed confidence that he could exercise influence over the Comyn government and use Comyn power in Scotland for his own purposes. In 1292, for example, he gave permission to John Comyn earl of Buchan to export lead from Man to cover eight towers at Cruggleton.[45] The marriage of John Comyn to Joan de Valence, daughter of William de Valence, cousin to Edward I, by ?1293,[46] was surely an attempt by Edward I to harness Comyn power. Even after war broke out between the Comyn-led Scottish government, acting on behalf of John Balliol, and Edward I's England in 1296, the Comyn network of castles and the political control which they symbolised had an influence on diplomacy as well as actual warfare during the years 1296 to 1314. Robert Bruce was as much influenced by them as Edward I.

The events of the Scottish Wars between 1296 and 1314 are sufficiently well known not to be repeated in detail.[47] This account will dwell on the Comyn perspective at crucial times in the conflict and analyse the changing relationships between the Comyns and the English kings Edward I and Edward II between 1296 and 1314. It will also examine the changing position of the Comyns in the Scottish political community in these years and especially the family's relationship with the Bruces.

The fact that the Comyns were not only a northern-based power was emphasised at an early stage of the military contest when John Comyn, earl of Buchan, and John Comyn the younger, the Guardian's son from the Badenoch line, took prominent roles along with six Scottish earls in the unsuccessful attack on Carlisle on 26th March 1296. At about this time an English army was gathering around Berwick and on 30th March the town was stormed and many townsmen (by one account, over 11,000) were butchered.[48] In revenge, the Scots based at Jedburgh (which had been under Comyn control in 1291 and in the early years of Balliol's reign) and under the leadership of the earls of Mar, Ross and Menteith raided Northumberland, especially Redesdale, Coquetdale and Tynedale, committing many atrocities.[49] On the way back from this raid they took Dunbar with the help of the Comyn countess of Dunbar who remained loyal to the Comyn-led Scottish government.[50] It was at Dunbar on 27th April that the first phase of the Scottish Wars took a decisive turn when the Scots army trying to relieve the siege of the town by English troops was routed and those within the castle surrendered.

The Scottish casualties at Dunbar were estimated at 10,000 dead. Despite the dangers of contemporary exaggeration of the size of the English force and the scale of Scottish casualties, other evidence seems to confirm the conclusiveness of the Scottish defeat. Key Scottish castles such as Roxburgh, Edinburgh and Stirling soon surrendered to the English, Stirling castle, in fact, being abandoned defenceless. Edward I marched north through Scotland via Perth, Montrose, Banff and Elgin, receiving fealty from Scottish nobles and knights. On 8th July at Montrose, King John Balliol formally submitted to Edward, resigning his kingdom to the English King and having his coat of royal arms stripped from his tabard in public, humiliating circumstances. According to a contemporary report, Edward I 'conquered the realm of Scotland, and searched it ... within twenty one weeks without any more'.[51] The ease of Edward's victory in 1296 has prompted much debate. To contemporary English chroniclers, the indiscipline of the Scottish knights who 'showed their heels so readily'[52] was a key factor. Modern commentators have added that the Scots were probably over-confident[53] and that they were poorly led by King John Balliol who inspired little support within Scotland.[54] It has also been suggested that the Scots 'were not strong enough to challenge Edward's army in open battle'.[55]

It seems clear that the full Scottish army was not involved at Dunbar. The Scottish military force at Dunbar represented the political reality in the Scotland of 1296 – a Comyn-led government with majority, but not full, support within Scotland. Seven Scottish earls had been involved in the Comyn-led raid from Annandale on Carlisle on 26th March 1296.[56] However, Patrick earl of March and Dunbar, Gilbert de Uphraville earl of Angus,[57] Robert Bruce the younger, earl of Carrick, as well as Robert Bruce the elder had done homage to Edward I and promised 'to serve him well and loyally against all mortal men'[58] on 24th March 1296. The followings of these magnates were, presumably, not in the Scottish host at Dunbar. The absence of the Bruces from the Scottish side at the first major confrontation of the Scottish Wars (or Wars of Independence) has caused some difficulty for the fourteenth- and fifteenth-century commentators Fordun and Bower to whom Robert Bruce was the ultimate hero and defender of Scottish nationhood against English imperialism. Fordun and Bower blamed Richard Siward, the commander at Dunbar, for betraying Dunbar to the English[59] but this criticism seems to have been based more on his adherence to Edward I after 1297 than his actions in 1296. He had been a castellan of royal castles for the Comyn-led government in the 1290s and, according to the Lanercost Chronicle, was 'a man renowned in war and expert in arms'.[60] He was treated as one of the leaders of the Scottish force after 1296, i.e, by imprisonment in England, rather than as a defector to the English cause.

Fordun, followed by Bower, tried to explain away the behaviour of the Bruces and also those who had apparently supported King John as recently as 23rd February 1296, when they sealed the treaty between Scotland and France. According to Fordun,[61] Edward I:

> promised and pledged himself faithfully to the said Robert [the
> grandfather] to promote him to the throne as having the better
> and stronger right, while the other [John Balliol] should be set
> aside and deprived for ever. By this promise ... he led him to
> write a letter himself to all his friends dwelling in Scotland,
> and advise them to surrender and deliver up to him all castles
> and fortified strongholds ... the Earls of Mar and Atholl, with
> the whole strength of their power, cleaved in the firm league
> of kinship, to the side of Robert Bruce ... It was for this reason
> – according to the general opinion – that the aforesaid earls
> with their troops, through goodwill and love of Bruce, fled
> scathless from the field on the day the aforesaid battle [Dunbar]
> was fought.

Like the attitude of Fordun to Richard Siward, his attitude to the earls of Mar and Atholl represents their later careers in close support of Bruce rather than the political reality of 1296. John de Strathbogie earl of Atholl (1284–1306) was certainly a friend of the Bruces and a near neighbour to them in the north where they were lords of part of Garioch. The earl was, however, a consistent supporter of the patriot cause without being a Comyn partisan and was amongst the Scottish prisoners taken at Dunbar. Donald earl of Mar, related to the Bruces and Atholl through marriage, had participated actively with the Scottish forces which had raided Northumberland and then captured Dunbar in 1296. The *Lanercost Chronicle* thought that the earl of Mar was one of the earls captured at Dunbar[62] but he appears to have been with John Balliol after the surrender at Dunbar[63] as he is mentioned, along with the king, John Comyn earl of Buchan and John Comyn of Badenoch, the king's closest advisers, coming to Edward I's mercy at Montrose between 8th and 10th July. It should be remembered that, despite his family links with the Bruces, Donald earl of Mar was a cousin of John Comyn earl of Buchan.

A retrospective Bruce viewpoint on 1296 can be a misleading one. A more contemporary and relevant question to ask is why the Comyns, forceful leaders of the Scottish political community in March 1296, capitulated so quickly. The answer to this question is probably as much a political as a military one. From the military point of view,

Dunbar may not have been a defeat for the full Scottish host – the forces of a number of Scottish earls did not participate and John Balliol himself does not seem to have taken part – but it was a decisive blow to the political establishment of Scotland in 1296, i.e. the Comyns and their allies. Although John Balliol has been criticised for poor leadership in 1296, it is clear that, in reality, he was a symbol for the Comyn-led government more than a leader of it. According to the *Lanercost Chronicle*,[64] 'it had been *laid down by the Scots to their king* [John] that he was neither to offer battle nor accept peace but that he should keep in hiding by constant flight'. After Dunbar, Balliol had fled, along with his closest advisers, John Comyn earl of Buchan, John Comyn lord of Badenoch and Donald earl of Mar, to the Comyn-dominated north. It was the Comyns who decided to change their policy, adopt a more pragmatic approach than aimless flight, and seek favourable surrender terms. Balliol had in fact reached Aberdeen, deep in Comyn territory, before being brought south to Montrose with his son, Edward, to surrender to Edward I.[65]

Edward I did seem, at first, willing to negotiate, after Dunbar, with those holding power and influence in Scotland. James Stewart had surrendered to Edward early in May 1296 and was soon employed to receive the surrender of the Comyn castle of Kirkintilloch about 10th June. A marriage alliance between James Stewart and the sister of one of Edward's closest supporters, de Burgh earl of Ulster, in 1296 was, no doubt, intended to consolidate Stewart's loyalty.[66] Even with John Balliol, Edward I initially sent Anthony Bek and Earl Warenne to negotiate terms,[67] a measure of the familiar relations which had been characteristic between a well-established Scottish government and representatives of the English government during the second half of the thirteenth century. The compromise proposed, that Edward would be granted Scotland while Balliol, in return, would receive an English earldom, was, however, no longer in accord with the tougher policy that Edward was now pursuing. He now intended to rule Scotland directly. Comyn fears that their leadership of the Scottish political community would be usurped by the Bruces with support from Edward proved to be unfounded. Just as the Comyns had used English influence to maintain and consolidate their political power in Scotland after 1286, the Bruces hoped to fulfil their long-held claims to Scottish kingship by being active in the service of Edward I before 1296. According to Fordun:[68]

> So after the victory gained over the Scots at Dunbar, the elder
> Robert of Bruce came up to the king of England and besought
> him to faithfully fulfil what he had long ago promised him, as to
> his getting the kingdom.

Edward's famous reply – '... in no little indignation ... "Have we nothing else to do but win kingdoms for thee" ' – showed that the king had another policy in mind than simply to replace Balliol by Bruce.

Though the Comyns were not replaced by their rivals, the Bruces, it is clear that Edward was determined to teach the rebellious Scottish government a lesson. He progressed round Scotland in July and August 1296, visiting royal centres such as Aberdeen, Banff and Elgin which had been under Comyn influence and sending commissions to 'search the district of Badenoch',[69] the lordship of the senior Comyn branch. Edward had also taken homages of the leading men of Scotland during his progress through Scotland, and this was to be followed by the swearing of fealty to Edward by every freeholder in Scotland. His takeover of Scottish government was demonstrated clearly by his removal of the Stone of Destiny, the most precious symbol of Scottish monarchy, from Scone abbey to Westminster abbey as well as by the seizure of other Scottish muniments and government records.[70] The removal of the mainstays of Scottish government, especially the Comyns, to England was part of the same plan.

John Comyn, lord of Badenoch, and John Comyn earl of Buchan, who, with Donald earl of Mar, submitted at the same time as John Balliol, were sent to England and ordered to stay south of the Trent.[71] Alexander Comyn of Buchan (John's brother) and John Comyn of Kilbride were also went to England and they joined those members of the Comyn family who were captured at Dunbar[72] – John Comyn, the younger, of Badenoch, son and heir of John the head of this senior branch of the family, Robert Comyn brother of the elder John of Badenoch, Alexander Comyn of Badenoch (another brother) and Edmund Comyn of Kilbride. Families supporting the Comyns and captured at Dunbar were also committed to prisons in England. Thus the earl of Ross (who had taken a leading role in the 1296 campaign) was sent to the Tower, as was Andrew de Moray (who had held the important post of justiciar of Scotia), John de Mowbray son of Geoffrey (Geoffrey de Mowbray had been

justiciar of Lothian), David de Graham, son of Patrick, the most senior
casualty at Dunbar (the Grahams were stalwarts of the Balliol/Comyn
government), Nicholas Randolph, son of Thomas Randolph (who had
been similarly prominent in Scottish government), and Richard Siward
(who had been castellan of royal castles in Scotland in the 1290s and was
castellan of Dunbar in 1296). Other prisons in England held members of
the Sinclair family (who had been justiciars of Galloway and sheriffs of
Dumfries, Edinburgh and Linlithgow); members of the Lochore family
(who had been sheriffs of Fife in the 1290s), members of the Cheyne
family (who had been sheriffs of Elgin and Kincardine), members of
the Ros family (who had been sheriffs of Lanark), a member of the
de la Hay family (who had been sheriffs of Perth), a member of the
Sinton family (who had been sheriffs of Selkirk), Robert Lovel who
had been sheriff of Inverness in King John's reign, and Hugh de Airth
who had been bailiff for John Comyn in the abthania of Dull. Other
families associated with the Comyns and Scottish government, Mowat
and Scot, were among the prisoners from Dunbar.

Edward I hoped to teach the Comyns and their supporters, at both
the centre of Scottish government as well as in the localities, a lesson.
He refused to fill the political vacuum, which he had created, with
the Bruces and their allies but instead gave responsibilities to his own
officials, the earl Warenne as lieutenant or keeper of Scotland, Hugh
Cressingham as treasurer and Walter Amersham as chancellor.[73] The
headquarters for Edward's administration in Scotland was established at
Berwick and the English pattern of administration was adopted with two
escheators for north and south of the Forth. He hoped to achieve stability
within Scotland by restoring lands to those who came to his fealty and had
not been involved in the war against him. Edward was even prepared to
show leniency to nobles such as Malise earl of Strathearn[74] who had
been involved in the attack on Carlisle in 1296. He too was allowed to
keep his lands and title though his two sons, Gilbert and Robert, were
sent to the Tower as hostages to ensure their father's good behaviour.

Despite the belief of Fordun and Bower that Edward I placed
much emphasis on continuity in Scottish administration at local
level,[75] local administration through castle control had been the
particular responsibility of the nobility, especially the Comyns and
their supporters, and in their absence change was inevitable. On 8th
September 1296 Henry de Percy had been appointed the English
warden of Ayr and Galloway.[76] Castles under Comyn influence in the

south-west, private (Kirkintilloch and Cruggleton), royal (Wigtown) or of allies (Buittle), were placed firmly under English control, as was the castle at Dumbarton which had been controlled by another key figure in Scottish government, James Stewart. It is uncertain, given the lack of evidence, how Edward sought to control Comyn castles in the north.[77] It is clear that he did not adopt the policy which Robert Bruce as king felt was necessary in 1308, the 'herschip' of Buchan. Edward may well have concentrated his resources south of the Forth to consolidate his new centre of administration in Scotland, Berwick. In the north, he seems to have used a mixture of English officials and Scots apparently cowed into acting on Edward's behalf by the imprisonment of family members in England.[78] There appear to have been English garrisons under Sir Henry Lathum at Aberdeen and William fitz Warin at Urquhart, a key strategic site guarding the north of the Great Glen. An experienced Scotsman, Reginald Cheyne, senior, was sheriff of nearby Inverness and it seems that the countess of Ross, and Gartnait, son of the earl of Mar, were also expected to act in Edward's interests in the north of Scotland.

Bower was probably correct in judging that Edward thought himself 'safe as a result of the abject submission of the Scots'[79] in 1296. The bending of the Scottish nobility to his will was a key part of Edward's policy. It even applied to the Comyns who were, after all, related to the king by marriage, and the other prominent Scots in captivity. Thus, on 12th October 1296 John Comyn of Badenoch, who was staying with his wife and family at the manor of Geddington, was given the privilege of taking twelve deer in the forest 'by gift of the king' as well as receiving permission to hunt fox, hare and cat in the same forest.[80]

The revolts of 1297 were to prove that Edward I's arrangements for exercising power in Scotland were flawed. The revolts have usually been seen as either aristocratic, inspired by supporters of the Bruce cause against the Balliol/Comyn party in the Great Cause,[81] i.e. James Stewart, Bishop Wishart and Robert Bruce, or 'the spontaneous act of middling and common folk'[82] with William Wallace and Andrew de Moray as the leaders. These views underestimate the wide-ranging support for the government and the policies which represented John Balliol's kingship. The Scottish government of 1292 to 1296, itself a continuation of previous Scottish governments, was based on patronage, especially that emanating from the Comyn family, and family networks. Families such as Comyn, Macdougall, Stewart and Moray had enjoyed the power which went with holding public office. It was unlikely that these families would consent to losing this willingly. Edward I, followed by later historians, underestimated the involvement of the Macdougall, Stewart and Moray families in 1297 as *representatives* of King John's government.

Revolt in Scotland started in the north early in 1297. Both Stewart and Macdougall power in the west and north-west as agents of Balliol's government was threatened by Edward's attempt to extend English influence in the area[83] by appointing Alexander Macdonald of Islay in April 1296 as baillie of Kintyre (formerly under James Stewart's jurisdiction) and baillie in the sheriffdoms of Lorn, Ross and the Isles (formerly under the control of Alexander Macdougall of Argyll). It is tempting to see the revolt of the Macdougalls in 1297 principally as a civil war with the Macdonalds, their rivals for political power in the north-west Highlands from the second half of the thirteenth century. It should be remarked, however, that the Macdougalls were as closely linked by marriage to the Comyns as the Balliols were and that they had been given political responsibilities in the north-west by the Comyn-led Scottish government. Edward I presumably thought that, with Alexander Macdougall of Argyll having done homage to him and being a prisoner in Berwick castle, the Macdougalls would not cause problems. The revolt of the Macdougalls, led by Alexander's son Duncan who had not sworn homage to Edward,[84] against Edward's agent Alexander Macdonald proved him wrong. The strategic Comyn castle of Inverlochy (and the two galleys outside)[85] were used in the resistance of Duncan to Macdonald's attempts to control the area.

The Stewarts had increased their political responsibilities in the west as well as the north-west in Alexander III's reign[86] and also under King John. An early submission to Edward in 1296 failed to preserve James Stewart's political status in the west, especially after September 1296 when Henry Percy was appointed English warden of Ayr and Galloway.[87] Stewart had lost political control (and power) in the west and north-west to both Edward's agents.

Further significant resistance to Edward I's administration came from another of Scotland's 'government' families, the Morays. A successful revolt in the north was led by Andrew de Moray,[88] son of Andrew de Moray of Petty who had been justiciar of Scotia during the Balliol kingship (to 1296) and was an important prisoner in the Tower of London. The younger Andrew, who himself had escaped from his imprisonment in Chester, had soon recaptured the English-held castles in the north, including Inverness, Urquhart, Banff, Elgin and Aberdeen, between May and mid-July 1297. This area had been very much under Comyn influence and it is worth noting the family relationship between Moray and Comyn – Andrew's father had married a daughter of John Comyn I of Badenoch.[89] It is clear that use of a combination of Edward's own men and relatives of those Scots in English prisons to suppress unrest had not been effective against Moray. Though the Comyns themselves were absent from Scotland, the involvement of members of the Macdougall, Stewart and Moray families could still be seen as the response of representatives of the Scottish government. The Morays and Macdougalls were part of the Comyn patronage system.

James Stewart played a significant role in a revolt in the south which soon ended ignominiously with surrender at Irvine in early July 1297.[90] Contemporary chroniclers as well as later historians have given close attention to this revolt, which has been seen as the official aristocratic revolt of 1297. The involvement of Stewart and Bishop Wishart who had acted as Guardians and had played active roles in the government of John Balliol certainly give it an 'official' character. From the surrender negotiations, it is clear that they regarded themselves as leaders and official representatives of the 'whole community of the realm of Scotland'. Yet the involvement of Robert Bruce, earl of Carrick, as one of the leaders along with Stewart and Wishart, confuses the issue. Robert Bruce had been exiled with his father by the Comyn/Balliol government; his father had not sworn fealty to Balliol and they had been on Edward's side at the outset of the war. The fact that Edward I showed no inclination to make the Bruces kings in Scotland may have persuaded the younger Bruce to join the revolt in Scotland *after* it had started. The *Guisborough Chronicle* believed that he was already aiming at the throne.[91] It seems more probable, however, that he was, as a first step, trying to use his military power as a Scottish earl and his family friendship with the Stewarts and Wishart to establish himself as one of the chief leaders of the Scottish political community in the absence of the Comyns and John Balliol.

Compared to the ineptitude of this aristocratic revolt in the south-west, the now famous revolt of William Wallace was outstandingly successful. Rather too much contrast has been made between the aristocratic revolt of Stewart, Wishart and Bruce and the 'popular' revolt of William Wallace. Wallace was himself from a knightly family in the feudal following of James Stewart[92] and also had links with Wishart. Again Stewart seems to be the focus for the involvement (for different reasons) of both Bruce and Wallace in revolt. The *Lanercost Chronicle*, supported by that of *Guisborough*, probably reflects the essence of the rising, planned by James Stewart and Bishop Wishart, who 'caused a certain bloody man, William Wallace, who had formerly been a chief of brigands in Scotland to revolt against the king and assemble the people in revolt'.[93] Neither chronicle, however, brings the revolts involving the Macdougalls (who had not sworn fealty to Edward either) and Moray into the general context of revolt in 1297. The revolts in 1297 were, above all, a reaction by remaining Scottish government representatives against Edward I's authority. They represented also a reaction in favour of the policies of the Scottish government, a resistance to Edward I's infringement of the rights of the kingdom and a defence of the ideas encapsulated in the Treaty of Birgham (1290): '... the rights, laws, liberties and customs of the same realm of Scotland to be preserved in every respect and in all time coming throughout the said realm and its borders, completely and without being impaired...'.[94] Such ideas represented the views of the Scottish political community in the warfare of 1296 and the revolts of 1297. As well as the reaction to an English takeover of Scottish government, there was opposition to Edward I's attempts in 1297, as in 1296, to recruit men from Scotland for his French wars.[95] However, Edward's demands included the seizing of 'all the middle people of Scotland to send them beyond the Scottish sea in his army' and greater demands from the population as a whole for money.[96] It was hardly surprising that there was a popular element in the revolts of 1297. Both William Wallace in the south, and Andrew Moray in the north, had popular support,[97] which no doubt was increased by their military success.

The Scots in prison in England were promised freedom if they served Edward I on his Flanders campaign. In early June 1297 Edward released John Comyn of Badenoch and John Comyn earl of Buchan, as well as other key members of the pre-1296 Scottish government,[98] Alexander de Balliol and Alexander earl of Menteith (the latter in July), after they promised to serve him overseas. Later in June, however, he asked the Comyns to help him quell the revolts in Scotland.[99] Alexander Macdougall was also released from Berwick on 24th May 1297, apparently on condition that he would help dissuade his son from continuing his revolt. Edward's policy towards Scotland seems to have been affected by the greater priority which he gave to the Flanders expedition and his apparent belief that, through the Comyns and their associates in government (duly chastened by their defeat and subsequent imprisonment in 1296), order could be restored to Scotland. The Comyns in the north, John earl of Buchan and his brother Alexander, were to help Henry Cheyne bishop of Aberdeen, Euphemia countess of Ross and Garnait son and heir of Donald earl of Mar to control the rebellion of Andrew de Moray.[100] John Comyn of Badenoch was commanded by Edward I to assist Brian fitz Alan in the custody of the kingdom and especially in the defence of Roxburgh.[101]

The news from Scotland in late July and early August 1297 cast doubt on either the ability or the willingness of the Comyns to promote Edward I's interests in Scotland. Hugh de Cressingham, the treasurer, wrote on 24th July: 'in some counties the Scotch have established and placed bailiffs and ministers so that no county is in proper order excepting Berwick and Roxburgh and this only lately';[102] on 4th August: 'we cannot yet raise any money in the land';[103] and on 5th August: 'the peace on the other side of the Scottish sea is still in obscurity, as it is said, as to the doings of the earls who are there'.[104] According to the *Guisborough Chronicle*, Earl John Comyn 'at first pretended to repress rebellion but in the end changed sides and became a thorn in our flesh'.[105] The Comyns did not come out openly in support of the revolt – the presence of John Comyn, the younger, of Badenoch,[106] and Edmund Comyn of Kilbride in Edward I's army in Flanders may have dissuaded the Comyns from an open stance – but the ability of the Scots to establish their own offices and for Moray to gather a large infantry force and join with Wallace's force in the south strongly suggests support from the Comyn patronage network in the north. The combined forces of Wallace and Moray won a famous victory at Stirling Bridge on 11th September 1297.[107] As late as 26th September 1297, the English still believed that the earl was loyal – his brother Alexander seems to have been consistently loyal to Edward – though by November/December the order for the king's bailiff to take the Tynedale lands of John Comyn of Badenoch into his hands indicates Edward's acceptance that the Comyns were in support of the Scottish revolt.[108]

It is difficult to establish the precise role of the Comyns during the ascendancy of William Wallace between the battle of Stirling Bridge and his defeat at the battle of Falkirk on 22nd July 1298. The victory of Wallace and Moray at Stirling Bridge in practice gave them leadership of the Scottish political community. They had re-established the Guardianship, this time a distinctly military regime with two proven military leaders replacing the traditional leadership of the Comyns and

Stewarts (which had been found wanting in battle in 1296 and 1297 and which had, in the case of the Comyns, been absent from Scotland for a year). Both Wallace and Moray (until his death late in 1297) acted, like Comyn, in the name of King John Balliol.[109] The military nature of the Guardianship is summed up by Wallace's description of himself as 'Guardian of the kingdom of Scotland and commander of its army, in the name of the famous prince the lord John, by God's grace illustrious king of Scotland, by consent of the community of the realm'.[110] The military Guardianship was conscious of the need for money to continue the war effort. This was shown by the letter of Moray and Wallace to the mayor and communities of Lübeck and Hamburg, assuring them of safe access to Scottish ports, and Wallace's raid on Northumberland.[111]

The relationship between Wallace and the Comyns is traditionally summed up by Fordun's memorable account of the Comyns' treachery in Wallace's defeat at the battle of Falkirk on 22nd July 1298.[112] Fordun refers to 'the ill-will, begotten of the spring of envy, which the Comyns had conceived towards the said William', as a result of which 'they, with their accomplices, forsook the field, and escaped unhurt'. After his defeat, Wallace resigned his office as Guardian, 'perceiving, by these and other strong proofs the glaring wickedness of the Comyns and their abettors'. The strength of such condemnation, of course, reflects the need of the nationalist narratives of the fourteenth and fifteenth centuries to condemn the Comyns specifically as rivals and enemies of their heroes, Robert Bruce and William Wallace. The *Lanercost Chronicle* blamed the inadequacy of the Scottish cavalry in general.[113] The accusation of treachery sits rather oddly with Fordun's recognition that Robert Bruce earl of Carrick fought on the English side at Falkirk, and 'was the means of bringing about this victory'.[114] It also sits slightly oddly with the Comyns' long-held support both of the customs and liberties of Scotland and John Balliol's kingship (to which Wallace also keenly adhered).

Yet there are a number of pieces of evidence to substantiate the fact that there was tension, even personal animosity, between Wallace and the Comyns. It was natural for the Comyns, in particular, but also for the aristocratic governing community in general, to feel that their traditional leadership role had been usurped. Wallace's actions, in power, probably increased this feeling. An earlier, more complete, text of the *Scotichronicon* referred to Wallace's suppression of the Comyns in Galloway.[115] The election of William Lamberton as bishop of St Andrews, at the behest of Wallace,[116] following the death of William Fraser in France in 1297, was a blow to the Comyns. William Fraser was from a family of Comyn supporters.[117] Comyn domination of Scottish politics in the second half of the thirteenth century had been supported by a line of pro-Comyn bishops of St Andrews. Gamelin (1255–71) had probably been a member of the Comyn family. It seemed that the Comyns had another family candidate in line for this highest ecclesiastical office in Scotland, and an office of great political significance. Master William Comyn, provost of St Andrews (1287–1329) and brother of John Comyn earl of Buchan, objected to his exclusion from the election process, and later, in 1306, it was asserted that he had, in fact, been elected but superseded by Lamberton.[118] This allegation, if correct, would certainly explain Comyn animosity towards Lamberton and Wallace. This animosity was openly displayed in an argument at a baronial council in Peebles in August 1299.[119] David Graham, a firm Comyn adherent, put forward a 'demand for Sir William Wallace's lands and goods, *as he was going abroad without leave*', and was met by the objections of Wallace's brother, Malcolm. During the argument, John Comyn earl of Buchan seized Lamberton bishop of St Andrews, obviously defending the Wallaces, while John Comyn of Badenoch took Robert Bruce by the throat. Comyn animosity towards Lamberton may have been further increased by Lamberton's identification with the Bruce following. Master William Lamberton appeared on a supplementary list of auditors acting on behalf of Robert Bruce, the Competitor during the Great Cause.[120] In 1299 he was identified as being in the Bruce following. The Comyns, it seems, had lost their traditional control over the highest ecclesiastical office, and one of the key political offices in the land. This was a vital blow to Comyn fortunes.

The stated cause of the argument in the baronial council of August 1299 showed that animosity between Wallace and the Comyns continued after Wallace's resignation from the Guardianship. He was out of sympathy with the traditional aristocratic leadership of the Scottish political community, although he continued to work abroad on behalf of John Balliol's kingship, returning to Scotland in 1303.[121] The view of Fordun, Bower, Wyntoun and Wallace's biographer, Blind Hary, that the Comyns were traitors to Wallace is rather at odds with the fact that the political community of the realm accepted John Comyn, the younger, as Guardian of Scotland 'in the same year' as Wallace's resignation and 'not long after' Falkirk.[122] The Comyns thus assumed their leadership role again, yet their year's exile had affected their position. Their leadership was no longer unquestioned. The new Guardianship of 1298 was a joint one between John Comyn the younger and Robert Bruce earl of Carrick.[123] In the Comyns' absence, Robert Bruce had benefited, gaining a much higher political profile despite his poor military showing in 1297. Though his father appeared on the English side at Falkirk, Robert Bruce the younger was in Ayrshire at the time of Falkirk and set fire to Ayr to prevent its use by the English. After Falkirk, Bruce was prepared, it seemed, to act on behalf of John Balliol, however unlikely this might have appeared given the Bruce rivalry with the Comyns and Balliols since 1286. The joint Guardianship was clearly a compromise, a government of national unity in which the military resources and patronage of the two most influential families in Scotland could be used in the interests of the political community as a whole. The Comyns' absence in England was, it seems, also exploited by a supporter of Bruce, Bishop Wishart of Glasgow.[124] John Comyn of Badenoch had asked Edward I in 1296 to order the Guardian of Scotland to put Mr Robert, Comyn's physician, in the church of Great Dalton (Dumfriesshire) 'from which he had been unlawfully ousted by the bishop of Glasgow'.

The years 1298–1304 saw many changes in the composition of the Guardianship but the presence of the Comyns is the one constant factor. Through their network of allies and castles, they simply had more political and military power in Scotland and greater powers of patronage (hence control) than any other family. In particular, they controlled Scotland north of the Forth. The English were not able to build on their success at Falkirk, Edward's difficulties in England forcing him to lead his army back there.[125] In these circumstances, the Scots and the administrative infrastructure so much influenced by the Comyns could be re-established. Yet at the centre the tensions between the Comyns on the one hand and Robert Bruce earl of Carrick and William Lamberton bishop of St Andrews on the other kept resurfacing, causing frequent changes in the leadership of the political community. During the quarrel between David Graham and Malcolm Wallace at the council of magnates in Peebles on 19th August 1299, John Comyn the younger 'leapt at the earl of Carrick and seized him by the throat, and the earl of Buchan turned on the bishop of St Andrews'.[126] The polarisation of support between the Comyns and Bruce is clear. A compromise was reached in which Lamberton, no doubt in his role as bishop of St Andrews, was given some seniority in a new triumvirate of guardians: 'the bishop of St Andrews should have all the castles in his hands as *principal captain*, and the earl of Carrick and John Comyn be with him as joint guardians of the kingdom'. Tension had occurred again by May 1300, however, and it is clear that John Comyn found it as difficult to work with Lamberton as with Bruce. At a parliament held at Rutherglen:[127]

> the bishop of St Andrews and sire John Comyn were at discord
> and the Stewart of Scotland and the earl of Atholl took the part
> of the bishop, and sir John Comyn said that he did not wish to be
> a guardian of the realm along with the bishop. But at length they
> were at accord and they had elected sir Ingram d'Umphraville
> to be one of the guardians of the realm in place of the earl of
> Carrick.

Bruce may have resigned at this parliament or just before. The new Guardianship was much more Comyn-orientated as Umphraville was a kinsman of Balliol and an ally of the Comyns.

A number of reasons have been put forward to explain the resignation and/or replacement of Bruce.[128] Bruce may have objected to the fact that the military activity in the Anglo-Scottish war was concentrated in the south-west in 1300; he may have been concerned that most of the Bruce lands there were in English hands. This latter fact, and the possibility that John Balliol would return to Scotland as king, made his position in Scotland increasingly untenable and a personal truce with Edward I an attractive alternative. All the Guardians since 1297, including Robert Bruce earl of Carrick, had acted on behalf of King John Balliol though Bruce's father had never sworn fealty to Balliol and the Bruces' active opposition to him since 1286 made the younger Bruce's position in Scotland untenable given the probability of Balliol's imminent return. The Scottish diplomatic efforts of Bishop Crambeth, William Wallace and others at the French court and the Papacy had won French support in particular, and French pressure secured Balliol's release from papal custody in the summer of 1301.[129] Balliol's subsequent return to his family lands in Picardy suggested that, with French support, he could soon return to Scotland. The Truce of Asnières, negotiated in France and ratified by King Philip, granted a truce to the Scots in the war with England to last from 26th January to 1st November 1302. According to the terms, the French were to hold certain lands in the south-west during the truce – these lands would probably include the earl of Carrick's castle at Turnberry as well as the Bruces' Annandale lands.[130]

In these circumstances Bruce returned to an alliance with Edward I by February 1302.[131] Edward consolidated this by a marriage alliance between Bruce and one of his chief magnate families, the de Burghs. Bruce took as his second wife Elizabeth, daughter of Richard de Burgh, earl of Ulster. The terms of Bruce's submission to Edward have been subject to much debate[132] because of their vagueness, but it seems that Bruce wanted Edward I's support for the Bruce landed rights in Scotland as well as his claim to the Scottish throne 'Because Robert ? fears that the ? realm of Scotland might be removed from the hands of the king, which God forbid, and delivered to John Balliol, or to his son, or that the right might be put in question, or reversed and repealed in a new judgement'.[133] The terms show the weakness of Edward I's position, faced with the possibility of Balliol's return to Scotland with a French army, and help to explain why tacit support for an alternative candidate for the Scottish throne was a feasible counter.

The growing confidence and influence of John Balliol in France and the imminence of his return were reflected in more changes in the leadership of the political community in Scotland. The triumvirate of guardians – Comyn, Lamberton and Umphraville[134] – lasted until early 1301 (certainly no later than May). At about this time, it seems, they were superseded by John de Soules, appointed by John Balliol directly as his agent in Scotland pending his return.[135] A number of official records between 10th July 1301 and 23rd November 1302 refer either to John de Soules acting in the name of (not on behalf of) King John or are royal acts issued by King John himself.[136] There is no doubting his special role in Scotland from 1301. There has, however, been much discussion concerning the relationship between John de Soules and John Comyn. It has been suggested that John de Soules was 'an effective substitute for the increasingly controversial Comyn leadership of the national cause',[137] and that the numerous changes in the Guardianship after 1297 inferred that 'John Comyn was an impossible man to get on with'.[138] John of Fordun clearly asserted, however, that 'John Comyn was guardian from 1298 to 1304' and that 'within that same time, John de Soules *was associated with him* by John of Balliol'.[139] This suggests that John de Soules was acting with Comyn rather than instead of him.[140] There is no evidence that two other members of the triumvirate of the Guardians, William Lamberton and Ingram de Umphraville, still acted as Guardians, but they were still actively involved on behalf of the Scottish government in 1302 on an embassy to France.[141] Similarly there is no official record evidence that John Comyn remained Guardian in 1301, but he was certainly sole Guardian in 1302 when John de Soules left Scotland to participate in the Scottish delegation to France.

John de Soules has been seen as a moderating influence between squabbling factions in Scottish politics. He was related to the Comyns but was also a neighbour and friend of the Bruces, members of the de Soules family appearing among the auditors of Bruce the Competitor. However, the Bruces were no longer among the leaders of the political community in Scotland in 1301, though it seems that the 'army of Carrick' was still at the disposal of de Soules and the Scottish patriots late in 1301. It is more probable that Soules, representing Balliol and perhaps appointed through French influence, was seen as the link between Balliol and the Comyn-led Scottish political community. Anyone who wanted to exert influence in the Scotland of the 1290s and 1300s had to seek accommodation with the Comyns because of their landed, political and military power. This was as true for John Balliol in 1301 as it had been for Edward I in the 1290s and as it would be for Robert Bruce in 1306. John de Soules' qualifications for his role as Balliol's special representative were his relationship with the Comyns and, importantly, his recent military success as commander of the Scottish forces which took Stirling in 1300.[142] Soules was an addition to the Scottish political scene rather than, simply, a replacement for Comyn.

John Comyn's active leadership of the political community, both politically and militarily, on behalf of John Balliol was notable between 1302 and 1304. John Comyn was sole Guardian in Scotland from the autumn of 1302 in John de Soules' absence in France. In early 1303 Comyn's role as 'leader and captain'[143] of the Scottish army was recognised when on 24th February, along with Simon Fraser, he defeated an English army at Roslin. After this victory, Comyn was described as Chief Guardian of Scotland. Edward I certainly saw John Comyn as the leader of the political community in Scotland when he made a retaliatory raid after Roslin. He seems to have singled out Lochindorb, a key Comyn of Badenoch base (John Comyn the elder died there c.1302), to use as his own base for imposing his own authority on the north of Scotland in 1303: 'after making some stay there, he received the submission of the northern districts, and appointed officers of his in all the castles and fortified towns surrendered to him'.[144] It is probable that the outer defence work at Lochindorb, a forewall on the south, was an addition of Edward I during this stay.

The Comyns' vast influence, especially in the north, also contributed to the ability of the Guardianships from 1298 to restore a semblance of government and administration in the area of Scotland under Scottish control. Both John Comyn of Badenoch and John Comyn earl of Buchan were holding courts in the north. As Guardian, John Comyn held a court in northern Scotland c.1299–1300 in a case between John de Mowbray and Malise earl of Strathearn.[145] In 1300 John Comyn earl of Buchan was justiciar of Scotia, 'holding pleas of his office near Aberdeen castle, in the place called Castelsyd'.[146] Present were John earl of Atholl, sheriff of Aberdeen, William Meldrum (an ex-sheriff of Aberdeen) and Alexander Comyn brother of the earl of Buchan, and sheriff of Aberdeen on behalf of Edward before 1304. The Guardianship's ability to govern was also indicated by the meeting of parliaments in Scotland. Parliaments were called at Rutherglen in 1300 and Aberdeen in 1302.[147] A range of governmental documents was also issued between 1298 and 1304 from places such as Govan, Torwood, Stirling, Rutherglen, Scone, St Andrews and Inchaffray.[148] Though records are scanty, officials such as chancellor were appointed and paid.[149] Sheriffs, key officials in local administration, were also appointed and are known to have been in existence at Aberdeen, Forfar, Stirling, Lanark and Roxburgh. In 1299 Ingram de Umphraville was appointed sheriff of Roxburgh (he was also to become Guardian at that time), even though there was an English officer in this post.

Control over sheriffdoms had been a key feature of Comyn political control in Scotland prior to 1296. It seems that a large measure of this control had returned between 1298 and 1304, and almost complete control north of the Forth. Control over sheriffdoms meant control over financial as well as military resources of the area. Military resources and the ability to use them successfully played an important part in the membership of the Guardianship in Scotland after 1297. The concentration by fourteenth- and fifteenth-century narratives on the military successes of Wallace and

Bruce between 1297 and 1314, and the cowardice of the Comyns at Falkirk, have prevented a balanced view of the Comyns' military role from 1296. English chroniclers have referred to the cowardliness of the Scottish cavalry in a more general way. It seems from 1296 and 1298 that the Scottish cavalry in general could not match English cavalry. This was again apparent in May 1300 at Cree when three Scottish cavalry brigades, led by John Comyn earl of Buchan, John Comyn of Badenoch and Ingram de Umphraville, took flight.[150] However, to an extent the lessons of Falkirk had been learned. More harrying tactics were adopted and these were quite successful in the period 1299 to 1303 when English control generally was reduced to south-east Scotland and parts of the south-west. The Scottish success in capturing Stirling in 1300 under John de Soules probably played a significant part in his promotion to Guardian in 1301. He continued to play a significant role as military leader until autumn 1302 when he went on an important delegation to France.

The Comyns, i.e. the earl of Buchan and John Comyn of Badenoch, the son, played important roles in the campaigns of 1299 to 1302 which concentrated mainly on the south-west of Scotland. Here the castles of the Comyns of Badenoch (i.e. Dalswinton and Kirkintilloch), of the Comyn earls of Buchan (Cruggleton) and of the Comyns of Kilbride (Kilbride) were important bases from which to attack the English. In 1299 the Scots leaders, including the earl of Buchan, gathered their forces in the north before crossing to Glasgow.[151] From 1300 inroads were made against the English in the south-west – Kirkintilloch and Dalswinton played important roles in the conflict and changed hands on a number of occasions between 1300 and 1302.[152] At one point in the summer of 1301 Dalswinton was used as a base for gathering Scottish support in the area.[153] John Comyn earl of Buchan was active alongside John de Soules in the summer of 1301, their forces lying at Loudoun.[154] When the earl of Buchan went as part of the powerful delegation to Paris in the autumn of 1302, along with John de Soules, James Stewart, Ingram de Umphraville and William Lamberton, John Comyn of Badenoch was left as sole Guardian but also as leader of the Scottish military forces. In this capacity he was very effective in defeating an English force at Roslin, a somewhat underestimated victory, though Fordun recognised its significance:[155]

... there never was so desperate a struggle, or one in which
the stoutness of knightly prowess shone forth so brightly. The
commander and leader in this struggle was John Comyn, the son
... John Comyn, then guardian of Scotland, and Simon Fraser
with their followers, day and night, did their best to harass and
to annoy, by their great prowess, the aforesaid kings officers
and bailiffs ... the aforesaid John Comyn and Simon, with their
abettors, hearing of their arrival at Roslyn and wishing to steal
a march rather than have one stolen upon them, came briskly
through from Biggar to Roslyn, in one night, with some chosen
men, who chose rather death before unworthy subjection to the
English nation; and all of a sudden they fearlessly fell upon
the enemy.

Comyn's success at Roslin was acknowledged by the Scots in Paris as
well as by Edward I. On 25th May 1303 the Scots magnates wrote words
of encouragement to Comyn the Guardian:[156] 'For God's sake do not
despair ... it would gladen your hearts if you would know how much
your honour has increased in every part of the world as the result of
your recent battle with the English [Roslin]'.

Edward's response was to launch the first English campaign against
northern Scotland since 1296. It is notable that this campaign concentrated
on the centre of Comyn power, i.e. north-eastern Scotland. Edward's
route took in key centres of Comyn influence – Aberdeen, Banff and the
private Comyn castles of Lochindorb (which he used as a base to receive
the submission of the north) and Balvenie (Mortlach).[157] It is interesting
to note that Edward did not use the Drumochter Pass, dominated by
Comyn castles. There is no record of resistance to Edward's progress
north although John Comyn was still campaigning in the south of
Scotland, in the autumn of 1303, with as many as 100 mounted men
and 1000 footsoldiers when he raided the Lennox as far as Drymen.[158]
Comyn then returned to his strongholds in the north.

John Comyn was recognised both politically and militarily as leader
of the community of Scotland from 1302 to 1304. It was John Comyn
who led negotiations for the wholesale Scottish submission in January
and February 1304.[159] The major English campaign of 1303 coincided
with the loss of Scotland's main ally, France, by May 1303. The French
army had been beaten by a Flemish force at Courtrai on 11th July
1302, and the ensuing Anglo-French peace, made on 20th May 1303,

excluded the Scots despite the diplomatic efforts of John de Soules, William Lamberton and John Comyn earl of Buchan in Paris. These factors plus the steady flow of important Scottish support to Edward – Robert Bruce in 1302, the Macdougalls (Comyn allies) in 1301, Alexander de Abernethy (also a Comyn ally) in 1302 and William earl of Ross (another Comyn supporter) in September 1303 when he was released from imprisonment in England – led John Comyn, again pragmatically, to try to negotiate the best possible terms from a position of relative military strength. John Comyn seemed to be acting for the Scots in France, i.e. the delegation to the French court, as well as those in Scotland.

The terms of the preliminary offer of submission set out by Comyn show him speaking on behalf of the community of Scotland, requiring, in return for submission, that all the laws, usages, customs and franchises should be kept in all points as they were in the time of King Alexander.[160] These terms have been recognised as being 'the language of the Treaty of Birgham'.[161] The Comyns had been consistently recognised as leaders of the political community in Scotland from the mid-thirteenth century. This leadership continued throughout the difficult years after 1286 and the policy of that leadership remained constant in that period. The Comyns were inextricably associated with the defence of the laws and customs of the Scottish realm. They were the spokesmen for the community of the realm.

NOTES

1. A full discussion of the military symbols of Comyn power, i.e. their castles, will be found in A. Young, 'The architectural lordship of the Comyns' in R. Oram and G. Stell (eds), *Architecture and Lordship in Scotland* 1000–1650 (Tuckwell Press) forthcoming.
2. Young, 'The Earls and Earldom of Buchan in the Thirteenth Century', p.178.
3. G.W.S. Barrow, 'Badenoch and Strathspey, 1130–1312 I Secular and Political', *Northern Scotland* (1988), p.6.
4. *Liber Insule Missarum*, pp.xxix–xxii; *Cal. Close Rolls* (1242–7), p.222.
5. *Chron. Bower* (Watt), V p.373.
6. Barrow, 'Badenoch and Strathspey', p.9; G.W.S. Barrow, 'The Highlands in the time of Robert Bruce', *Kingdom of the Scots*, pp.377–8. A charter of John Comyn II, dated 1289 at Ruthven, refers to his land in the Blair Atholl area (*Coupar Angus Chrs* I pp.134–5).
7. Barrow, 'Badenoch and Strathspey', p.8. John Comyn II died at Lochindorb c.1302. *Chron. Wyntoun* (Laing), II pp.311–12.

8. Barrow, 'The Highlands in the time of Robert Bruce', *Kingdom of the Scots*, p.378.
9. Young, 'The Earls and Earldom of Buchan', pp.187–8.
10. *Aberdeen Reg.* II pp.276–7.
11. *Ibid.* pp.30–34 – the charter, dated 1272, mentions a constable at Kingedward.
12. Young, 'The Earls and Earldom of Buchan', p.185.
13. *Ibid.* pp.188–9.
14. *Ibid.* pp. 1174, 185.
15. S.R.O. RH 6/59.
16. Geoffrey Barrow appropriately described Balvenie as a 'Comyn stepping stone' in 'The Highlands in the lifetime of Robert the Bruce' in *Kingdom of the Scots*, p.378.
17. Ian A.G. Shepherd, *Exploring Scotland's Heritage: Grampian* (1986), no.29, p.89.
18. John Comyn I, lord of Badenoch, was the first 'Red Comyn', a title generally used by the head of the senior, Badenoch, branch of the family. The soubriquet seems to have been derived from the heraldic colour of the Badenoch branch of the family.
19. *Chron. Bower* (Watt), V p.181.
20. *Cal. Docs. Scot.* I no.2678; Annals of Furness in Anderson, *Scottish Annals from English Chroniclers*, p.382.
21. Barrow, *Badenoch and Strathspey*, pp.8–9; *Coupar Angus Chrs* I pp.134–5; S. Cruden, *The Scottish Castle* (1960), pp.57–62; D. Macgibbon and T. Ross, *Castellated and Domestic Architecture* (1887), I pp.70–78; J. Lewis, 'Inverlochy Castle', *Discovery and Excavation, Scotland* (1989), pp.28–9.
22. *Reg. Aberdeen*, I pp.30–34, II pp.276–7.
23. A.E. Truckell and J. Williams, 'Medieval pottery in Dumfriesshire and Galloway;, *Trans. Dumfriesshire Galloway Natural History and Antiquarian Soc.*, 3rd Series, 44 (1966–7), p.133.
24. Young, 'Earls and Earldom of Buchan', p.197; for total value of de Quincy lands in Scotland see G.G. Simpson, 'An Anglo-Scottish Baron of the Thirteenth Century: The Acts of Roger de Quincy, Earl of Winchester and Constable of Scotland' (Edinburgh University Ph.D. thesis, 1965, pp,214–16).
25. *Cal. Docs. Scot.* II no.421; *Cal. Docs. Scot.* I no.2366.
26. Stevenson, *Documents*, I p.393; the thanages of Formartine and Belhelvie granted to Comyn earl of Buchan by John Balliol were worth 250 marks a year, *Aberdeen Reg.* I p.55.
27. *Cal. Docs. Scot.* III no.233.
28. *Ibid.* III no.512. Tarset itself was said to be worth £200 in 1296.
29. *Cal. Pat. Rolls* (1258–66) pp. 198, 551; *Cal. Liberate Rolls* V p.198.
30. G. Stell, 'The Balliol Family and the Great Cause of 1291–2' in Stringer, *Essays on the Nobility of Scotland*, p.157. Edward I demanded a relief of £3,290 for John Balliol's succession to his mother's Scottish lands. The *Lanercost Chronicle* described Dervorguilla de Balliol, King John's mother, on her

death c.1290 as 'a woman eminent for her wealth and possessions both in England and Scotland' (*Chron. Lanercost*, p.72).

31. S. Cruden, *The Scottish Castle*, p.61.
32. See note 21.
33. J.S. Richardson and M.E.B. Simpson, *The Castle of Balvenie, Banffshire* (1961); Ian A.G. Shepherd, *Exploring Scotland''s Heritage: Grampian* (1986), no.29 p.89.
34. *R.C.A.H.M.S.* (1982) p.21 no.59; J. Horne (ed.), *Kirkintilloch by select contributors*, pp. 26, 30, 33.
35. J. Horsley (1732) in *R.C.A.H.M.S.* p.21.
36. *Cal. Docs. Scot.* V p.185.
37. D. Macgibbon and T. Ross, *The Castellated and Domestic Architecture of Scotland*, III p.233.
38. James Ferguson, 'On the House of Comyn', *Buchan Field Club*, Vol. XI (1914) p.76.
39. R.C.A.H.M.S. (Roxburghshire) Vol. I (1956) p.233 no.466.
40. *Cal. Docs. Scot.* II nos. 766, 823, 1816.
41. See note 23.
42. *Exchequer Rolls* I pp.1–51.
43. Stevenson, *Documents*, I pp.247–8, 275, 312; *Rotuli Scotiae* I pp.12b, 17a. Bridburgh appears to be Barburgh where there is a motte and bailey castle (NX892901), referred to as Dinning Motte in *R.C.A.H.M.S.* (Dumfriesshire), no.65. I am most grateful to Mr A.M.T. Maxwell-Irving for this information.
44. *R.C.A.H.M.S.* II pp. 186, 196, 198, 223; III pp. 173, 177, 191; S. Cruden, *The Scottish Castle*, pp.58–62 notes the similarities between Dunstaffnage and the Comyn castles of Lochindorb and Inverlochy.
45. Stevenson, *Documents*, I p.329.
46. P.R.O. SC 1/3/37.
47. G.W.W. Barrow, *Robert Bruce*; E.M. Barron, *The Scottish War of Independence* (2nd edition, 1934).
48. Prestwich, *Edward I*, p.471.
49. Barrow, *Robert Bruce*, p.71.
50. *Ibid.* p.72. Patrick earl of Dunbar married a daughter (Marjorie) of Alexander Comyn earl of Buchan.
51. Stevenson, *Documents*, II p.31.
52. *Chron. Lanercost* p.140 – a theme repeated at the Battle of Falkirk (*ibid.* p.166).
53. Barrow, *Bruce*, p.69.
54. Prestwich, *Edward I*, p.473.
55. *Ibid.* p.471.
56. According to the *Guisborough Chronicle* (p.273), this army numbered 500 cavalry and 40,000 footsoldiers.
57. Gilbert de Umphraville, like Patrick earl of Dunbar, was married to a daughter of Alexander Comyn earl of Buchan. He had attended the royal

court of King John Balliol. He was nevertheless an Englishman. Ingeram de Umphraville was a consistent supporter of the Balliol/Comyn cause.

58. Stones, *Anglo-Scottish Relations*, p.137.
59. *Chron. Fordun* II p.319.
60. Stevenson, *Documents*, I pp.285–6; *Chron. Lanercost* p.131.
61. *Chron. Fordun* II pp. 317–19.
62. *Chron. Lanercost* p.140.
63. Stevenson, *Documents*, p.28.
64. *Chron. Lanercost* p.145. (my italics)
65. *Chron. Fordun* II p,320.
66. Stevenson, *Documents*, II pp.111–12.
67. Prestwich, *Edward I*, p.473. John Balliol had married Isabel, second daughter of John de Warenne earl of Surrey, in February 1281. (Stell, 'The Balliol Family and the Great Cause of 1291–2' in Stringer, *Essays on the Nobility*, p.160.) Edward I undoubtedly sought to use marriage alliances with his own family and those of his key English supporters to influence major baronial families such as Comyn, Balliol, Bruce and Stewart.
68. *Chron. Fordun* II p.319.
69. Stevenson, *Documents*, II p.29.
70. Barrow, *Bruce*, pp.73–4; this was a direct contravention of the rights of the Scots agreed in the Treaty of Birgham, 'the relics, charters, privileges and other muniments which concern the royal dignity and realm of Scotland shall be deposited in a secure place within the realm of Scotland...' Barrow, 'A Kingdom in Crisis', *S.H.R. LXIX* p.139.
71. *Cal. Docs. Scot.* II nos. 839, 848; *Chron. Guisborough* p. 284.
72. *Cal. Docs. Scot.* II no.742.
73. Stevenson, *Documents*, II p.31.
74. C. Neville, 'The Political Allegiance of the Earls of Strathearn during the War of Independence', *S.H.R. LXV* p.138.
75. *Chron. Fordun* II pp.320–1.
76. *Cal. Docs. Scot.* II p.225; Stevenson, *Documents*, II p.100.
77. For full discussion of the English administration in Scotland after 1296 see Fiona Watson, *Scotland under Edward 1296–1307*, unpublished Ph.D. thesis, University of Glasgow, 1991.
78. *Rotuli Scot.* I p.42; Stevenson, *Documents*, II pp. 209–13, 232–3.
79. *Chron. Bower* VI p.81.
80. Stevenson, *Documents*, II p.113.
81. Barrow, *Robert Bruce*, p.80. According to the *Lanercost Chronicle* (p.163), James Stewart and Bishop Wishart were behind William Wallace's revolt.
82. Duncan, 'The Community of the Realm of Scotland and Robert Bruce', *S.H.R.* XLV p.193.
83. *Rotuli Scotiae* I pp.22–3; *C.D.S.* II no.853.
84. Stevenson, *Documents*, II p.190.

85. *Ibid.*
86. Young, 'Noble Families and Political Factions' in Reid (ed.), *Scotland in the Reign of Alexander III*, pp.14–15.
87. *Cal. Docs. Scot.* II no.853 pp.224–5.
88. Barrow, *Bruce*, pp.85–6.
89. Andrew de Moray married the widow of William Comyn of Kilbride before 1289 (*Cal. Docs. Scot.* II no.376).
90. Stevenson, *Documents*, pp.192–4.
91. *Chron. Guisborough* p.295; Barrow, *Bruce*, pp.83–4.
92. Barrow, *Bruce*, p.81.
93. *Chron. Lanercost*, p.163.
94. Barrow, 'A Kingdom in Crisis', *S.H.R.* LXIX (1990) p.137.
95. Stevenson, *Documents*, II pp.167–9.
96. *Ibid.* p.198; Prestwich, *Edward I*, p.476.
97. Stevenson, *Documents*, II pp. 202, 212.
98. *Ibid.* II p.175.
99. *Ibid.* II pp.211–12.
100. *Ibid.*
101. *Rotuli Scotiae* I p.50.
102. Stevenson, *Documents*, II p.207.
103. *Ibid.* p.219.
104. *Ibid.* p.226.
105. *Chron. Guisborough* p.297 as cited in Barrow, *Bruce*, p.344 n.23.
106. John Comyn, the younger was among the Scots who deserted Edward's army c.March 11298 and went to the King of France to plead for his help (Barrow, *Robert Bruce*, pp. 98, 345 n.41.
107. Barrow, *Bruce*, pp.86–9; W. Seymour, *Battles in Britain*, I 1066–1547 (1975), pp. 69–75.
108. Barrow, *Bruce*, p.334 n.23.
109. *Chron. Guisborough* p.306; *Acts. Parl. Scot.* I pp.453–4.
110. *Chron. Guisborough* p.306.
111. *Documents Illustrative of Sir William Wallace, his life and times* (Maitland Club 1841) (Wallace Papers) facsimile as frontispiece; Barrow, *Bruce*, pp.92–3; C.J. McNamee, 'William Wallace's Invasion of Northern England in 1297', *Northern History* XXVI (1990) pp.40–58.
112. *Chron. Fordun* II pp.321–4.
113. *Chron. Lanercost* p.166.
114. *Chron. Fordun* II p.323. Fordun seems, in fact, to have confused the younger Robert Bruce with his father who was with Edward I at Falkirk.
115. *Chron. Bower* (Watt), VI p.240 notes.
116. M. Ash, 'William Lamberton, Bishop of St Andrews, 1297–1328' in G.W.S. Barrow (ed.), *The Scottish Tradition*, Essays in Honour of Ronald G. Cant (1974), p.45.

117. Stones and Simpson, *Edward I and the Throne of Scotland*, II pp.84–5.
118. Ash, 'William Lamberton, Bishop of St Andrews', p.45; *Cal. Docs. Scot.* II no.1017.
119. *Cal. Docs. Scot.* II no.1978.
120. Stones and Simpson, *Edward I and the throne of Scotland*, II p.83.
121. Andrew Fisher, *William Wallace* (1986), pp.86–99; for a letter from the King of France (7th November 1300) recommending Wallace to the Pope, PRO SC 1/30/81, *National Manuscripts of Scotland* I p.XL.
122. *Chron. Fordun* II p.324.
123. S.R.O. GD 137/3679, *Acts. Parl. Scot.* I p.454.
124. *Cal. Docs. Scot.* V no.169.
125. Prestwich, *Edward I*, pp.482–3.
126. *Cal. Docs. Scot.* II no.1978. (my italics)
127. G.O. Sayles, 'The Guardians of Scotland and a Parliament at Rutherglen in 1300', *S.H.R.* Vol XXIV (1927), pp.245–50; *Cal. Docs. Scot.* V no.220.
128. For discussion see N. Reid, 'The kingless kingdom: the Scottish guardianships of 1286–1306', *S.H.R.* Vol LXI p.111; Barrow, *Bruce*, pp.109–12.
129. Barrow, *Bruce*, pp.113–20; Prestwich, *Edward I*, pp.490–6.
130. Barrow, *Bruce*, pp.121–2; Palgrave, *Documents*, I pp.243–4.
131. E.L.G. Stones, 'The Submission of Robert Bruce to Edward I, c.1301–2', *S.H.R.* Vol. 34 (1955), pp.122–34.
132. M. Prestwich, *Edward I*, pp.496–7; Barrow, *Bruce*, pp.121–4.
133. Stones, *Anglo-Scottish Relations*, pp.237–9.
134. *Acts. Parl. Scot.* I p.454 (act of 13th November 1299).
135. Barrow, *Bruce*, p.114.
136. S.R.O. GD 137/3680; *Acts. Parl. Scot.* I p.454; Walter Scott, *Minstrelsy of Scottish Border* (1812) III p.254; Stevenson, *Documents*, II pp.449–50; Stevenson and Wood, *Scottish Heraldic Seals* (1940) I no.22 where the seal of John de Soules appears as a counter seal.
137. M. Lynch, *Scotland, a New History*, p.122.
138. Barrow, *Bruce*, p.114.
139. *Chron. Fordun* II p.324. (my italics)
140. For full discussion of John de Soules' role as either sole or Chief Guardian see Barrow, *Bruce*, pp.114–21; N. Reid, 'The kingless kingdom: the Scottish guardianships of 1286–1306; *S.H.R.* LXI pp.111–13.
141. Barrow, *Bruce*, p.124.
142. *Acts. Parl. Scot.* I p.454.
143. *Chron. Fordun* p.326.
144. *Ibid.* p.328.
145. *Cal. Docs. Scot.* II no.1592.
146. *Arbroath Liber* I no.231.
147. A.A.M. Duncan, 'The early parliaments of Scotland', *S.H.R.* (1966) p.48.
148. Simpson, *Handlist of the Acts of Alexander III. Guardians and John*, nos.415–22.

149. Barrow, *Bruce*, pp. 104–5, 119; *Cal. Docs. Scot.* II nos. 439, 1608, 1978.

150. Barrow, *Bruce*, p.113; for detail of the campaigns see Fiona Watson, *Scotland under Edward I* 1296–1307 (unpublished Ph.D. thesis, Glasgow, 1991), pp.90–91.

151. Stevenson, *Documents*, II p.302; for dating see Barrow, *Bruce*, p.347 n.97.

152. For a detailed survey of the campaigns 1299–1302 see Fiona Watson, *Scotland under Edward I* 1296–1307, unpublished Ph.D. thesis, pp.90–193; for Dalswinton pp. 169–71, 292–3, and Kirkintilloch pp. 188, 194, 301–2.

153. Barrow, *Bruce*, p.121.

154. Stevenson, *Documents*, p.431.

155. *Chron. Fordun* II pp.325–8.

156. *Acts. Parl. Scot.* I pp.454–5 as cited in Barrow, *Bruce*, p128.

157. *Chron. Fordun* II p.328; Barrow, *Bruce*, p.125.

158. Stevenson, *Documents*, II p.486.

159. *C.D.S.* V no.346; Palgrave, *Documents*, 278–88.

160. Palgrave, *Documents*, p.287.

161. Barrow, *Bruce*, p.129.

CHAPTER EIGHT

The Comyn Murder, Bruce Kingship and the Battle of Bannockburn, 1304–1314

On 10th February 1306 Robert Bruce murdered John Comyn in the Greyfriars' church at Dumfries and six weeks later was inaugurated at Scone as king of Scots.[1] The English reaction to these events eventually culminated in the battle of Bannockburn on 23rd–24th June 1314. Bannockburn confirmed Robert Bruce as Scottish king and established his reputation as a military hero against the English. This reputation was further bolstered by the fourteenth- and fifteenth-century narratives of Fordun, Bower, Wyntoun and Barbour who heightened Bruce into a hero of epic proportions, 'a saviour and champion',[2] and emphasised Bannockburn as the climax of a holy war. As a counterpoint to Bruce's role as an epic hero, the Comyns, as rivals of Robert Bruce, were seen as traitors to Bruce in 1306 and disgraceful allies of Edward II. The political reality in 1304 was very different.

It was only in the course of the fourteenth and fifteenth centuries, through the naturally patriotic fervour of post-Bruce writers and after long periods of warfare between England and Scotland, that relations with English kings tended to be seen in simple, polarised terms – heroic resistance or traitorous complicity. In reality, pragmatism, family ambitions and patriotism all played roles for those families involved in the complex power politics of Scotland in the late thirteenth and early fourteenth centuries. These considerations were not mutually exclusive. It was realistic for those in power in Scotland (and wanting to keep it), i.e. the Comyns, as well as those aspiring to political power (and wanting to win it), i.e. the Bruces, to reach mutually beneficial agreements with the

English king and to use the generally recognised military superiority of the English kingdom for their own ends.[3] It is in this contemporary light that the roles of the Comyns and Bruces should be set in 1304 and during the decade after.

In 1304 Robert Bruce had been an ally of Edward I since early 1302,[4] actively participating in Edward I summer campaign of 1303, commanding a garrison at Ayr castle on behalf of the English king in 1303 and early 1304, and sending siege weapons to help the English in the assault on Stirling, the capture of which set the seal on the English military victory in July 1304. The Comyns, on the other hand, were acknowledged in Scotland in 1304 as leaders of the Scottish political community. This was a continuation of a role which they acquired by the middle of the thirteenth century and consolidated further between 1258 and 1286 when they became pillars of Alexander III's monarchy, partners in an alliance of mutual dependence and benefit. After 1286 they naturally defended this position and the position of the monarchy; any infringement of the rights of the Scottish kingdom posed a threat to the dominant political position of the Comyns within that kingdom. It was natural that the Comyns should be behind the more precise and clear definitions of the political and legal rights of that kingdom in both the Treaty of Birgham (1290) and the terms of submission to Edward I in 1304.

The Comyns were pragmatists, however, and not simply patriots. Their survival at the forefront of Scottish political life, through the minority of Alexander III's reign and through the crises following Alexander III's death in 1286, is a remarkable story. In the course of this long period, realism rather than idealism marked their relationship with English kings. The Comyns led Scotland into war with England in 1296 but it is noticeable that the submissions of 1296 and 1304 were completed without the wholesale defeat of the Comyns in battle and without the destruction of their castles, symbols of their political and administrative control of large areas of Scotland, especially north of the Forth. In 1296 it was the Comyns who brought King John Balliol south from Aberdeen to submit to Edward I in July of that year. There was no resistance to Edward I's progress through Scotland after the capture of key members of the Balliol/Comyn government at Dunbar in April 1296. In 1303, the Comyns again did not resist Edward I's next major military expedition north of the Forth which received little opposition after Brechin.

It seems that the Comyns sought to secure the best terms from Edward, starting negotiations in the autumn of 1303 and finally submitting at Strathord on 9th February 1304. John Comyn was negotiating from a position of relative military strength having won a famous victory over the English at Roslin in February 1303. However, the Scottish resistance had lost the potential military support from the French alliance and a number of important Comyn allies had chosen to come to terms with Edward I between 1301 and 1304, for example the Macdougalls in 1301, Alexander de Abernethy in 1302, Alexander de Balliol in 1301 and William earl of Ross in 1303.[5] They joined Richard Siward, who had been in Edward I's service, whether reluctantly or not, since 1297, in the English king's peace.[6] Another important Scot, not a Comyn partisan but a significant supporter of the Scottish war effort, John earl of Atholl, was received to the king's peace in January 1304.[7] The loss of important allies and the loss of the French alliance should be set alongside Comyn concern over Robert Bruce's submission to, and possible political manoeuvrings with, Edward I after February 1302 as well as William Wallace's return to Scotland in 1303.[8] Together, these factors prompted Comyn's final negotiations for the wholesale submission of the Scots in February 1304.

The terms which Comyn sought were not the surrender terms of a defeated leader. They included the well-known demand that the laws, usages, customs and franchises should be kept exactly as they were in the time of Alexander III. An important supplement to this negotiating position was that amendment to these laws, usages, customs and franchises could only be made with the advice of the 'bones gentz' of the land.[9] The Comyns were trying to ensure the continuance of their own influence and the political status quo. This was threatened as Edward was already in practice introducing a patronage system of his own in 1303.[10] The Comyns were in danger of losing their ability to dispense patronage and control important offices of administration.

The Comyns were also in danger of losing their lands and even their freedom, as had happened in 1296. Edward was under pressure from his English supporters in the Scottish wars since 1298 to grant out the lands of his Scottish enemies. In 1301 Edward had, for example, granted to one of his leading military commanders, his cousin Aymer de Valence, £1000 of land in Scotland, i.e. the castle and barony of Bothwell and all the lands belonging to William de Moray.[11] Some of the terms put forward by John Comyn early in 1304 show that Comyn landed interests were as much a part of the negotiations as the interests of the Scottish kingdom. Indeed the first clause of the preliminary terms of submission put forward by Comyn concerned securing life and limb, freedom from imprisonment and the confirmation of lands and property in Scotland, England and Ireland.[12] The Comyns and other Scottish nobles, consistent in their opposition to Edward since 1296, had suffered much from confiscation of their lands. To the Comyns, their lands were the key to their political power in Scotland. The seeking of pardons for acts committed during the war and the request that no hostages should be taken to secure the peace were also issues which were particularly felt by the Comyns and their close adherents who had actively engaged in the war with England since 1296. That John Comyn sought to protect his own family interests and those of his closest allies, the Mowbrays, in the peace negotiations is demonstrated by one particularly blatant clause: John Comyn and John de Mowbray asked Edward I to grant them the lands which John Balliol as king had given to both themselves and their fathers before them.[13]

Edward's reactions to John Comyn's negotiating stance in 1304 is interesting and needs to be set in the context of the Comyns' relationship with the English king since 1296. Edward I refused the particular demands of John Comyn and John de Mowbray, pointing out that they 'have been more concerned to harm and travail the king and his people and have done worse than the others, wherefore they should be more humble: it does not seem at all to the king that they should receive the conditions they ask'.[14] Yet, considering this recognition that the Comyns and their allies had formed the backbone of resistance to Edward I since 1296, Comyn was treated not ungenerously; in fact, he was treated more generously than some. The general terms for the Scots agreed by Edward I were that there would be no loss of life or limb, no imprisonment or disinheritance. For John Comyn there was added the special condition that 'he should retain the lands of his ancient heritage, provided that he be exiled for one year outside Scotland ... for reverence and honour of the king, and to come closer to his good will ... he would not hold land nor anything else without the good wish and will of his liege lords'.[15] Other individuals received harsher terms. James Stewart and John de Soules, in their absence, were to receive two years' exile outside Scotland and south of the Trent; Simon Fraser and Thomas Bois were to receive an exile period of three years not only outside Britain and Gascony but outside the lordship of the King of France. In addition, Wishart the bishop of Glasgow 'for the great evils he has caused'[16] was to be exiled for two or three years outside Scotland. Conditions for the surrender of William Wallace were vague. He was to be received 'to the king's will and ordinance'[17] but it is unlikely that the general conditions agreed by Edward would apply to him.

Negotiations for submission and Edward I's decisions on general and individual terms took place over a period of several months. While John Comyn was leading negotiations for a general submission in January and February 1304, several matters had still to be settled. Scots on the Continent should have submitted by 12th April but James Stewart, John de Soules and Ingram de Umphraville had not yet done so. Stirling castle, under William Oliphant, did not surrender until 24th July 1304. Edward's patience was clearly being stretched by this, and other, lingering resistance. William Wallace was back in Scotland in 1303 and actively resisting. On the day after the siege of Stirling had ended, Edward I ordered John Comyn, Alexander de Lindsay, David Graham and Simon Fraser, all with sentences of exile pending, to prove their loyalty to him in very practical terms. They were told 'to make an effort between now and the twentieth day of Christmas 13th January 1305 to take Sire William Wallace and hand him over to the king *so that he can see how each one bears himself whereby he can have better regard towards the one who takes him, with regard to exile or ransom or amend of trespass or anything else in which they are obliged to the king*'.[18] It was not until October 1305, i.e. after Wallace's capture and death, that final details covering the submission of the Scots were agreed by Edward I. Terms of exile on his most important Scottish opponents who had submitted were replaced by a system of fines. Those who had submitted with Comyn, i.e. in February 1304, were to pay the value of the rents of their lands for three years; those who submitted before Comyn were to pay the value of rents for two years; the Scottish clergy were to pay the value of rents for one year. There were a number of exceptions. Bishop Wishart of Glasgow had to pay three years' rent; Ingram de Umphraville, because of his very late submission to Edward, had to pay five years' rents, and the two knights who returned from the Continent with him, William de Balliol and John Wishart, were to be fined four years' rents.

In terms of property and land, the Comyns had emerged very favourably from the surrender negotiations in 1304 and 1305. Despite their leadership of Scottish resistance to Edward since 1296 and despite their disloyalty to Edward in 1297 when they rejoined Scottish resistance after agreeing to help Edward to curb it, the Comyns were confirmed in their vast landed heritage after payment of a fine. The lands of the Comyn earls of Buchan had been granted to Henry de Percy by Edward I on 29th March 1304 but they were restored to Comyn and his family with the exception of Slains and Balvenie castles on 10th May 1304.[19] James Stewart's lands were not restored to him until November 1305.[20] Unlike William Wallace and Simon Fraser, fellow military leaders fighting on behalf of John Balliol's kingship, the Comyns were never declared outlaws. It can be argued that the Scots who were singled out for harsher treatment in the submission terms were those such as Simon Fraser, Thomas Bois, Herbert Morham and Alexander Lindsay who had been in Edward I's service and had betrayed that trust. The Comyns, however, had also betrayed Edward I's trust. John Comyn lord of Badenoch and John Comyn earl of Buchan, having freed themselves from imprisonment by agreeing to join Edward I's Flanders campaign in 1297, failed to carry out Edward I's instructions to help quell resistance to him in Scotland in the summer of 1297 and rejoined the Scots. John Comyn, the younger, of Badenoch who was on Edward I's Flanders campaign, deserted early in 1298 and sought refuge at the French king's court. Edmund Comyn of Kilbride was also regarded as a traitor in 1298. Among the charges levelled against William Wallace in 1305 was that he convened parliaments in Scotland[21] and that he sought to encourage support for the Franco-Scottish alliance. The Comyns as leaders of the Guardians from 1298 to 1304 had considerable political control at both central and local levels in this period and a number of parliaments were held; they were also to the fore when the alliance with France was initiated in 1295, and John Comyn earl of Buchan was actively involved in seeking the maintenance of the alliance in 1302 and 1303.

Not only in 1304 does there appear to have been a special relationship between Edward I and the Comyns. The Comyns, as dominant figures within the Guardianship which faced the prospect of a civil war stirred up by Robert Bruce, the elder, in 1286, had appealed to Edward I for help then.[22] They had worked with Edward to secure a marriage alliance linking the Maid of Norway to Edward I's heir and appeared to Edward to be the dominant group in Scotland and the one best able to deliver, with his help, a stable country for that union. Following the Maid's death, the Comyns, still dominant within the Guardianship, again sought Edward I's assistance. Such appeals to England should be seen in the context of the practical politics and general co-operation which governed relationships between the two countries in the period up to 1290 rather than in the post-Bruce context of patriotism and nationalism. Edward I, through his agent Anthony Bek, seemed to support the choice of Balliol, the Scottish government's official candidate for the Scottish crown. Even after Comyn resistance to Edward's overly harsh interpretation of his overlordship and infringement of the terms of the Treaty of Birgham after Balliol's enthronement, Edward still sought to influence the Comyns as the power in Scottish government. The marriage of John Comyn, junior, of Badenoch to Joan de Valence, daughter of William de Valence, cousin of Edward I, was surely a part of this strategy. Edward I used marriage alliances with the de Burgh family, his close allies, to cement James Stewart's submission to him in 1296 and Robert Bruce's submission in 1302.[23]

The brother of John Comyn earl of Buchan, Alexander Comyn of Buchan, was also married to Joan, sister of William Latimer,[24] of another English noble family close to Edward I. Manipulation of the Scottish nobility seems to have been a prominent part of Edward I's policy towards Scotland after Alexander III's death. It is perhaps no coincidence that Alexander Comyn of Buchan was one of the most consistent supporters of Edward's cause in his capacity as sheriff of Aberdeen from c.1297–1304. His survival, however, in the heart of an area controlled by his brother and others resisting English control in the area north of the Forth must have been partly condoned by John Comyn earl of Buchan.[25] Even after John Comyn the younger of Badenoch came out openly in favour of Scottish resistance to English government in Scotland, Edward I maintained some contact with him through his cousin, John's wife, Joan. In 1298, Edward ordered his cousin and her son to return to England but in 1299 gave Joan permission to visit her husband in Scotland.[26] It is interesting to note that when John Comyn was negotiating for the submission of the Scots in early 1304, he was negotiating with, among others, his own brother-in-law, Aymer de Valence.[27]

There were, in fact, a number of important factors which contributed to Edward's preference to work with the dominant political force in Scotland, the Comyns, rather than attempt to destroy them. The English king's war with France was undoubtedly at times a greater priority in terms of military and financial resources. His anxiety to commence a campaign in Flanders in 1297 perhaps encouraged Edward to seek Comyn help to quell the rebellions against his English administration in Scotland. In 1298, Edward I was not able to devote military resources to Scotland and follow up the military victory at the battle of Falkirk because of problems in England.[28] The years 1298 to 1302 had allowed the Scots and especially the vast Comyn network of influence to regain political and administrative control over Scotland north of the Forth. It made practical sense for Edward I to seek some *modus operandi* with the dominant governing group in Scotland, the Comyns, in 1304 after he had forced submission by a military march through Scotland. This explains the relative leniency towards the Comyns and their allies in the terms of submission in 1304.

Edward I had not achieved a total military victory over Scottish forces in 1296 or 1303. The north of Scotland, Comyn-dominated territory, was largely out of English control between 1297 and 1303.[29] To attempt a total military conquest of Scotland, a large permanent English presence and new English fortifications, similar to those built in north Wales in the 1270s and 1280s, would be needed. In 1300 Edward I was 'not in a financial position to build new fortifications in Scotland on a scale that he had done in Wales'.[30] The commutation of provisional sentences of exile for Edward's Scottish enemies into large fines based on value of land rents showed his financial priorities. The Comyns had a network of castles throughout Scotland but especially dominating the main communication lines across northern Scotland. It was sensible for Edward to influence the Comyns and use these castles for his own interests instead of building new structures.

As part of the submission of 1304, the Scots had to agree to the ordinances of Edward regarding the settlement of Scotland. The lessons of the period 1298 to 1303, when the administrative system run by the Scottish Guardians, especially in northern Scotland, had been far more effective than Edward's own structure, had been learned. Edward started to appoint more Scots to his new administration in Scotland in 1303 and 1304, rewarding those such as Alexander de Abernethy, William earl of Ross and John earl of Atholl who had come early to his peace.[31] Of the seventeen sheriffs known in 1304, thirteen were Scottish.[32] In the final settlement of 1305, Scots were once more involved in Edward's government and administration.[33] Robert Bruce, Wishart bishop of Glasgow and John de Mowbray were asked to be advisers in the consultation process for the new Scottish constitution. Following their advice, ten representatives were to be elected by the Scottish community of the realm as advisers to the English parliament in framing the ordinances.

According to the 1305 Ordinances, a council of twenty-one Scots – four bishops, four abbots, five earls and eight barons – were to act as the council for Edward's new lieutenant of Scotland, John of Brittany. This council would act alongside the chancellor and chamberlain and the justiciars. Pairs of justiciars, one Englishman and one Scotsman, would be responsible for four areas, Lothian, Galloway, the area between Forth and the Mounth, and the area beyond the Mounth. In the ordinances of 1305 eighteen Scots were named as sheriffs and only two Englishmen. The sheriffs were to be appointed or removed by the lieutenant of Scotland or the chamberlain. Sheriffs had to be 'sufficient men and most profitable for the king and people, and the maintenance of peace'.

The new Scottish constitution could be said to fulfil key aspects of Comyn's submission demands in 1304[34] such as the retention of the laws, customs, usages and franchises of Scotland as they had been in Alexander III's time and that amendments of them could be made only with the advice of the 'bones gentz' of the land. Yet Scotland was no longer regarded in 1305 as a kingdom; it was consistently referred to in the 1305 Ordinances as 'the land of Scotland',[35] and in this sense it could be claimed that there were 'few, if any benefits to the Scots'.[36] The fact is that the settlement was forestalled by Bruce's murder of John Comyn on 10th February 1306 which signalled Bruce's coup. The obvious question to ask in order to understand the events of 1306 is how Comyn and Bruce, in particular, but also other influential families, were affected by the process of Edward I's reorganisation of the government of Scotland?

It is clear that the Ordinances, despite the involvement of Scots at a number of levels, had replaced Scottish kingship and had given Englishmen the reins of real power through the offices of lieutenant chancellor and chamberlain. The main involvement of Scots was at local administrative level through sheriffs. In effect, this meant that Edward had taken over the local administrative system of the Guardians. The aristocratic governing community which had, in tandem with the Scottish monarchy, governed Scotland at both national and local levels from the second half of the thirteenth century onwards and which continued after Alexander III's death under the Guardianship, had come to an end. Names which had dominated Scottish government in this period, Comyn, Stewart, Moray, later joined by Bruce and Soules, were not involved in key executive posts like justiciarships or sheriffdoms. The justiciarships had been the virtual preserve of the

Comyns and their allies in the thirteenth century under Alexander III, King John and the Guardianships. It is interesting to note that of the Scottish co-justiciars in 1305, Reginald Cheyne had already shown his support for Edward I after 1296[37] although the Cheyne family had long been associated with the Comyns. The English co-justiciar with Reginald Cheyne for the area beyond the Mounth was John de Vaux of Northumberland. A John de Vaux was present in John Comyn's council at the 1304 submission at Strathord.[38] The pairing of Cheyne and Vaux would, it seems, have looked favourably on Comyn interests in an area always dominated by the Comyns in the thirteenth century. Other Scots who held the post of co-justiciar in 1305 were Robert Keith, the Marischal, who had submitted to Edward I in 1303, Adam Gordon who had been warden of the west march for the Scots in 1300 and Roger Kirkpatrick, a close associate of Robert Bruce in 1306[39] and a man perhaps who could represent Bruce interests in the south-west. It was very noticeable that Alexander Comyn of Buchan, who had been perhaps the most consistently loyal of Edward I's officials in the north since 1297, held neither a co-justiciarship nor even a sheriffdom in 1305 despite holding the sheriffdom of Aberdeen until 1304.[40]

In reviewing the holders of sheriffdoms in 1305, it is apparent that there is a return to the local families who held these offices under the Guardians. A number were prominent members of Comyn's council at the time of the submission of 1304.[41] Two members of the Ros family were in Comyn's council, Geoffrey and James. Geoffrey, who had experience as sheriff of Lanark under King John, was sheriff of Ayr in 1305 (incidentally replacing Robert Bruce in this office). Two members of the Airth family were in Comyn's council of 1304, Hugh and William. This family, long associated with the Comyns of Badenoch, were rewarded in 1305 with the sheriffdom of Forfar.[42] Walter Barclay, also in Comyn's council of 1304, gained the sheriffdom of Banff in 1305, a sheriffdom long associated with the Comyns of Buchan. It does seem, however, that the Comyns lost control of Aberdeen perhaps as a form of reprimand. Alexander Comyn of Buchan was replaced as sheriff of Aberdeen by Norman Leslie, a loyal supporter of Edward in the north. In the February parliament of 1305, Leslie appealed to the king against the forfeiture of his lands by John Comyn as Guardian and the granting of these lands to Philip de Mowbray, a close Comyn associate.[43] Yet, this apart, many other names closely associated with the Comyns and Comyn-led governments appear in the list of sheriffs of 1305. Thus the

Lochore family, long associated with the sheriffdom of Fife under the Guardianship and John Balliol, were once more sheriffs of Fife through Constantine Lochore. Richard Siward, a loyal supporter of Edward I since 1297 but also a prominent member of the Comyn government prior to 1296, held the sheriffdom of Dumfries in 1305. The Sinclair family, associated with a number of sheriffdoms under the Guardians, were represented in 1305 by Henry Sinclair as sheriff of Lanark. He replaced Robert Bruce in this post. The Mowat family, long associated with the Comyns in the north, retained their hereditary sheriffdom of Cromarty in 1305.

Edward I was determined, however, to ensure that key Scottish castles in the south-east such as Berwick, Roxburgh and Jedburgh were held by his most important English officials.[44] In addition, of the two English sheriffs named in the 1305 Ordinances, Ivo de Aldeburgh held the sheriffdoms of Edinburgh, Haddington and Linlithgow and Robert de Hastings was sheriff of Peebles. Edward also chose to reward loyalty by such as John de Menteith (who captured William Wallace, and became sheriff of Dumbarton in 1305), Norman Leslie, Reginald Cheyne and Richard Siward. Edward seemed content to reinstate the largely Comyn-influenced administration in the north of Scotland.

As for the Council of Ten,[45] Comyn influence was present there too though it should be remembered that this body simply offered advice to the English parliament. John Comyn earl of Buchan was on this council along with John de Mowbray, one of the Comyns' closest supporters in government and one of the three Scottish advisers to Edward I in February 1305. Also present were a number of individuals who had played roles in the Scottish 'cause' against Edward I, for example the bishops of St Andrews and Dunkeld, Robert de Keith, Adam de Gordon and John de Inchmartin, as well as John of Menteith (who replaced the pro-English Patrick earl of Dunbar) and the abbots of Coupar Angus and Melrose. Similarly the lieutenant of Scotland's council of twenty-one barons is perhaps more important for Edward's recognition of who comprised the political community of Scotland in 1305 than for what the council was empowered to do. The lieutenant's council[46] reflected the strong presence of the Comyn family with John Comyn of Badenoch, John Comyn earl of Buchan and their family associates William earl of Ross, John de Mowbray and Alexander Macdougall lord of Argyll.[47] The list included Henry Cheyne, bishop of Aberdeen and from a family associated with the Comyns. Amongst the fourteen secular lords represented in the list, the earls of Buchan, Atholl, Ross and Carrick had been actively involved for most or part of the period after 1296 in opposition to English overlordship though the earl of Dunbar had been consistently on the English side. Of the eight Scottish nobles, John Comyn, John de Mowbray, Alexander of Argyll, Robert de Keith, Adam de Gordon and John de Inchmartin had been mainstays of the Scottish opposition to Edward and Duncan de Frendraught had been one of Edward's officials north of the Forth while John de Menteith had won favour (with the English at least) for capturing William Wallace.

Undoubtedly, both the 1304 submission itself and Edward I's arrangements for a new constitution in the period 1303 to 1305 affected Scottish families in different ways. The Comyns had retained their vast landed inheritance but had lost political power, i.e. decision-making authority at the centre of government, though through their associates they retained local administrative influence especially in the north. Not all Scots welcomed the submission itself. The Scots had not, as in 1296, succumbed to a great military defeat. John de Soules, perhaps the strongest defender of the Balliol kingship after 1301, 'refused the conditions'[48] and does not appear to have returned to Scotland from France. The submission did mean, in practice, an acceptance of English overlordship and an end to the fight (at least for the immediate future) for the Balliol kingship. Robert Wishart, bishop of Glasgow, despite being involved as adviser to Edward in 1305, was punished rather more harshly than others in the surrender terms[49] and may not have supported Comyn's leadership in the submission. He was noticeably absent from the list of ten representatives of the Scottish community of the realm advising the English parliament in 1305 and from the new lieutenant of Scotland's council of advisers. Simon Fraser, having at one stage been declared an outlaw, was still sent into exile after his eventual submission.[50] James Stewart did not have his lands restored to him until November 1305. A number of Scottish nobles had been rewarded by posts of responsibility after submitting between 1301 and 1303, only to be deprived of any responsibility in the final Ordinances of 1305. This applied to Alexander de Abernethy, William earl of Ross, John earl of Atholl and Robert Bruce earl of Carrick. A number of Scottish families, therefore, had grievances of some kind against the new English regime in Scotland.

Robert Bruce had submitted to Edward c.February 1302, almost exactly two years before John Comyn had led the vast majority of

Scots to submission. Bruce had fought for Edward I after 1302, and been made sheriff of Ayr and Lanark in 1303. Although he had been one of the three preliminary advisers used by Edward I to help the English king in the arrangements for a new Scottish constitution, he had no position of responsibility in the Ordinances of 1305 for the government of Scotland, even losing the sheriffdoms of Ayr and Lanark. Bruce was not even recognised as one of the ten representatives of the Scottish community of the realm to the English parliament of 1305 but was one of the twenty-one Scots in the lieutenant of Scotland's council. The Ordinances, as well as confirming Bruce's lack of official authority in Scotland, suggested, too, in one curious clause, a certain lack of faith in Bruce's loyalty: 'Further it is agreed that the earl of Carrick be ordered to put the castle of Kildrummy in the keeping of a man for whom he himself is willing to answer'.[51] Lack of faith in Bruce was already demonstrated in 1303 and 1304 by the greater responsibilities given to John earl of Atholl, William earl of Ross and Alexander de Abernethy after their rather late submissions. Bruce was not even rewarded with land for the support he had given Edward I in the war since 1302.

It is very significant, too, that Bruce's personal circumstances changed dramatically on 21st April 1304 when his father died.[52] He now owned the lordship of Annandale as well as the earldom of Carrick and part of Garioch (see Map 4). He was also acting guardian for his neighbour Donald the young earl of Mar. He had inherited his family claim to the Scottish throne which had been such a strong factor in the internal politics of Scotland since 1286. Bruce inherited this right at a time when the Scottish support for John Balliol's kingship had collapsed with the submission negotiated by John Comyn in 1304.

Hopes of a Balliol kingship may have collapsed but the power behind Balliol, the Comyns and their associates, had by no means been destroyed by Edward I. Edward I's main aim in Scotland, as seen in the 1305 Ordinances, was 'the keeping of the peace and the quiet of the land'[53] and he showed more leniency to the Comyns because he needed their tacit support to help him in the administration of northern Scotland. There had been signs of unrest in Scotland after the submission of 1304. On 11th June Robert Bruce made a secret bond of mutual alliance with Bishop William Lamberton, promising 'to be of one another's counsel in all their business and affairs at all times and against whichever individuals'.[54] Plots were in the air. When William Wallace was captured, documents were found in his possession showing that he had been plotting with the magnates of Scotland. It is not known if Bruce was involved but Bruce's pact with Lamberton showed that Bruce was seeking wider support. The weakness of the Bruces' position in Scotland since 1286 was that they had not a sufficiently wide power-base. The Comyns' position had not collapsed in 1304 and any conspiracy would have to take their power into account. Bruce's plotting and the savage execution of William Wallace on 23rd August 1305,[55] which undoubtedly raised the political temperature in Scotland, form the background to the infamous murder of John Comyn by Robert Bruce in the Greyfriars' church at Dumfries on 10th February 1306.

According to tradition, first recounted by Scottish chroniclers of the fourteenth and fifteenth centuries, Bruce approached John Comyn 'who was then the most powerful man in the country' with his own 'kind hearted plan' to end 'the endless tormenting of the people'.[56] Robert gave Comyn the choice of two courses of action: either Comyn should reign with Bruce gaining all of Comyn's lands or Bruce should become king with all Bruce's lands going to Comyn. According to Fordun, Comyn preferred the latter course and a solemn covenant was made between them but 'John broke his word; and, heedless of the sacredness of his oath, kept accusing Robert before the king of England, through his ambassadors and private letters, and wickedly revealing that Robert's secrets'.[57] After being confronted with his treachery in the Greyfriars' church at Dumfries, 'the evil-speaker is stabbed and wounded unto death'. According to tradition in both Scotland and England, John Comyn was killed in two stages, with Bruce's men returning to the church to finish off the deed. According to Walter Bower,[58] Bruce returned to Lochmaben castle and reported to his kinsmen, James Lindsay and Roger Kirkpatrick, 'I think I have killed John the Red Comyn'. Bruce's men returned to the church to end any doubt that the deed had, in fact, been done, with Roger Kirkpatrick, according to a wholly fabulous tale, exclaiming 'I mak siccar'.[59] The murder of John Comyn was such a dramatic and important event in Scottish history and in its effect on Anglo-Scottish relations that it is hardly surprising that both Scottish and English traditions developed. The Scottish traditions emphasised Comyn's treachery[60] while English propaganda emphasised that the murder was premeditated. According to Thomas Gray, Bruce 'plotted with his two brothers that they should kill the said John Comyn on the way [from Dalswinton to Dumfries].'[61] Comyn, in this tradition, was portrayed (for a short time) as a martyr. More contemporary, though still biased, English accounts certainly give a different angle to the murder and the narrative of Walter of Guisborough deserves some precedence.[62] According to Guisborough, Bruce feared that Comyn would hinder him in his attempt to gain the Scottish throne and sent two of his brothers, Thomas and Nigel, from his castle at Lochmaben to Comyn's castle at Dalswinton, ten miles away, asking Comyn to meet him at the Greyfriars' church, Dumfries to discuss 'certain business'. It seemed that Bruce wanted to put a plan to Comyn, no doubt involving the revival of Scottish kingship with Bruce on the throne. After initially friendly words, Bruce turned on Comyn and accused him of treacherously reporting to Edward I that he (Bruce) was plotting against him. It seems probable that their bitter antagonisms of the past – they had come to blows at a baronial council in 1299 – were instantly revived and in a heated argument mutual charges of treachery were made. It is unlikely that the murder was premeditated. Bruce struck Comyn with a dagger and his men attacked him with swords. Mortally wounded, Comyn was left for dead. Comyn's uncle, Robert, was killed by Christopher Seton when he attempted to defend his nephew. According to both English and Scottish traditions, John Comyn was killed in two stages.

Both English and Scottish sources stress that John Comyn was a major obstacle to Robert Bruce's ambitions in 1306. The situation had been the same, in fact, since 1286. English sources such as the *Guisborough Chronicle* emphasise Bruce's ambitions for the crown[63] and Comyn's faithfulness to the English king to whom he had just done homage. In his report to the pope concerning the English king's charges against William Lamberton, Edward I reported 'Bruce rose against king Edward as a traitor and murdered Sir John Comyn, lord of Badenoch, in the church of the Friars Minor of the town of Dumfries, by the high altar, because Sire John would not assent to the treason which Robert planned to perpetrate against the king of England, namely, to resume war against him and make himself king of Scotland'.[64] John Comyn had come to terms with Edward I in 1304 without suffering military defeat. It is not known if he had lingering ambitions to renew the campaign for the Balliol kingship though he probably did not feel in 1304 that a military campaign against the full force of Edward I's army could be a success without significant support from the king of France. As a practical and pragmatic politician, John Comyn, 'perceiving that he could not withstand the might of the King of England',[65] perhaps realised that the Comyns had more to lose than any other family in Scotland from full-scale war with England. If he had ambitions to renew the fight for the Scottish monarchy in the name of Balliol or even his own family, the time was not yet right. Given the long-term ambition of the Bruces to topple the Comyns from their position in Scottish politics, it is unlikely that the Comyns would co-operate with any plan that Bruce might have for fulfilling his family's long-held claims to the Scottish throne. It is unlikely that loyalty to Edward I was primarily responsible for Comyn's refusal to co-operate with Bruce. The Comyn stance was dictated by the Bruce threat, present since 1286, to their political dominance in Scotland.[66] It was only in the post-Bruce era that the Comyns could be seen as betraying the cause of Scottish independence in 1306. In 1306 Robert Bruce did not have general support in Scotland for his ambitions; he did not yet represent the community of the realm of Scotland, and John Balliol was not dead.

It was most probable that in 1306, or earlier, Robert Bruce was seeking either the support or the compliance of the Comyns. He obviously had plans, no doubt developed with Wishart and Lamberton,[67] to usurp the throne in the light of the failure of the Balliol kingship. These were probably brought forward somewhat because of Comyn's murder. It is unlikely that an enthronement at Scone could be organised six weeks after Comyn's murder unless some preliminary planning had been done. Fordun[68] was probably nearer the truth than Gray[69] when he commented that 'not only did he [Bruce] lift his hand against the king of England ... but he also launched out into a struggle with all and sundry of the kingdom of Scotland, except a very few well wishers of his, who, if one looked at the hosts of those pitted against them, *were as one drop of water compared with the waves of the sea*, or a single grain of any seed with the multitudinous sand'. No doubt Fordun understated Bruce's support to heighten the achievement of his hero, but the events of 1306 show the continuing strength of Comyn power and support in Scotland.

The importance of John Comyn's murder was recognised in both Scotland and England. The fact that the Comyns, to Edward, represented stability in Scotland is reflected in his description of John Comyn's murder as an act 'by some people who are doing their utmost to trouble the peace and quiet of the realm of Scotland'.[70] By 5th April 1306 Edward had appointed Aymer de Valence, Comyn's brother-in-law, as his special lieutenant in Scotland with wide-ranging powers against Bruce and particular responsibility in the east of the country.[71] Henry de Percy was given similar responsibilities in the west. Edward I's personal links with John Comyn were emphasised when he ordered Joan de Valence (his cousin) to send her son, John, John Comyn's son and heir, to England where he was to be in the care of Sir John Weston, master and guardian of the royal children[72]. The alliance between the Comyns and the English kings continued effectively until the battle of Bannockburn. In the Scotland of 1306 the main issue was civil war rather than an Anglo-Scottish one.[73] It was simply a stage beyond the situation in 1286 when the Comyn-led Guardianship appealed to Edward I against the *threat* of a Bruce-induced civil war. In 1306 Robert Bruce had staged a successful coup – the threat was a reality. Bruce, however, still had to assert his authority over the Comyns and their associates. Very few of those put in positions of authority by the 1305 Ordinances supported Bruce in 1306. Of the seventeen sheriffs named in the Ordinances, only three, Walter Barclay, William Mowat (a family long associated with the Comyns in northern Scotland) and Malcolm Innerpeffry joined Bruce in 1306.[74] Comyn support was soon actively involved with Aymer de Valence in the civil war against Bruce.[75] John Comyn earl of Buchan, John de Mowbray, Alexander de Abernethy, Ingram de Umphraville, Edmund Comyn of Kilbride, Richard Siward and William de Balliol were to the fore, as was Adam Gordon and David son of the earl of Atholl. The family support of William earl of Ross and Alexander Macdougall, lord of Argyll, would become prominent in the Comyn cause later in the year.[76]

As in 1286, the Bruces' first military activity was to strengthen their south-west base. Thus the royal castles of Dumfries and Ayr were taken, the Comyn castle of Dalswinton was captured, also the Siward castle of Tibbers.[77] Even in the south-west, however, Bruce was unable to cause the people of Galloway (long influenced by Balliols and Comyns) to support him. He did have early support from Robert Boyd of Cunningham and Robert Wishart, bishop of Glasgow, who 'gave him absolution fully for his sins'[78] and promised him support. At Bruce's coronation there was significant support, according to the *Guisborough Chronicle*, from 'four bishops, five earls and the people of the land'.[79] The traditional role in the ceremony conducted by the earl of Fife was taken by his aunt, Isabel wife of John Comyn earl of Buchan, a notable desertion from the Comyn cause. At the ceremony[80] were the earls of Atholl, Lennox and Menteith and possibly the young earl of Mar (in Bruce's guardianship at the time). Bishops in support of Bruce at that time were certainly the bishops of St Andrews and

Glasgow and probably the bishops of Dunkeld and Moray. Support for Bruce in 1306[81] was also received from Simon Fraser, no doubt aggrieved by his treatment at the hands of Edward I; John de Soules who had shown disenchantment with the submission of 1304; and James Stewart, through his family links with Bruce. In 1306 Bruce also forced support from Malise earl of Strathearn, brother-in-law of John Comyn, earl of Buchan. Other important landowners forfeited by Edward I in 1306 for giving support to Robert Bruce were Walter Logan, Alexander Menzies, Reginald Crawford, Gilbert de la Hay (from a family linked to the Comyns by marriage but, significantly, in fear of loss of land in 1305), Thomas Randolph, Alexander Lindsay and Alexander Scrymgeour (who had served all the Guardians). It is clear that Bruce's support was not just confined to the south-west and that individuals or families dissatisfied with English overlordship or the settlement of 1305 were drifting to Bruce's side. Nevertheless, the fact remained that Bruce had little support from the north where Comyn support was still supreme and where the resources and castles of the earldoms of Buchan, Ross and Sutherland and the lordships of Badenoch (with Lochaber) and Argyll were formidable. These resources when combined with English dominance in the south, and further supported by Comyns and their associates in the south and south-west, gave the Comyn/English alliance military superiority. Edward I moved north to add his support. Obviously a sick man, he stayed for a while in the Comyn town of Newbrough near Hexham.[82]

The English and Comyn forces achieved early success. Bishop Lamberton, who apparently made overtures of surrender in June 1306, was arrested along with Bishop Wishart and imprisoned in southern England.[83] Aymer de Valence routed Bruce's forces at Methven near Perth in June 1306.[84] Bruce met a second defeat at Dalry in the borders of Argyll by John Macdougall of Argyll. Kildrummy castle (Mar) was captured in September. Bruce's wife and other royal ladies were captured by William earl of Ross. Also captured were John earl of Atholl, Simon Fraser and Neil Bruce. Fraser was drawn, hanged and quartered in London and his head placed on a pole beside that of Wallace at London Bridge. The earl of Atholl, Neil Bruce and many others suffered similar fates.[85] Robert Bruce's sister, Mary, and Isabel countess of Buchan were lodged in cages within the towers of Roxburgh and Berwick.[86]

Bruce's military resistance had to be abandoned and he fled the mainland to spend over four months in exile, possibly in Ireland, the island of Rathlin and the Hebrides.[87] Although the renewed military campaign opened badly in 1307 with the capture of his brothers Thomas and Alexander Bruce in Galloway – they were hanged and beheaded at Carlisle[88] – Bruce's fortunes were revived in April and May by victories over English forces at Glen Trool and Loudoun Hill, near Kilmarnock.[89] These victories, rather like the victories of Andrew de Moray and William Wallace in 1297, seem to have brought Bruce immediate popular support. On 15th May a Scottish lord on the English side wrote:

> I hear that Bruce never had the good will of his own followers
> or of the people generally so much with him as now. It appears
> that God is with him, for he has destroyed the King Edward's
> power among English and Scots. The people believe that Bruce
> will carry all before him ... I fully believe, as I have heard
> from Reginald Cheyne, Duncan of Frendraught and Gilbert of
> Glencarnie, who keep the peace between the Mounth and on
> this side, that if Bruce can get away in this direction or towards
> the parts of Ross he will find the people all ready at his will
> more entirely than ever, unless King Edward can send more
> troops for there are many people living loyally in his peace so
> long as the English are in power. May it please God to prolong
> King Edward's life, for men say openly that when he is gone the
> victory will go to Bruce.[90]

The *Lanercost Chronicle* too commented that, despite the cruel repression of Bruce's followers in 1306, 'the number of those willing to strengthen him in his kingship increased daily'.[91] On 13th March 1307 Edward I himself showed an awareness of the possible reasons behind support for Bruce: 'As some persons, he understands, interpret his late ordinance for settling Scotland as too harsh and rigorous, which was not his intention, he commands him to proclaim throughout Scotland, that all who have been compelled by the abettors of Robert de Brus to rise against the king in war, or to reset Robert innocently by his sudden coming among them, shall be quit of all manner of punishment therefor'.[92]

The movements of the increasingly confident Bruce after September 1307 – encouraged no doubt by his own victories and Edward I's death on 7th July 1307 at Burgh-on-Sands – were aimed at the strongholds of the Comyns and their associates in northern Scotland. As previous Scottish kings had discovered, their kingship could not be secure without control over northern Scotland. Bruce and his army headed first towards Inverlochy, in late September 1307.[93] Inverlochy was, perhaps, the most advanced of Comyn's northern castles architecturally and held a key strategic site at the south end of the Great Glen. Bruce attacked it by land and sea and the castle was taken sometime in October, the process no doubt aided by the truce agreed between Bruce and the Comyns' main allies in the north, the Macdougalls. Inverness and Castle Urquhart were then taken. Castle Urquhart had been under the control of Alexander Comyn in 1304. William earl of Ross, another Comyn associate, was also frightened into a truce by the rapid movement of Bruce's forces. Bruce's progress in the north was apparently aided by the absence of Reginald de Cheyne, warden beyond the Mountains. Bruce then moved north to attack Elgin and Banff. His progress was halted by illness and by the forces of John Comyn, earl of Buchan, John Mowbray and David of Strathbogie, earl of Atholl[94] who came to the aid of Duncan Frendraught sheriff of Banff. The earl of Buchan's force met Bruce's force at Slioch near Huntly on 31st December 1307 but withdrew because of the apparent strength of Bruce's army.[95] Bruce then moved towards the key Comyn of Buchan castle of Balvenie which linked the lordship of Badenoch with the earldom of Buchan. Bruce next attacked the Cheyne castle of Duffus and then moved further west to Tarradale castle in the Black Isle. (Alexander Comyn of Buchan had held this castle, with Urquhart, in 1304.) John Mowbray rescued Elgin from a second attack by Bruce. On 22nd May Bruce defeated the earl of Buchan at the battle of Inverurie[96] (between Inverurie and Oldmeldrum). According to Fordun, 'when the rout was over, and the enemy was overthrown and scattered, King Robert ravaged the earldom of Buchan with fire'. This was the famous 'herschip' of Buchan, made well known by Balfour's description:[97]

> Now ga we to ye king agayne
> Yat off his wictory was rycht fayn,
> And gert his men bryn all Bowchane
> Fra end till end, and sparyt nane,
> And heryit tham on sic maner
> Yat eftir yat weile fyfty zer
> Men menyt ye herschip off Bouchane.

Presumably the 'herschip' paid particular attention to the visible symbols of Comyn lordship at Dundarg, Slains,[98] Cairnbulg, Rattray, Kingedward and Ellon, the manor house at Kelly and the abbey at

Deer. Bruce's campaign in Buchan was matched by his brother Edward's campaign in Galloway.[99] Bruce had won the north (except for Banff, and for a time, Aberdeen) and the earl of Buchan was forced to flee south. William earl of Ross submitted to Bruce and promised to serve him faithfully.[100] Both the earl of Ross and the Macdougalls of Argyll[101] seem to have lost the support of their barons in the face of Bruce's successes. The Macdougalls were defeated at the battle of the Pass of Brander c.August 1308 and eventually surrendered the castle of Dunstaffnage and other castles including Loch Awe. The Macdougalls eventually fled to seek aid from the English.[102] The opposition to Bruce, the Comyns and their associates, had been driven out of their main bases in Buchan, Badenoch, Argyll and Galloway and were now dependent on the English in their Lothian base.

It would be a mistake to suggest that the Scottish civil war was over by 1309 and that the years 1309[103] to 1314 saw a concentration in Scotland on the war with England building up to the decisive battle of Bannockburn. The opposition to Bruce, largely the remnants of the Comyn party, was still in existence and could claim to be the community of the realm in 1309.[104] David, earl of Atholl, Alexander de Abernethy, John Macdougall of Argyll, Ingram de Umphraville, David Graham and Edward Comyn of Kilbride, on behalf of John Comyn, attended the English parliament 1312–13, on the affairs of Scotland. This was, very much, the core of the Comyn government in exile.[105]

Robert Bruce, however, could, by 1309, begin to use his control of Scottish government to strengthen the national and international acceptance of his own kingship. Opposition to his kingship and the fact that John Balliol was still alive (he died in 1313) meant he *needed* to justify his position. The king of France still acknowledged John Balliol as king of Scotland in April 1308 though he recognised Robert Bruce as king by July 1309.[106] From 1308, when there is first evidence of Robert Bruce's *acta*, there is a conscious attempt by Bruce to refer to himself as successor to Alexander III and completely ignore any reference to John Balliol.[107] Bruce had, of course, issued acts in the name of King John, during his joint Guardianship with John Comyn in 1299. In 1309, it was still politic either to ignore the Balliol kingship completely or explain it away as the declarations of the St Andrews parliament, Bruce's first parliament, of 1309 tend to do.[108] The St Andrews parliament solemnly upheld Robert Bruce's right to the throne and saw a declaration of support for Bruce from both magnates and clergy. The Declaration of the Clergy was, above all, a propaganda document for Bruce and against Balliol.[109] For the first time, it was declared that Balliol was imposed by English force on the Scots, a belief perpetuated and strengthened by the powerful patriotic narratives of the later fourteenth and fifteenth centuries. The 1309 Declaration turned Balliol into a villain: 'the realm of Scotland was lost by him and reduced to servitude ... for lack of a captain and a faithful leader'. In contrast Bruce 'by right of birth and by endowment with other cardinal virtues is fit to rule, and worthy of the name of king and the honour of the realm'. It should be pointed out that this St Andrews Parliament lacked the presence of families who had been the mainstays of Scottish government in Alexander III's reign and after, the Comyns, and their associates in the 1290s, Mowbray, Abernethy, Balliol, the earls of Atholl and Angus, David of Brechin and Adam Gordon.[110]

It is in this context that the relationship between the Comyns, representing a government in exile, and the English between 1308 and 1314 should be studied. After the murder of John Comyn of Badenoch, the most senior member of the Comyn family was John Comyn earl of Buchan. When Robert Bruce attacked the earldom of Buchan, the Comyns of Buchan and their supporters were acting as representatives of Edward II.[111] Buchan had been a Scottish royal base from c.1212 but in 1308 it was one for the English king. This made the 'herschip' of Buchan even more inevitable after Comyn's defeat at Inverurie. After the Comyn hold over northern Scotland had been removed, John Comyn earl of Buchan was appointed by Edward as joint warden of the western marches, Annandale, Carrick and Galloway, in June 1308.[112] He died shortly afterwards between 11th August and 3rd December.[113] The deaths of the two senior members of the Comyn family in 1306 and 1308 and the removal of Comyn dominance over northern Scotland in 1308 meant, in effect, the end of the Comyns as a political force in Scotland.

The years after 1308 merely underlined this fact as the vast amount of land held by the Comyns in Scotland, the basis of their political influence for nearly one hundred years, was divided up among Bruce's supporters. Key Bruce supporters received the biggest share. Thus the lordship of Badenoch was included in Thomas Randolph's earldom of Moray (1312); Thomas Randolph also received the lordship of Nithsdale.[114] Walter Stewart and Robert Boyd divided Dalswinton between them while Walter Stewart also gained the barony of Kilbride.[115] James

Douglas gained Bedrule in the Teviot valley;[116] Malcolm Fleming, the barony of Kirkintilloch; Walter fitz Gilbert, Machan in the Clyde Valley; William Oliphant, the lands of 'Gaskenes' (Findogask) and 'Uchtertyre' (Ochtertyre) in Perthshire.[117] The significance of the earldom of Buchan was emphasised by Bruce's infeftments for military service of key supporters and government officers including Robert Keith the marischal and Gilbert Hay the constable. Not all of the earldom of Buchan was forfeited to the crown. Margaret Comyn and her husband John of Ross, brother of Hugh earl of Ross (a brother-in-law of Robert Bruce), gained half of the earldom as Margaret was one of Earl John Comyn's two co-heirs, daughters of his brother, Alexander. This part later became the baronies of Kingedward and Philorth.[118] The other half of the earldom was forfeited to the crown as the other co-heiress, Margaret's sister Alice, had married Sir Henry Beaumont and thus became thoroughly English in allegiance. The main grants of forfeited land made by Robert Bruce as king were the barony of Aden, to Robert Keith the marischal; the barony of Kelly to the marischal's brother, Edward Keith; the barony of Crimond or Rattray to Archibald Douglas; and the barony of Slains to Gilbert Hay.[119] The vast estates of the Comyns of Buchan elsewhere in Scotland were likewise divided up amongst Bruce supporters. Alexander Seton gained the lands of Myles, Elphinstone and Tranent in the sheriffdom of Edinburgh; Thomas Hay received a third part of the land of Leuchars; John de Kynmonth was granted the lands of Kirk in the sheriffdom of Dumfries; Isabel countess of Atholl and Alexander Bruce, her son, received the lands of Culvend and the tenement of 'Sannaykis' in Kelton; Robert Wallace gained Durris in the sheriffdom of Kincardine; and John of Strathhenry received the lands of 'Bellachis' in Fife.[120]

With the vast estates of the Comyns of Buchan, Badenoch and Kilbride distributed among Bruce's supporters, Robert Bruce could afford to be lenient with lesser landowners who had supported the Comyns and even lesser members of the Comyn family itself. Robert Bruce granted land to Walter Comyn, a lesser-known member of the family, possibly the Walter Comyn of Peeblesshire referred to in 1296.[121] Bruce, after 1314, ensured that the widow of Edmund Comyn of Kilbride was provided for 'until she can recover her rightful dower according to the assize of the land'.[122] She was granted the lands of 'Cullenachy' and 'Salhope' in Aberdeenshire.

The political circumstances of 1306 and 1308 drove several members of the Comyn family to England where they gained some compensation for their losses in Scotland. In 1312 Edward II, 'considering the services of John Comyn of good memory to his late father, that he was slain for his fidelity and that John his son had served the late king and now himself constantly, whereby his lands have been ruined by the rebels in Scotland', granted him the manor of Mansfield in Nottingham, the soke and farm of Lindeby and the mills of Carbelton (£54 4s), the manor of Harewell in Berkshire (£30) and the manor of Geddington in Northampton (£52) 'in aid of his expenses and sustenance'.[123] It was undoubtedly with English military aid that John Comyn, son of the John Comyn killed in 1306, was still in possession of his castle at Dalswinton between 1311 and 1312.[124] As for the Buchan branch of the family, Joan, widow of Alexander Comyn of Buchan (Earl John's brother), was granted the manor of Flaxflete in Yorkshire in 1311 'in aid of her maintenance'. This land had been granted to her 'as her lands in Scotland were lost through the war'.[125] Sometime shortly after 1311 Joan, hearing that the manor was to be taken out of her hands, petitioned the king, saying that she had nothing else to live on, and begging him to give it to her for four or five years for its extent. She also begged help, at his pleasure, for the loss of her lands in Scotland, more than £500 yearly for her support for she would rather lose them than live among the king's enemies there.[126] Edward did, in fact, grant her the lands in lease. As for Alice Comyn, one of the two co-heiresses of John Comyn, earl of Buchan, she and her husband Henry Beaumont received their share of the Buchan inheritance in England.[127] Henry Beaumont also received custody of the property of the other Buchan co-heiress, Margaret, in Whitwick (Leicestershire) and all her other lands in 1312. He was also considered in England to be the rightful constable of Scotland in right of his wife, Alice.[128]

Edmund Comyn of Kilbride still held lands in Hertfordshire in 1310 but he had been ousted from his Scottish lands 'by the enemy' and was living on his Northumberland lands near Berwick in 1313.[129] All three branches of the Comyn family depended totally on English support after 1308, if their land and power in Scotland were to be restored. It has been noted how closely connected the Comyns were by marriage to the English royal family and leading English noble families by the end of the thirteenth century. John Comyn of Badenoch (d.1306) was married to Joan de Valence, daughter of William de Valence (and sister to Aymer de Valence) and cousin to the English king. Alexander Comyn of Buchan married Joan, sister of William Latimer. Aymer de

Valence and William Latimer were at the forefront of English military campaigns against Scotland. Alice, niece and co-heiress of John Comyn earl of Buchan, also married Henry Beaumont. The English certainly recognised the importance of the Comyns in the 1290s and were actively pursuing a policy of trying to bind the family to English interests through marriage alliances.

It is a mistake to regard the outcome of Bannockburn as inevitable and from a Comyn perspective a last vain hope for them to resume their place in Scottish political society. It is apparent that Bruce had little faith in defeating English forces in a pitched battle. The years before 1314 were filled with dour fighting rather than preparation for a decisive pitched battle.[130] The Comyn castle of Kirkintilloch was in English hands in 1309 and Dalswinton was in either English or John Comyn's hands after Robert Bruce's defeats and flight in 1306 until 1311–12. The Macdougalls were encouraged to use their fleet against the Hebrides and Argyll and were made 'admiral and captain' of a special fleet in 1311.[131] Philip Mowbray held Stirling in 1313 and it was in the attempt to relieve the siege of Stirling that Edward II gathered a large army in the summer of 1314. In this army there were Aymer de Valence and Henry Beaumont, both Comyn relatives; Scots present included John Comyn, son and heir of the murdered Comyn of Badenoch, Edmund Comyn of Kilbride and the Comyn associate and former Guardian Ingram de Umphraville, as well as Robert de Umphraville earl of Angus.

The battle of Bannockburn was fought over two days, on 23rd–24th June 1314 and, as is well known, resulted in a decisive defeat for the English forces. According to the *Lanercost Chronicle*: 'In the leading division were killed the Earl of Gloucester, Sire John Comyn, Sir Pagan de Typtoft, Sir Edmund de Mauley and many other nobles besides footsoldiers who fell in great numbers'.[132] John Comyn's prominence in the English army is clear. Edmund Comyn of Kilbride was also killed in the battle.[133] The death of the chief of the Badenoch line of the Comyn family, followed two years later, in 1316, by the death of his son and heir, Adomar,[134] while still a child, meant the end of the male line of the Comyns of Badenoch. With hindsight, we can see that Bannockburn saw the end of English attempts to conquer Scotland and an end to Comyn ideas of returning to territorial and political power in Scotland. The situation was not quite so clear-cut at the time. In 1315 Joan widow of Alexander Comyn of Buchan was granted the manor of Malton to be held 'till she recovers her lands in Scotland'.[135] She did, in fact, go to Scotland in 1320 'to treat for restitution of her lands'.[136] On Edmund Comyn's death in 1314, the king allowed Maria his widow her terce from his lands of Magna Fakenham in Suffolk, Savecampe in Hertfordshire and Newham near Bamburgh in Northumberland.[137] Her lands were seized, however, and granted to William de la Beche 'as the widow adheres to the Scots'.[138] Maria later petitioned the king for the return of her lands, saying that she was obliged to leave Northumberland and dwell among her friends in Scotland to save herself from starvation.[139]

Comyn political fortunes from the mid-twelfth century had rested on their landed acquisitions. The family's Tynedale lands acquired c.1150 were the family's first major territorial acquisitions, and from this base in Northumberland the family acquired landed power in southern Scotland and especially northern Scotland to become the most powerful nobles in thirteenth-century Scotland. In 1316 their Tynedale lands were an excellent barometer of their faded fortunes. The inquisition on the death of Adomar Comyn, the last of the male Badenoch line, in 1316, found that Adomar 'died seized of the manors of Tyrsete, Hethyneshlach, Thorntoun and Walwyck ... They return nothing at present but were once worthy 500 marks per annum'.[140] Landed wealth had been the essential foundation for the Comyns' lengthy spell at the forefront of thirteenth-century Scottish politics. The 'harrying' of Buchan had brought an end to Comyn viceregal powers in northern Scotland. Their cause was weakened by the untimely deaths of leading members of the family in 1306, 1308, 1314 and 1316. The battle of Bannockburn and its aftermath destroyed any hopes of a revival in the family's political fortunes, and in that sense was more important for its impact on the Scottish civil war than the Anglo-Scottish war.

Bannockburn effectively ended the Comyn century in Scottish history from c.1212 to 1314 though it did not end opposition to Bruce or the need for Bruce to use propaganda to secure his position further. The great narratives of the fourteenth and fifteenth centuries further heightened the achievements of Robert Bruce, and the Comyns have suffered the most from this. Their political leadership from the mid-thirteenth century helped to develop and strengthen the territorial, political and constitutional position of the Scottish monarchy. Their partnership with that monarchy – an alliance of mutual self-interest – naturally led to their leadership of the Scottish political community after Alexander

III's sudden death. They helped to bring the notion of the community of the realm into the open after 1286 and especially in 1290 at the Treaty of Birgham when that concept was given political value and real definition. Comyn leadership of the Scottish political community continued in exceptionally difficult political circumstances, despite challenge in near civil war as well as in warfare with England. It was, perhaps, Robert Bruce's greatest achievement to overcome a well-entrenched and Comyn-led political establishment in Scotland and thus bring to an end the Comyn century. Bannockburn and the subsequent patriotic narratives of the fourteenth and fifteenth centuries have had the effect of enhancing Bruce's reputation to the point where the Comyns' significant contribution to Scottish political identity and nationhood has been overshadowed and neglected. The Comyns were rather more than treacherous rivals of Robert Bruce.

NOTES

1. T.M. Smallwood, 'An unpublished early account of Bruce's murder of Comyn', *S.H.R.* LIV (1975) 1–10; *Chron. Guisborough* pp.366–7; *Chron. Fordun* II p.333.
2. *Chron. Fordun* II p.330.
3. A similar recognition was made by Comyns and Durwards in the 1250s – see ch.3; Bruce Webster, review article 'Anglo-Scottish Relations, 1296–1389: Some recent essays', *S.H.R.* LXXIV, April 1995 p.105.
4. *Cal. Docs. Scot.* II nos. 1303, 1356, 1465, 1548; Barrow, *Bruce*, pp.141–2.
5. *Cal. Docs. Scot.* II nos. 1204, 1226, 1395, 1463, 1631.
6. *Ibid.* no.1307.
7. *Ibid.* II no.1440.
8. A. Fisher, *William Wallace*, pp.100–111.
9. Palgrave, *Documents*, p.287.
10. *Cal. Docs. Scot.* II nos. 1287, 1395, 1420, 1437, 1631, 1694. For full discussion of Edward I's settlement of Scotland, 1303–5, see Fiona Watson's forthcoming essay in *Thirteenth Century England* VI. I am most grateful to Dr Watson for letting me see this essay in advance of publication.
11. *Ibid.* II no.1214.
12. Palgrave, *Documents*, p.286.
13. *Ibid.* p.287.
14. *Ibid.* p.278.
15. *Ibid.* p.280.
16. *Ibid.* p.284.
17. *Ibid.*
18. *Ibid.* p.276. (my italics)
19. *Cal. Docs. Scot.* II no.1487; Palgrave, *Documents*, pp.288–91.
20. Stevenson, *Documents* II pp.454–6.

21. Barrow, *Bruce*, p.137.
22. See chapter 5, passim.
23. Barrow, *Bruce*, pp.113–14, 141.
24. *Cal. Docs. Scot.* III no.233.
25. Alexander Comyn of Buchan held land in the sheriffdom of Edinburgh 'by gift of John earl of Buchan', his brother, *Cal. Docs. Scot.* IV no.1399. He also held 'Inrafan' in the north from his brother, *Cal. Docs. Scot.* II no.1617. 'Inrafan' was evidently Inverfeoran, i.e. Dingwall. See E. Beveridge, *The Abers and Invers of Scotland* (1923), p.68. This land went with Tarradale; see note 40 below. I am most grateful to Professor G.W.S. Barrow for supplying this information on 'Inrafan'.
26. *Cal. Pat. Rolls.* (1292–1301), pp. 337, 395.
27. *Cal. Docs. Scot.* no.1393.
28. Prestwich, *Edward I*, ch.18, only ; *The Scottish Wars* 1296–1307, pp.483 ff.
29. In general see Fiona Watson, *Scotland under Edward I* 1296–1307, unpublished Ph.D. thesis (Glasgow Univ., 1991).
30. Prestwich, *Edward I*, pp.497–8.
31. *Cal. Docs. Scot.* II nos. 1395, 1440, 1592, 1631, 1682, 1689, 1694.
32. *Cal. Docs. Scot.* II nos. 1474, 1514, 1586, 1646 – for full discussion see Fiona Watson, *Scotland under Edward I* 1296–1307 (unpublished Ph.D. thesis), pp.390–92.
33. Stones, *Anglo-Scottish Relations*, pp.241–59; Palgrave, *Documents*, p.293.
34. Barrow, *Bruce*, p.133.
35. Stones, *Anglo-Scottish Relations*, pp. 245, 25, 255, 257.
36. Prestwich, *Edward I*, p.515.
37. *Cal. Docs. Scot.* II no.1737.
38. *Ibid.* II no.1741. Both John Comyn of Badenoch and John de Vaux were Northumberland landowners (Stones, *Anglo-Scottish Relations*, p.245). The John de Vaux present at Strathord may have been the lord of Dirleton.
39. *Chron. Bower* (Watt), VI p.311.
40. *Cal. Docs. Scot.* II no.1617. Alexander also held the important castles of Urquhart and Tarradale in 1304 and was granted control of Aboyne before David, earl of Atholl, objected (*ibid.* no.1633). Alexander seems to be dead by 1308.
41. *Ibid.* II no.1741.
42. For sheriffs of 1305, Stones, *Anglo-Scottish Relations*, p.247.
43. *Memo. de Parliamento no.* 296. The case is discussed in Watson, *Scotland under Edward I* 1296–307, p.261.
44. Stones, *Anglo-Scottish Relations*, p.249. Berwick would be the English headquarters and the king's lieutenant himself would control Roxburgh and Jedburgh.
45. *Ibid.* pp.241–2.
46. Palgrave, *Documents*, p.293.
47. Patrick, earl of Dunbar, was also related to the Comyns by marriage.
48. Gray, *Scalacronica*, p.127.
49. Palgrave, *Documents*, pp. 276, 284.
50. *Ibid.* p.281.

51. Stones, *Anglo-Scottish Relations*, p.255.
52. Barrow, *Bruce*, pp.142–3. Barron argued that Bruce had fallen from favour. E.M. Barron, *The Scottish War of Independence* (1934), pp.172 ff.
53. Stones, *Anglo-Scottish Relations*, p.255.
54. Palgrave, *Documents*, pp.323–5; Barrow, *Bruce*, p.131. There was unrest in Scotland after the submission of John Comyn in February 1304. James Stewart, John de Soules and Ingram de Umphraville had not submitted by 12th April (*ibid.*, 276). Stirling castle was not captured until July 1304. When Wallace was captured, documents were found on him linking him in 'confederations' with unspecified Scottish nobles (Barrow, *Bruce*, p.139.)
55. Barrow, *Bruce*, pp.136–7.
56. *Chron. Fordun* II p.330. According to Bower, this approach took place in 1304. (*Chron. Bower* (Watt), VI p.303); see also Barbour's *Brus* I, 484 cited in A.A. Duncan, 'The War of the Scots', *Transactions of the Royal Historical Society* (1992), p.135. Comyn could also put forward a claim to the throne.
57. *Chron. Fordun* II p.331.
58. *Chron. Bower* (Watt), VI pp.311–13.
59. Barrow, *Robert Bruce*, p.148.
60. Bower emphasised Comyn treachery to Bruce but added the interesting detail, 'I have found elsewhere that John the Red Comyn was the first to persuade the said Robert Bruce to assume royal power' (*Chron. Bower* (Watt), VI p.309).
61. Gray, *Scalacronica*, p.29.
62. *Chron. Guisborough*, pp.366–7.
63. *Ibid.* p.366.
64. Palgrave, *Documents*, p.335, translated in Barrow, *Bruce*, pp.140–41.
65. Gray, *Scalacronica*, p.25.
66. Bruce questioning of the Comyn leadership of the political community of the realm was clearly stated in the Appeal of the Seven Earls (1290–91). Stones, *Anglo-Scottish Relations*, pp.89–101.
67. *Ibid.* pp.271–9.
68. *Chron. Fordun* II p.333. (my italics)
69. According to Gray, *Scalacronica*, p.28, Robert Bruce 'retained a strong following through kinsmanship and alliance'.
70. *Cal. Docs. Scot.* II no.1747.
71. M. Prestwich, *Edward I*, p.506.
72. *Cal. Docs. Scot.* II no.1798.
73. A.A.M. Duncan, 'The War of the Scots', *T.R.H.S.*, pp. 125–7, 135–6.
74. Palgrave, *Documents*, pp.301–19.
75. Stones, *Anglo-Scottish Relations*, pp.261–9; Gray, *Scalacronica*, p.31; *Chron. Lanercost*, pp.176–7.
76. *Chron. Fordun* II pp.334–5.
77. Stones, *Anglo-Scottish Relations*, pp. 261, 267.

78. *Ibid.* p.267.
79. *Chron. Guisborough* p.367.
80. *Ibid.*; Barrow, *Robert Bruce*, pp.150–2.
81. *Ibid.* pp.154–9, 325–8; C. Neville, 'The Political Allegiance of the Earls of Strathearn', *S.H.R.* LXV, pp.142–4.
82. *Chron. Lanercost*, p.181.
83. *Ibid.* p.178; Stones, *Anglo-Scottish Relations.* pp.271–9.
84. *Chron. Fordun* pp.334–5.
85. *Chron. Lanercost* p.179; Gray, *Scalacronica*, pp.32–3; *Chron. Fordun* p.335.
86. Gray, *Scalacronica*, p.31; M. Prestwich, *Edward I*, pp.508–9.
87. *Chron. Fordun* II p.335. 'left alone in the islands'; *Chron. Lanercost* p.178, 'lurking in the remote isles of Scotland'; Barron, *The Scottish War of Independence*, ch.XXII, 'The Mystery of the Island of Rathlin', pp.248–59; Barrow, *Bruce*, pp.164–71.
88. Gray, *Scalacronica*, p.34.
89. Barrow, *Bruce*, p.172.
90. *Ibid.* pp.172–3; *Cal. Docs. Scot.* II no.1926.
91. Barrow, *Bruce*, p.173; *Chron. Lanercost* p.182.
92. *Cal. Docs. Scot.* II no.1909.
93. Barrow, *Robert Bruce* 175 ff; Patricia M. Barnes and G. W. S. Barrow 'The Movements of Robert Bruce between September 1307 and May 1308' *S.H.R.* XLIX (1970) pp.46-59.
94. Barrow, *Bruce* p.176.
95. *Chron. Fordun* II p.336.
96. *Ibid.* p.337.
97. Barbour's *Bruce* M. P. McDiarmid and J. A. C. Stevenson (Scottish Text Society, 1980-5) pp.221-2.
98. It is notable that when John earl of Buchan had his lands restored to him in 1304, the castles of Balvenie and Slains were excluded, presumably a mark of their importance (Palgrave, *Documents* p.288).
99. *Chron. Lanercost* p.185; *Chron. Fordun* II p.337.
100. Barrow, *Bruce* p.177.
101. *Ibid.* p.178–81.
102. *Chron. Fordun* II p.338.
103. Barrow, *Bruce* pp.187, 190; Duncan, 'War of the Scots' T.R.H.S. p.144; A. Grant, *Independence and Nationhood*, Scotland 1306-1469 (1984) p.4–5.
104. Barrow, *Bruce* p.186.
105. *Cal. Docs. Scot* III no. 303.
106. Barrow, Bruce p.183.
107. Reid, 'Crown and Community under Robert Bruce' in Grant and Stringer *Medieval Scotland: Crown, Lordship and Community* p.203-7.
108. Barrow, *Bruce* pp.183-5; Reid 'Crown and Community under Robert Bruce' p.205.

109. Stones, *Anglo-Scottish Relations* pp.281–7; the complaint against 'the divers strategems and tricks of Robert's rivals' (p.281) diverts attention from the obvious need for Robert Bruce to justify the overthrow of his rivals, the Comyns, the accepted leaders of the political establishment in Scotland since the 1250's.

110. Barrow, *Bruce* p.186.

111. *Cal. Docs. Scot* III no.43.

112. *Ibid.* no.47.

113. *Cal. Pat. Rolls* (1307-1313) pp.92,95.

114. *Registrum Magni Sigilli Regum Scotorum* (ed. J. M. Thomson and others, Edinburgh, 1882-1914) (hence Reg. Mag. Sig) I App I no.31; Barrow, Bruce p.277.

115. *Ibid.* I App II nos. 305, 315, 323; I App II nos. 220, 529.

116. *Ibid.* I No. 12, App II no.26.

116. *Ibid.* I no.12; App II no.26.

117. *Ibid.* I nos. 72, 80; App II no.657; App II no.448.

118. Young, 'The Earls and Earldom of Buchan', p.82; *Reg. Mag. Sig.* I App II no.49.

119. Young, 'The Earls and Earldom of Buchan', p.188; *Reg. Mag. Sig.* I no.602; App I no.47; *Regesta Regum Scottorum* V no.347; *Reg. Mag. Sig.* I App I no.66.

120. *Reg. Mag. Sig.* I Appl II nos. 220, 308, 319, 361, 497, 529, 632, 676, 876.

121. *Ibid.* I no.24; *Cal. Docs. Scot.* II no.82 pp. 202, 209.

122. *Reg. Mag. Sig.* I App. I no.6; App II no.51.

123. *Cal. Docs. Scot.* III no.293; *Cal. Pat. Rolls* (1307–1313) p.510. In 1314 Edward committed the three manors to Margaret widow of John Comyn 'for the support of herself and their son Adomar' (*Cal. Docs. Scot.* III no.385).

124. Barrow, *Bruce*, p.182; *Cal. Docs. Scot.* III no.278, V nos. 566, 614.

125. *Cal. Close Rolls* (1307–1313) pp. 391, 412; *Cal. Fine Rolls* II p.112; *Cal. Docs. Scot.* III no.233.

126. *Cal. Docs. Scot.* III no.233.

127. *Cal. Pat. Rolls* (1307–1313) p.267; *Cal. Close Rolls* (1307–1313) pp. 409, 497.

128. *Cal. Close Rolls* (1307–1313) p.341; B. M. Add Chrs 35662.

129. *Cal. Docs. Scot.* III no.321.

130. Barrow, *Bruce*, p.190.

131. *Ibid.* p.192.

132. *Chron. Lanercost* p.208.

133. *Cal. Docs. Scot.* III nos. 627, 1041.

134. *Ibid.* III no.512.

135. *Cal. Fine Rolls* II p.267; *Cal. Docs. Scot.* III no.503.

136. *Cal. Docs. Scot.* III no.706.

137. *Ibid.* III no.398.

138. *Ibid.* no.595.

139. *Ibid.* nos. 627, 1041.

140. *Ibid.* no.512. The Comyn lands in Tynedale were occupied by the Scots in 1315 (*ibid.* no.460).

BIBLIOGRAPHY

A. PRIMARY
1. *Manuscript Sources*

Edinburgh, National Library of Scotland

N.L.S. Adv. MSS. 15.1.18 Nos. 1, 31, 65, 68
N.L.S. Adv. MSS. 15.1.23
N.L.S. Adv. MSS. 16.1.10
N.L.S. Adv. MSS. 16.2.29
N.L.S. Adv. MSS. 29.4.2
N.L.S. Adv. MSS. 33.2.38
N.L.S. Adv. MSS. 34.1.9
N.L.S. Adv. MSS. 34.1.10
N.L.S. Adv. MSS. 34.2.1
N.L.S. Adv. MSS. 34.3.4
N.L.S. Adv. MSS. 34.3.25
N.L.S. Adv. MSS. 34.4.2
N.L.S. Adv. MSS. 34.4.7
N.L.S. Adv. MSS. 34.5.1
N.L.S. Adv. MSS. 34.6.24
N.L.S. Adv. MSS. 35.2.4
N.L.S. Adv. MSS. 35.3.13
N.L.S. Adv. MSS. 35.4.9
N.L.S. Adv. MSS. 35.4.12
N.L.S. Adv. MSS. 35.4.16
N.L.S. Adv. Chr. A.2
N.L.S. Chrs. 6001, 6004, 6005

Edinburgh, Scottish Record Office

S.R.O. G.D. 1/17
S.R.O. G.D. 4/2
S.R.O. G.D. 28/6
S.R.O. G.D. 45/26/4. Dalhousie Muniments – Transcripts and Notes of Crown Charters
S.R.O. G.D. 45/3036
S.R.O. G.D. 52/388
S.R.O. G.D. 86/1
S.R.O. G.D. 101/1; 101/2
S.R.O. G.D. 137/3679 and 3680
S.R.O. G.D. 175 Docs. 7,8,11,22,24
S.R.O. G.D. 205 Box I (Deed Box 248)/1
S.R.O. G.D. 212. Maitland Thomson Notebooks Nos. 6,7,17,28,30,32,90
S.R.O. G.D. 254/1
S.R.O. Crown Office Writs No.6
S.R.O. R.H. 1/1 Transcripts and Photostats etc. from Royal Charters, 1124–1370
S.R.O. R.H. 1/2/12; 1/2/31; 1/2/32
S.R.O. R.H. 2/2/1; 2/2/3; 2/2/4; 2/2/5; 2/2/11; 2/2/12; 2/2/13; 2/2/14
S.R.O. R.H. 5/27; 5/42; 5/59; 5/65/5/66; 5/140; 5/187; 5/189; 5/190–195
S.R.O. R.H. 6/25; 6/28; 6/52; 6/58; 6/59; 6/69; 6/75; 6/99; 6/159

London, British Museum Department of Manuscripts

B.M. Add. MSS. 28,024 fos. 116v–117r (Cartulary of the Earls of Warwick)
B.M. Add. MSS. 33245
B.M. Add. Chr. 35665
B.M. Campbell Charters XXX, 6
B.M. Cotton Charters XLVIII, No.3
B.M. Cotton Tib. E.V. fos. 37v, 38v, 43 r-v, 76r, 126r. (Cartulary of St. James, Northampton)
B.M. Harl. Chrs. 43 B9; 43 B11
    48 G. 33-9
B.M. Harl. MS. 4693 (fos. 35v-36r)

B.M. Lansdowne MS. 415 fol. 36r (Cartulary of Garendon Abbey)

London, Public Record Office

P.R.O. C. 47/22/8
P.R.O. Inq. Post Mortem C.134 File 197(2)
P.R.O. De Banco Rolls Nos. 286,287
P.R.O. D.L.10 Nos. 205–7 – (Royal Charters)
P.R.O. D.L.36 – (Cartae Miscellaneae)
P.R.O. D.L.25/L.81
P.R.O. E.39 Scots Docs. 99(61) 100(110)
P.R.O. E.40/4766
P.R.O. E.101 Bundle 6 Nos. 34,36
P.R.O. E.199 Bundle 33 No.2
P.R.O. E.326 (Ancient Deeds B), 11343
P.R.O. SL.C.I 4/105
P.R.O. S.C.I 7/205
P.R.O. S.C.I 8/139
P.R.O. S.C.I 12/49; 12/50; 12/87; 12/119; 12/131; 12/132
P.R.O. S.C.I 14/58; 14/67;
P.R.O. S.C.I. 16/33; 16/92; 16/93; 16/94
P.R.O. S.C.I 18/147
P.R.O. S.C.I 20/147; 20/149; 20/158
P.R.O. S.C.I 21/21; 21/172
P.R.O. S.C.I 23/85
P.R.O. S.C.I 26/30
P.R.O. S.C.I 30/81; 30/84; 30/114; 30/190
P.R.O. S.C.I. 31/137
P.R.O. S.C.I 37/107
P.R.O. S.C.I 45/135
P.R.O. S.C.I 47/93
P.R.O. S.C.I 55/57
P.R.O. S.C.I 62/37
P.R.O. S.C.I 63/43; 63/120
P.R.O. S.C.8 File 10 No.456
P.R.O. S.CL.8 File 93 No.4650
P.R.O. S.C.8 File 197 No.9816

Northumberland Record Office

Swinburne (Capheaton) MSS. 1/43

2.*Printed Sources*
(a) *Record Material*

Abbrevatio Placitorum (Record Commission, 1811)
Abbrevatio Rotulorum Originalium (Record Commission, 1805)
Registrum Episcopatus Aberdonensis 2 vols. (Spalding and Maitland Clubs, 1845)
Illustrations of the Topography and Antiquities of the Shires of Aberdeen and Banff (Spalding Club 1847–1869)
Acts of the Parliaments of Scotland, ed. T. Thomson and C. Innes (Edinburgh 1814–1875)
Liber Sancte Marie de Aberbrothoc, 2 vols. (Bannatyne Club 1848–1856)
Liber Sancte Marie de Balmorinoch (Abbotsford Club 1841)
Antiquus Cartularis Ecclesie Baiocensis – Bourienne
Registrum Episcopatus Brechinensis, 2 vols. (Bannantyne Club, 1856)
Calendar of Chancery Rolls (Various) 1277–1326 (London 1912)
Calendar of Chancery Warrants (London, 1927)
Calendar of Charter Rolls (1226–) 6 vols. (London, 1903–1919)
Calendar of Close Rolls (1227–) (London, 1892–)
Calendar of Documents preserved in France illustrative of the History of Great Britain and Ireland, ed. J.H. Round (1899)
Calendar of Documents relating to Scotland, I–V, ed. J. Bain et al. (Edinburgh, 1881–1986)
Calendar of Entries in the Papal Registers relating to Great Britain and Ireland: Papal Letters, ed. W.H. Bliss and others (London, 1893).
Calendar of Fine Rolls (1272) (London, 1911)
Calendar of Inquisitions Post Mortem and other analogous Documents (H.III–) (London, 1904–)
Calendar of Inquisitions Miscellaneous (Chancery) (London, 1916–)
Calendar of Liberate Rolls (1226–) (London, 1916–1964)
Calendar of Patent Rolls (1216–) (London, 1893–)
Registrum Monasterii S. Marie de Cambuskenneth (Grampian Club, 1872)
Cartae Antiquae Rolls 1–10, 11–20 (Pipe Roll Society New Series Nos. 9 and 10, 1939 and 1957)
A Descriptive Catalogue of Ancient Deeds (London, 1890–)
Chartulary of the Cistercian Priory of Coldstream (Grampian Club, 1879)
Charters of the Hospital of Soltre, of Trinity College, Edinburgh, and other

Collegiate churches in Mid-Lothian (Bannatyne Club, 1861).

Charters of the Abbey of Coupar Angus, 2 vols., ed. D.E. Easson (Scottish History Society, 1947)

Register of Cupar Abbey, ed. Rev. Charles Rogers

Curia Regis Rolls of the Reigns of Richard I and John (London, 1922–1961)

Liber S. Marie de Dryburgh (Bannatyne Club, 1847)

Chartularies of St Mary's, Dublin, ed. K. Gilbert (2 vols.) (Rolls Series No.80) (London, 1884)

Registrum de Dunfermelyn (Bannatyne Club, 1842)

Durham Episcopal Charters, ed. H.S. Offler (Surtees Society No.179, 1962)

Exchequer Rolls of Scotland, ed. J. Stuart and others (Edinburgh, 1878–1908)

Book of Fees (1198–1293) 3 vols. (London, 1920–1931)

Feudal Aids (Inquisitions and Assessments relating to) 6 vols. (London, 1899–1920)

Feet of Fines, 7 and 8 Richard I; Pipe Roll Society Vol. XX (London, 1896)

Foedera, Conventiones, Litterae e Cuiuscunque Generiis Acta Publica, ed. T. Rymer, Record Commission edition (London, 1816–1869)

Formulary E: Scottish Letters and Brieves 1286–1424 (University of Glasgow, Scottish History Department, Occasional Papers, 1976), ed. A.A.M. Duncan

Facsimiles of Scottish Charters and Letters prepared by Sir William Fraser (Edinburgh, 1903)

Registrum Episcopatus Glasquensis, 2 vols. (Bannatyne and Maitland Clubs, 1843)

The Priory of Hexham – its Chronicles, Endowments, Annals, title deeds, etc. 2 vols. – Surtees Society Nos. 44 and 46 (1863–1864)

Highland Papers, ed. J.R.N. Macphail (Scottish History Society, 4 vols., 1914–34)

Reports of the Royal Commission on Historical Manuscripts, Nos. 3, 5, 10, 15 (London, 870–)

Liber Cartarum Sancte Crucis (Bannatyne Club, 1840)

Charters, Bulls and other Documents relating to the Abbey of Inchaffray (Scottish History Society, 1908)

Liber Insule Missarum (Bannatyne Club, 1847)

Charters of the Abbey of Inchcolm, ed. D.E. Easson and A. MacDonald (Scottish History Society, 1938)

Llanthony Prima et Secunda Irish Cartularies – Brooks

Chartulary of the Abbey of Lindores (Scottish History Society, 1903)

Cartulaire de Louviers – Bonnin (1888)

Liber Sancte Marie de Lundoris (Abbotsford Club, 1841)

Registrum Malmesburiense, 2 vols. (Rolls Series 72, 1879–1880)

Liber Sancte Marie de Melrose (Bannatyne Club, 1837)

Registrum Honoris de Morton (Bannatyne Club, 1853)

Registrum S. Marie de Neubotle (Bannatyne Club, 1849)

Northumberland and Durham Deeds (Newcastle upon Tyne Record Series)

Northumberland Pipe Rolls – Hodgson, J., *A History of Northumberland* Part III Vol. III (Newcastle upon Tyne, 1825)

National Manuscripts of Scotland (Facsimiles) (3 vols., Southampton, 1867–71)

The History and Antiquities of North Durham (Appendix to), ed. J. Raine (London, 1852)

Registrum monasterii de Passelet (Maitland Club, 1832; New Club, 1877)

Palgrave, F. (ed.), *Documents and Records Illustrating the History of Scotland*, 2 vols. (London, 1837)

Pipe Rolls 5 H II – Publications of the Pipe Roll Society. Old and New Series 1884–

Placita de Quo Warranto (Record Commission, 1818)

Red Book of the Exchequer (3 vols. ed. H. Hall, Rolls Series 95 (London, 1896)

Regesta Regum Anglo-Normannoram I ed. Davis (Oxford, 1913); II ed. Johnson and Cronne (Oxford, 1956); III ed. Cronne and Davis (Oxford, 1968)

Regesta Regum Scottorum I (Acts of Malcolm IV 1153–65), ed. G.W.S. Barrow (Edinburgh, 1960), II (Acts of William I, 1165–1214), ed. G.W.S. Barrow (Edinburgh, 1971)

Regesta Regum Scottorum V (Acts of Robert I 1306–1329), ed. A.A.M. Duncan (Edinburgh, 1988)

Regesta Regum Scottorum (handlists): Acts of Alexander II, ed. J.M. Scoular (Edinburgh, 1959); Acts of Alexander III, the Guardians and John, ed. G.G. Simpson (Edinburgh, 1960–)

Registrum Magni Sigillii Regum Scottorum, ed. J.M. Thompson and others (Edinburgh, 1882–1914)

35th Report of the Deputy Keeper, Public Record Office (London, 1874)

Rievaulx Cartulary (Surtees Society No.83, 1887)

Robertson, J. (ed.), *Conciliia Scocie: Statuta Ecclesiae Scoticanae* (Bannantyne

Club, 1866)

Robertson, W. (ed.), *An Index drawn up about the year 1629 of many records of charters* (Edinburgh, 1798)

Rotuli Hundredorum (Record Commission, 1812–)

Rotuli Litterarum Clausarum (Record Commission, 1833–4)

Rotuli Normanniae in Turri Londinensi, ed. T. Hardy (London, 1835)

Rotuli de Oblatis et Finibus in Turri Londinensi, ed. T. Hardy (London, 1835)

Rotuli Scotiae in Turri Londinensi et in Domo Capitulari Westmonasterii Asservati i–ii, ed. D. Macpherson and others (London, 1814–1819)

Royal Letters and other Historical Illustrations of the reign of Henry III, ed. Shirley (2 vols.), Rolls Series (London, 1862–1866)

Liber Cartarum Prioratus Sancti Andree in Scotia (Bannatyne Club, 1841)

Liber Ecclesie de Scon (Bannatyne and Maitland Clubs, 1843)

Stevenson, J. (ed.), *Documents illustrative of the History of Scotland 1286–1306*, 2 vols. (Edinburgh, 1870)

Stones, E.L.G. (ed.), *Anglo-Scottish Relations 1174–1328* – some selected documents (London, 1963)

Stuart, J., 'The Erroll Papers', *Spalding Club Miscellany ii* (Aberdeen, 1842)

Tanqueray, F.J. (ed.), *Recueil de lettres anglo-francaise* (Paris, 1916)

Theiner, Augustin (ed.), *Vetera Monumenta Hibernorum et Scotorum 1216–1547* (Rome, 1864)

Documents illustrative of Sir William Wallace, his life and times (Maitland Club, 1841)

Worcester Cartulary, Pipe Roll Society Vol. LXXVI, New Series XXXVIII (1962–3)

(b) Narrative Sources (Chronicles, Annals, etc.)

Anderson, A.O. (ed.), *Early Sources of Scottish History, 500–1286*, 2 vols. (Edinburgh, 1922, reprinted 1990)

Anderson, A.O. (ed.), *Scottish Annals from English Chroniclers 500 to 1286* (London, 1908, reprinted 1990)

Annales Monastici, Rolls Series 36 (London, 1864–1869)

Barbour, J., *The Brus*, ed. W.M. Mackenzie (London, 1909)

Materials for a History of Archbishop Thomas Becket, ed. W. Campbell, 7 vols., Rolls Series 60 (London, 1873–1885)

Buik of the Chroniclis of Scotland or a Metrical Version of the History of Hector Boece by William Stuart (ed. William B. Turnbull), Rolls Series 6 (London, 1858)

Extracta e Variis Cronicis Scocie (Abbotsford Club, 1842)

Fordun, John of, *Johannes de Fordun, Chronica Gentis Scottorum*, 2 vols., ed. W.F. Skeme (Edinburgh, 1871–2)

Chronicle of Walter of Guisborough, ed. H. Rothwell (Camden Soc. Vol. LXXXIX, London, 1957)

Blind Hary, *The Wallace*, ed. M.P. McDiarmid (2 vols., Edinburgh, 1968)

The Chronicle of the Reigns of Henry II and Richard I (commonly known as Benedict of Peterborough, Rolls Series 49 (London, 1867)

Chronica Magistri Rogeri de Houedene, ed. W. Stubbs (Rolls Series, 4 vols., 1868–1871)

Chronicon de Lanercost (Bannatyne Club, 1839)

Chronicle of Lanercost, 1272–1346, trans. by Sir Herbert Maxwell (Glasgow, 1913)

Chronicle of Pierre de Langtoft (2 vols.), ed. T. Wright, Rolls Series 47, London, 1866–8)

Lawrie, A.C. (ed.), *Annals of the Reigns of Malcolm and William, Kings of Scotland* (Glasgow, 1910, reprinted 199)

Lawrie, A.C. (ed.), *Early Scottish Charters prior to 1153* (Glasgow, 1905, reprinted 199)

William of Malmesbury, *Gesta Pontificum*, Rolls Series 52 (London, 1870)

Chronica de Mailrus (Bannatyne Club, 1835)

The Chronicle of Melrose, translated by J. Stevenson in *Church Historians of England* (London, 1835–8)

The Chronicle of Melrose (Facsimile Edition), ed. A.O. Anderson and others (London, 1936)

Chronica Johannis de Oxenedes, ed. Sir Henry Ellis, Rolls Series 13 (London, 1859)

Matthew Paris, *Historia Anglorum*, 3 vols., ed. F. Madden, Rolls Series 44 (London, 1866–9)

Matthew Paris, *Chronica Majora*, 7 vols., ed. Luard, Rolls Series 57 (London, 1872–1883)

Chronicles of the Picts: Chronicles of the Scots, ed. W.F. Skene (Edinburgh, 1867)

Liber Pluscardensis, ed. F.J.H. Skerne, 2 vols. (Edinburgh, 1877–80)

Scalacronica by Sir Thomas Gray of Heton Knight (Maitland Club, 1836)

Scalacronica by Sir Thomas Gray, trans. by Sir Herbert Maxwell

Chronicles of the reigns of Stephen, Henry II and Richard I, ed. R. Howlett, Rolls Series, 4 vols. (London, 1884–9)

Scotichronicon by Walter Bower, general editor D.E.R. Watt (Aberdeen and Edinburgh, 1987–)

Symeonis monachi opera omnia, ed. T. Arnold, Rolls Series, 2 vols. (London, 1882–5)

Historia Anglicana, Thomas Walsingham, Rolls Series 28, ed. H.T. Ridley (London, 1863–4)

Wyntoun, Andrew, *Orygynale Cronykil of Scotland*, 3 vols., ed. D. Laing (Edinburgh, 1872–9)

Historians of the Church of York and its Archbishops (ed. Raine), Rolls Series 71 (London, 1879–94)

B. SECONDARY

1. *Books*

Appleby, J. C. and Dalton, P.   *Government, Society and Religion in Northern England 1000–1700* (Stroud, 1997)

Baldwin, J.R.   *Exploring Scotland's Heritage: Lothian and the Borders* (Edinburgh, 1989)

Barron, E.M.   *The Scottish War of Independence* (Inverness, 1934)

Barrow, G.W.S.   *The Anglo-Norman Era in Scottish History* (Oxford, 1980)

Barrow, G.W.S.   *Feudal Britain* (London, 1956)

Barrow, G.W.S.   *The Kingdom of the Scots* (London, 1973)

Barrow, G.W.S.   *Robert Bruce* (3rd edition, Edinburgh, 1988)

Barrow, G.W.S.   *Scotland and its Neighbours in the Middle Ages* (London, 1992)

Barrow, G.W.S. (ed.)   *The Scottish Tradition, Essays in Honour of R.G. Cant* (Edinburgh, 1974)

Bates, C.L.J.   *Border Holds of Northumberland* (Newcastle upon Tyne, 1891)

Birch, Walter de Gray   *History of Scottish Seals* (Stirling, 1905–7)

Bishop, T.A.M.   *Scriptores Regis* (Oxford, 1961)

Bjorn, C., Grant, A. and Stringer, K.J. (eds.)   *Nations, Nationalism and Patriotism in the European Past* (Copenhagen, 1994)

Bjorn, C., Grant, A. and Stringer, K.J. (eds.)   *Social and Political Identities in Western History* (Copenhagen, 1994)

Caldwell, David H. (ed.)   *Scottish Weapons and Fortifications, 1100–1800* (Edinburgh, 1981)

Cowan, I.B. and Easson, D.E. *Medieval Religious Houses: Scotland* (London, 1976)

Close-Brooks, J. *Exploring Scotland's Heritage: the Highlands* (Edinburgh, 1986)

Coss, P. (ed.) *Thomas Wright's Political Songs of England* (Cambridge, 1996)

Cruden, S. *The Scottish Castle* (Edinburgh, 1960)

Cumming-Bruce, M.E. *Family Records of the Bruces and Cummings* (Edinburgh, 1870)

Davies, R.R. *Domination and Conquest: the experiences of Ireland, Scotland and Wales, 1100–1300* (Cambridge, 1990)

Dickinson, W.C. *Scotland from the Earliest Times to 1603* (Edinburgh, 1961)

Dunbar, J.G. *The Historic Architecture of Scotland* (London, 1966)

Duncan, A.A.M. *Scotland, the Making of the Kingdom* (Edinburgh, 1975)

Farrer, W. *Honours and Knights' Fees* (3 vols.) (London and Manchester, 1923–5)

Fawcett, R. and Breeze, D. *Inchmahome Priory* (Edinburgh, 1986)

Fisher, A. *William Wallace* (Edinburgh, 1986)

Frame, R. *The Political Development of the British Isles, 1100–1400* (Oxford, 1990)

Fraser, C. *A Life of Anthony Bek* (Oxford, 1957)

Fraser, W. *The Red Book of Menteith* (Edinburgh, 1880)

Godsman, J. *Kingedward, the story of a parish* (1952)

Grant, A. *Independence and Nationhood: Scotland 1306–1469* (London, 1984)

Grant, A. and Stringer, K.J. (eds.) *Medieval Scotland: Crown, Lordship and Community, Essays presented to G.W.S. Barrow* (Edinburgh, 1993)

Hailes, Lord, Sir David Dalrymple *Annals of Scotland from the Accession of Malcolm III to the Accession of the House of Stewart*, 3 vols. (Edinburgh, 1819)

Hedley, W.P. *Northumberland Families*, 2 vols. (The Society of Antiquaries, Newcastle upon Tyne, 1968–1970)

Haskins, C.H. *Norman Institutions* (1918)

Hodgson, J. *History of Northumberland* in 3 parts (Newcastle upon Tyne, 1827–)

Holt, J.C. *The Northerners* (Oxford, 1961)

Horne, J. (ed.)   *The History of Kirkintilloch* (Kirkintilloch, 1910)

Labarge, M.W.   *A Baronial Household of the Thirteenth Century* (London, 1965)

Lynch, M.   *Scotland, a New History* (Edinburgh, 1991)

Macgibbon, D. and Ross, T.   *The Castellated and Domestic Architecture of Scotland from the Twelfth to Eighteenth Century*, 3 vols. (Edinburgh, 1887–92).

Macgibbon, D. and Ross, T.   *The Ecclesiastical Architecture of Scotland* (Edinburgh, 1896–7)

Mackenzie, A.M.   *The Kingdom of Scotland* (Edinburgh, 1948)

McNeil, P. and Nicholson, R.   *An Historical Atlas of Scotland c.400–c.1600* (St Andrews, 1975)

Moore, M.   *Lands of the Scottish Kings in England* (London, 1915)

Nicholson, R.   *Scotland, the Later Middle Ages* (Edinburgh, 1974)

A History of the County of Northumberland (Bamburgh – Northumberland County History Committee, 1893–1940)

Origines Parochiales Scotiae (Bannatyne Club, 1851–5)

Painter, S.   *Studies in the History of the English Feudal Barony* (Baltimore, 1943)

Poole, A.L.   *Domesday Book to Magna Carta* (1951, 2nd Edition 1955)

Powicke, M.   *The Thirteenth Century* (Oxford, 1962)

Powicke, M.   *King Henry III and the Lord Edward*, 2 vols. (Oxford, 1947)

Pratt, J.B.   *Buchan* (Aberdeen, 1859)

Prestwich, M.   *Edward I* (London, 1988)

Reid, N. (ed.)   *Scotland in the Reign of Alexander III, 1249–1286* (Edinburgh, 1990)

Richardson, J.S. and Simpson, M.E.B.   *The Castle of Balvenie, Banffshire* (1961)

Ritchie, G. and Harman, M.   *Exploring Scotland's Heritage: Argyll and the Western Isles* (Edinburgh, 1985)

Ritchie, R.L.G.   *The Normans in Scotland* (Edinburgh, 1954)

Royal Commission on the Ancient and Historical Monuments of Scotland, *An Inventory of the Monuments … in the County of Wigtown* (Edinburgh, 1912)

Royal Commission on the Ancient and Historical Monuments of Scotland, *An Inventory of the Monuments … in the County of Dumfries* (Edinburgh, 1920)

Royal Commission on the Ancient and Historical Monuments of

Scotland, *An Inventory of the Monuments ... in the County of Roxburghshire* (Edinburgh, 1956)

Royal Commission on the Ancient and Historical Monuments of Scotland, *An Inventory of the Monuments ... in the County of Peeblesshire* (Edinburgh, 1967)

Rounds, J.H. *Family Origins and other Studies*, ed. William Page (London, 1930)

Salter, M. *The Castles of Lothian and the Borders* (Malvern, 1994)

Scammell, G.V. *Hugh de Puiset, Bishop of Durham* (Cambridge, 1956)

Seymour, W. *Battles in Britain, 1066–1547* (London, 1975)

Shepherd, I.A.G. *Exploring Scotland's Heritage: Grampian* (Edinburgh, 1986)

Simpson, W.D. *Dundarg Castle*, Aberdeen University Studies no.131 (Aberdeen, 1954)

Skene, W.F. *Celtic Scotland: a History of Ancient Alban*, 3 vols. (Edinburgh, 1886–90)

Stell, G. *Exploring Scotland's Heritage: Dumfries and Galloway* (Edinburgh, 1986)

Stevenson, J.B. *Exploring Scotland's Heritage: the Clyde Estuary and Central Region* (Edinburgh, 1985)

Stevenson, J.H. and Wood, M. *Scottish Heraldic Seals* (Glasgow, 1940)

Stuart, Margaret *Scottish Family History* (Edinburgh, London, 1930)

Stenton, F.M. *The First Century of English Feudalism, 1066-1166* (Oxford, 1932)

Stones, E.L.G. and Simpson, G.G. *Edward I and the Throne of Scotland 1290-1296* (Oxford, 1978)

Stringer, K.J. *Earl David of Huntingdon 1152-1219*, a Study in Anglo-Scottish History (Edinburgh, 1985)

Stringer, K.J. (ed.) *Essays on the Nobility of Medieval Scotland* (Edinburgh, 1985)

Tocher, J.F. *The Book of Buchan* (1910

Tuck, A. *Crown and Nobility 1272-1461*

Treharne, R.F. *The Baronial Plan of Reform* (Manchester, 1932)

Walker, B. and Ritchie, G. *Exploring Scotland's Heritage: Fife and Tayside* (Edinburgh, 1987)

Young, A. *William Cumin: Border Politics and the Bishopric of Durham 1141-1144* Borthwick Paper 54, University of York (York, 1978)

2. *Articles*

Anderson, A.O., 'Anglo-Scottish Relationships from Constantine II to William' S.H.R. XLII (1963)

Ash, M. 'William Lamberton, Bishop of St. Andrews, 1297-1328' in G.W.S. Barrow (ed) *The Scottish Tradition* (1974) pp 44–45

Barrow (ed.) 'The Scottish Tradition' (1974) pp.44–55

Barrow, G.W.S. 'The Beginnings of Feudalism in Scotland', Bulletin of the *Institute of Historical Research* (1956) pp.1–31

Barrow, G.W.S. 'The Border' *Durham University Inaugural Lecture*, 1962

Barrow, G.W.S. 'Northern English Society in the 12th and 13th Centuries' *Northern History* IV (1969)

Barrow, G.W.S. 'The Earliest Stewart Fief', *The Stewarts* X (1956) pp.162–78

Barrow, G.W.S. 'The Scottish Clergy and the War of Independence' *S.H.R.* XXXXI (1962) pp.1-22

Barrow, G.W.S. 'Hidden Record II: An unremembered Scottish family' *Scottish Record Society* (1994)

Barrow, G.W.S. 'The Scottish Judex in the 12th and 13th Centuries' *S.H.R.* XLV (1966) pp.16–26

Barrow, G.W.S. 'Some Problems in Twelfth and Thirteenth Century Scottish History: a Genealogical Approach' *Scottish Genealogist* XXV No.4 Dec. 1978 pp.97–112

Barrow, G.W.S. 'Wales and Scotland in the Middle Ages', *Welsh Historical Review X*, 1980-1 pp.302-19

Barrow, G.W.S. 'Badenoch and Strathspey, 1130-1312' I Secular and Political' *Northern Scotland* VIII (1988) pp.1-15

Barrow, G.W.S. 'Frontier and Settlement: Which influenced which? England and Scotland, 1100-1300' in R. Bartlett and A. Mackay (eds.), *Medieval Frontier Societies* (Oxford, 1989) pp.3–21

Barrow, G.W.S. 'The Anglo-Scottish Border: Growth and Structure in the Middle Ages' in *Grenzen and Grenzregionem* (Publications of the Kommission fur Saarlandischen Landersgeschichte und Volksforschung, no.22, Saarbrucken, 1994.

Barrow, G.W.S. 'A Kingdom in Crisis: Scotland and the Maid of Norway' *S.H.R.* LXIX 2, no.188 Oct. 1990 pp.120–41

Barnes, P. and Barrow, G.W.S. 'The Movements of Robert Bruce between September 1307 and May 1308', *S.H.R.* XLIX (1970), pp.46–59

Barrow, G.W.S. 'A Kingdom in Crisis: Scotland and the Maid of Norway', *S.H.R.* LXIX 2, no.188 Oct. 1990, pp.120–41

Dixon, P. 'From Hall to Tower: the Change in Seigneurial Houses on the Anglo-Scottish Border after c.1250', in P.R. Coss and S.D. Lloyd (eds.), *Thirteenth Century England* IV (Proceedings of the Newcastle upon Tyne Conference, 1991)

Dunbar, J. 'The Medieval Architecture of the Scottish Highlands', in L. Maclean (ed.), *The Middle Ages in the Highlands* (Inverness Field Club)

Duncan, A.A.M. 'The Earliest Scottish Charters', *S.H.R.* XXXVII (1958)

Duncan, A.A.M. 'The Early Parliaments of Scotland', *S.H.R.* XLV (1966), pp.36–58

Duncan, A.A.M. 'The Nation of Scots and the Declaration of Arbroath' (*Historical Association* G.75, London, 1970)

Duncan, A.A.M. 'The Earldom of Atholl in the 13th Century', *Scottish Genealogist.* Vol. VIII No.2, April 1960

Duncan, A.A.M. 'The Community of the Realm of Scotland and Robert Bruce', *S.H.R.* XLV (1966), pp.184–201

Duncan, A.A.M. 'The War of the Scots', *Transactions of the Royal Historical Society* (1992), pp.125–51

Ferguson, J. 'The House of Comyn (1124–1314–1914)', *The Buchan Field Club*, Vol. XI (1915–1917)

Ferguson, J. 'The Old Baronies of Buchan', *The Buchan Field Club*, Vol. X (1909)

Ferguson, J. 'The Old Castles of Buchan', *The Buchan Field Club*, Vol. X (1909)

Fisher, A. 'Wallace and Bruce', *History Today*, Feb. 1989, pp.18–23

Goldstein, R.J. 'The Scottish Mission to Boniface VIII in 1301: a Reconsideration of the Context of the "Instructiones and Processus",' *S.H.R.* IXX (1991)

Green, J. 'Anglo-Scottish Relations 1066–1174', in M. Jones and M. Vale (eds.), *England and Her Neighbours, 1066–1453*, pp.53–72

Keen, M. 'William Wallace and the Scottish Outlaws', in *The Outlaws of Medieval Legend* (1961), pp.64–77

Keeney, B.C. 'The Medieval Idea of the State: the Great Cause, 1291–92', *University of Toronto Law Journal* VIII, pp.48–71

Lewis, J. 'Inverlochy Castle', *Discovery and Excavation, Scotland* (1989)

Lloyd Lewis, C. 'The Origins of some Anglo-Norman Families', *Harl. Soc. 103*

Malcolm, C.A. 'The Office of Sheriff in Scotland – origins and early development', *S.H.R.* XX (1922–3)

Miller, E. 'War in the North', *The Anglo-Scottish Wars of the Middle Ages* (University of Hull, 1960), pp.3–22

Mitchell, J. 'An Historical Account of the Comyns Earls of Buchan', N.L.S. MSS2099 (nineteenth century)

Munro, J. 'The Lordship of the Isles', in L. Maclean (ed.), *The Middle Ages in the Highlands* (Inverness Field Club, 1981)

Murray, H.K. and Murray, J.C. 'Old Rattray, burgh and castle', *Discovery and Excavation, Scotland* (1986)

Neville, C.J. 'The Political Allegiance of the Earls of Strathearn during the War of Independence', *S.H.R.* LXV (1986), pp.133–53

Prestwich, M. 'England and Scotland During the Wars of Independence', in M. Jones and M. Vale (eds.), *England and Her Neighbours, 1066–1453: Essays in Honour of Pierre Chaplais* (Hambledon, 1989), pp.181–97

Prestwich, M. 'Colonial Scotland: The English in Scotland under Edward I', in R.A. Mason (ed.), *Scotland and England, 1286–1815* (Edinburgh, 1987

Prestwich, M. 'Edward I and the Maid of Norway', *S.H.R.* LXIX (Oct. 1990)

Pryde, G.S. 'Two Burgh Charters', *S.H.R.* XXIX (1950)

Reid, N. 'Margaret "Maid" of Norway and Scottish Queenship', *Reading Medieval Studies* VIII, 1982, pp.75–96

Reid, N. 'The Kingless Kingdom: the Scottish Guardianship of 1286–1306', *S.H.R.* LXI (1982), pp.105–29

Reid, N. 'Crown and Community under Robert I', in A. Grant and K.J. Stringer (eds.), *Medieval Scotland, Crown, Lordship and Community* (Edinburgh, 1993), pp.203–22

Richardson, H.G. and Sayles, G.O. 'The Scottish Parliaments of Edward I, *S.H.R.* XXV (1928), pp.300–317

Round, J.H. 'Bernard, the King's Scribe', *E.H.R.* Vol. XIV, 1899

Round, J.H. 'The Cumins of Snitterfield' *Ancestor* Vol. IX.

Round, J.H. 'The Origins of the Comyns' *Ancestor* Vol. X, 1904

Round, J.H. 'Comyn and Valoignes' *Ancestor* Vol. XI

Sayles, G.O. 'The Guardians of Scotland and a Parliament at Rutherglen in 1300' *S.H.R.* XXIV (1927)

Simpson, G.G. 'Why was John Balliol called "Toom Tabard"' *S.H.R.* XLLVII (1968) pp.196-199

Simpson, G.G. 'The claim of Florence Count of Holland to the Scottish Throne, 1291-2' *S.H.R.* XXXVI (1957) pp.111–123

Simpson, G.G. 'The Declaration of Arbroath, revitalised' *S.H.R.* LVI (1977) pp.11–33

Simpson, G.G. and Webster, B. 'Charter Evidence and the Distribution of Mottes in Scotland' in K.J. Stringer (ed.) *Essays on the Nobility of Medieval Scotland* (Edinburgh, 1985)

Simpson, W.D. 'Slains Castle' *Transactions of the Buchan Field Club*, XVI (1940)

Simpson, W.D. 'Cairnbulg Castle, Aberdeenshire' *Proceedings of the Society of Antiquaries of Scotland* XLVIII (1948-9)

Smallwood, T.M. 'An unpublished early account of Bruce's murder of Comyn' *S.H.R.* LIV (1975) pp.1–10

Stell, G. 'The Balliol Family and the Great Cause of 1291–2' in K.J. Stringer (ed.) *Essays on the Nobility of Medieval Scotland* (Edinburgh, 1985) pp.151–7

Stell, G. 'The Scottish Medieval Castle: Form, Function and "Evolution"' in K.J. Stringer (ed.) *Essays on the Nobility of Medieval Scotland* (Edinburgh, 1985)

Stones, E.L.G. 'The Submission of Robert Bruce to Edward I c.1301-2' *S.H.R.* XXXIV (1955) pp.122–134

Stones, E.L.G. 'English Chroniclers and the Affairs of Scotland 1286-1296' in R.H.C. David and J.M. Wallace-Hadrill (eds.) *The Writing of History in the Middle Ages* (Oxford 1981)

Truckell, A.E. and Williams, J. 'Medieval Pottery in Dumfriesshire and Galloway' *Transactions of the Dumfriesshire and Galloway Natural History and Antiquarian Society* 3rd series, 44, (1966–7)

Watt, D.E.R. 'The Minority of Alexander III of Scotland' *Transactions of the Royal Historical Society* 5th series XXI (1971) pp.1–23

Webster, B. Review Article: Anglo–Scottish Relations, 1296–1389: some recent essays *S.H.R.* LXXIV, 1, No.197, April (1995) pp.99–108

Young, A. 'The Political Role of Walter Comyn, Earl of Menteith, during the Minority of Alexander III in Scotland', in K.J. Stringer (ed.), *Essays on the Nobility of Medieval Scotland* (Edinburgh, 1985), pp.131–49

Young, A. 'Noble Families and Political Factions', in N. Reid (ed.), *Scotland in the Reign of Alexander III, 1249–1286* (Edinburgh, 1990), pp.1–30

Young, A. 'The Earls and Earldom of Buchan in the Thirteenth Century', in A. Grant and K.J. Stringer (eds.), *Medieval Scotland: Crown, Lordship and Community* (Edinburgh, 1993), pp.174–99.

Young, A. 'The Bishopric of Durham in Stephen's Reign', in D. Rollason, M. Harvey and M. Prestwich (eds.), *Anglo-Norman Durham, 1093–1193* (Woodbridge, 1994), pp.353–68

Young, A. 'The North and Anglo-Scottish Relations in the Thirteenth Century', in J.C. Appleby and P. Dalton (eds.), *Government, Society and Religion in Northern England, 1000–1700* (Stroud, 1997) pp.77–89

Young, A. 'The Architectural Lordship of the Comyns', in R. Oram and G. Stell (eds.), *Architecture and Lordship in Scotland, 1100–1650* (1998) (forthcoming)

BOOKS OF REFERENCE

Cockayne, G.E. *The Complete Peerage*, revised by V. Gibbs and others (London, 1910–1959)

Davis, G.R.C. *Medieval Cartularies of Great Britain* (London, 1958)

Paul, J.B. (ed.) *The Scots Peerage* (Edinburgh, 1904–14)

Powicke, F.M. and Fryde, E.B. (eds.) *Handbook of British Chronology* (London, 1961)

Sanders, I.J. *English Baronies: A Study of their Origin and Descent, 1086–1327* (Oxford, 1960)

Watt, D.E.R. *Fasti Ecclesia Scoticanae Medii Aevi*, 2nd Draft (St Andrews, 1969)

THESES

Reid, N. 'The Political Role of the Monarchy in Scotland, 1249–1329' (unpublished Ph.D. thesis, University of Edinburgh, 1984)

Simpson, G.G. 'An Anglo-Scottish Baron of the Thirteenth Century. The Acts of Roger de Quincy Earl of Winchester and Constable of Scotland' (unpublished Ph.D. thesis, University of Edinburgh, 1965)

Watson, F. 'Scotland under Edward I, 1296–1307' (unpublished Ph.D. thesis, University of Glasgow, 1991)

INDEX

❖

Index

Eviot (Uviet, Vinet) family, 46, 52

Fakenham, Magna (Suffolk), 209
Falaise, Treaty of (1174), 18
Falkirk, battle of (1298), 7, 168
Fechil (Buchan), 23
Fedarg, Philip de (Meldrum), 29
Ferendraught, Duncan de, 195, 202–3
Fergus, earl of Buchan, see Buchan, earls of
Fiddich, river, 149
Fife, 100
Fife, earls of
   Duncan (d.1289), 92, 96, 100–1, 103, 135
   Malcolm, 56, 59, 71, 123
   Macduff, brother of Duncan, 123
Fife, sheriffdom of, 69, 114, 156, 162
   see Lascelles; Lochore
Findogask (Perthshire), 151, 206
Fithkil (Fife), 26
fitz Alan, Brian, Guardian of Scotland,
   112, 167
fitz Gilbert, Walter, 20, 206
fitz Warin, William, 163
Flanders, 166
Flint castle, 151
Flaxflete (Yorkshire), 207
Fleming, Malcolm, 206
Florence, Count and Great Cause, 115
Fordoun (Mearns), 26
Fordun, John of, chronicler, ch.1 *passim*
Forfar, 20
   sheriffdom of, 69, 156, 174, 193
   Mowat family and, 69
   Bethun, David de and, 99, 126
France, war with England, 136
   alliance with Scotland (1295), 139, 140
   defeat at Courtrai (1302), 176
   Anglo-French peace 1303, 176–7
   and Bruce, 204
Fraser family, 73, 85, 100, 114, 169
   Andrew, 100, 124, 125
   Richard, 125
   Simon elder, 67
   Simon younger, 100, 125, 173, 176, 187–9, 195, 201
   William, bishop of St. Andrews, Guardian (d.1297), 92, 96–7, 108–9, 112, 125, 133, 138, 140, 169
Freskin, William II, 21

Galloway, 100–2, 154
   rebellions in, 35–6, 112, 130
Galloway, William de, 126
Gamelin, Bishop of St. Andrews, Chancellor of Scotland, 51–2, 56, 59, 69–70, 169
Garioch, 115, 159
Gascony, 97
Geddington (Northampton), 163, 207

Giffard, William, 21, 47, 71
Glasgow, bishops of
   William Bondington, 52
   Robert Wishart, see Wishart
Glencarnie, Gilbert of, 202
glens
   Great Glen, 148, 163, 203
   Glen Fiddich, 149
   Glen Trool, battle of, 202
   Glen Rinnes, 149
   Glen Spean, 148
Gloucester, earl of, 208
Gordon, Adam de, 193–4, 200, 205
Gourlay, Hugh, 52, 70
   William, 52, 70
Govan, 174
Graham family, 29, 46, 85, 114
   Henry de, 46
   David de, 52, 69
   Patrick de, killed at Dunbar (1296), 69, 99, 124, 133, 135
   David, son of Patrick, 162, 169–70, 188, 204
The 'Great Cause' (1291–2), 91, 95, 112ff
Guardians of Scotland (1286–92), 92ff, 97–134
   seal of the Guardians, 93
   request for English help, 102, 104
   Edward I's attitude to, 104, 106, 111
   Guardians compromise Scotland's independence, 111–12
   Brian fitz Alan joins the Guardians, 112
   The Council of Twelve (1295) a return to Guardianship? 140
   Wallace and Moray re-establish Guardianship 1297, 167ff
   joint Guardianship of Comyn and Bruce 1298–1300, 170
   Guardianship 1298–1304, 170ff
   triumvirate: Lamberton, Bruce and Comyn, 171–2
   resignation of Bruce, replacement by Umphraville, 171–2
   role of John de Soules, 172ff
   John Comyn as sole Guardian 1302–4, 173–7

Haddo (now Kelly), 149
Harewell (Berkshire), 207
Harlech castle, 151
Hastings, Robert de, 194
Hay family, 56, 85, 114, 126, 162
   Gilbert de (la), 29, 46, 58, 71–2
   Gilbert (1306), 201, 206
   Nicholas, 99, 126
   Thomas, 206
   Henry, Earl, 15, 16, 17
   Henry I, 15, 19